Notes and Lectures Upon Shakespeare and Some of the Old Poets and Dramatists

NOTES AND LECTURES UPON

SHAKESPEARE

AND SOME OF THE OLD POETS

AND DRAMATISTS

WITH OTHER LITERARY REMAINS

OF S. T. COLERIDGE

EDITED BY MRS. H. N. COLERIDGE

VOL. II.

LONDON
WILLIAM PICKERING
1849

CONTENTS.

VOL. II.

A COURSE OF LECTURES.

A COURSE OF LECTURES.

PROSPECTUS.

HERE are few families, at present, in the higher and middle classes of English society, in which literary topics and the productions of the Fine Arts, in some one or other of their various forms, do not occasionally take their turn in contributing to the entertainment of the social board, and the amusement of the circle at the fire side. The acquisitions and attainments of the intellect ought, indeed, to hold a very inferior rank in our estimation, opposed to moral worth, or even to professional and specific skill, prudence, and industry. But why should they be opposed, when they may be made subservient merely by being subordinated? It can rarely happen, that a man of social disposition, altogether a stranger to subjects of taste, (almost the only ones on which persons of both sexes can converse with a common interest) should pass through the world without at times feeling dissatisfied with himself.

2   B

The best proof of this is to be found in the marked
anxiety which men, who have succeeded in life
without the aid of these accomplishments, shew in
securing them to their children. A young man
of ingenuous mind will not wilfully deprive himself
of any species of respect. He will wish to feel himself on a level with the average of the society in
which he lives, though he may be ambitious of distinguishing himself only in his own immediate pursuit or occupation.

Under this conviction, the following Course of
Lectures was planned. The several titles will best
explain the particular subjects and purposes of
each: but the main objects proposed, as the result
of all, are the two following.

1. To convey, in a form best fitted to render
them impressive at the time, and remembered afterwards, rules and principles of sound judgment,
with a kind and degree of connected information,
such as the hearers cannot generally be supposed
likely to form, collect, and arrange for themselves,
by their own unassisted studies. It might be presumption to say, that any important part of these
Lectures could not be derived from books; but none,
I trust, in supposing, that the same information
could not be so surely or conveniently acquired
from such books as are of commonest occurrence,
or with that quantity of time and attention which
can be reasonably expected, or even wisely desired,
of men engaged in business and the active duties
of the world.

2. Under a strong persuasion that little of real value is derived by persons in general from a wide and various reading; but still more deeply convinced as to the actual mischief of unconnected and promiscuous reading, and that it is sure, in a greater or less degree, to enervate even where it does not likewise inflate; I hope to satisfy many an ingenuous mind, seriously interested in its own development and cultivation, how moderate a number of volumes, if only they be judiciously chosen, will suffice for the attainment of every wise and desirable purpose; that is, in addition to those which he studies for specific and professional purposes. It is saying less than the truth to affirm, that an excellent book, (and the remark holds almost equally good of a Raphael as of a Milton) is like a well chosen and well tended fruit tree. Its fruits are not of one season only. With the due and natural intervals, we may recur to it year after year, and it will supply the same nourishment and the same gratification, if only we ourselves return to it with the same healthful appetite.

The subjects of the Lectures are indeed very different, but not, (in the strict sense of the term) diverse; they are various, rather than miscellaneous. There is this bond of connexion common to them all,—that the mental pleasure which they are calculated to excite, is not dependent on accidents of fashion, place, or age, or the events or the customs of the day; but commensurate with the good sense, taste, and feeling, to the cultivation of which

they themselves so largely contribute, as being all
in kind, though not all in the same degree, productions of genius.

What it would be arrogant to promise, I may
yet be permitted to hope,—that the execution will
prove correspondent and adequate to the plan. Assuredly, my best efforts have not been wanting so
to select and prepare the materials, that, at the
conclusion of the Lectures, an attentive auditor,
who should consent to aid his future recollection by
a few notes taken either during each Lecture, or
soon after, would rarely feel himself, for the time
to come, excluded, from taking an intelligent interest in any general conversation likely to occur in
mixed society.

Syllabus of the Course.

1. January 27, 1818.—On the manners, morals,
literature, philosophy, religion, and the state of society in general, in European Christendom, from
the eighth to the fifteenth century, (that is from
A.D. 700, to A.D. 1400), more particularly in reference to England, France, Italy, and Germany;
in other words, a portrait of the so called dark ages
of Europe.

II. January 30.—On the tales and metrical ro-
mances common, for the most part, to England,
Germany, and the north of France, and on the
English songs and ballads, continued to the reign

of Charles I. A few selections will be made from the Swedish, Danish, and German languages, translated for the purpose by the Lecturer.

III. February 3.—Chaucer and Spenser; of Petrarch; of Ariosto, Pulci, and Boiardo.

IV. V. VI. February 6, 10, 13.—On the dramatic works of Shakspeare. In these Lectures will be comprised the substance of Mr. Coleridge's former courses on the same subject, enlarged and varied by subsequent study and reflection.

VII. February 17.—On Ben Jonson, Beaumont and Fletcher, and Massinger; with the probable causes of the cessation of dramatic poetry in England with Shirley and Otway, soon after the restoration of Charles II.

VIII. February 20.—Of the life and all the works of Cervantes, but chiefly of his Don Quixote. The ridicule of knight errantry shewn to have been but a secondary object in the mind of the author, and not the principal cause of the delight which the work continues to give to all nations, and under all the revolutions of manners and opinions.

IX. February 24.—On Rabelais, Swift, and Sterne: on the nature and constituents of genuine Humour, and on the distinctions of the Humorous from the Witty, the Fanciful, the Droll, and the Odd.

X. February 27.—Of Donne, Dante, and Milton.

XI. March 3.—On the Arabian Nights' Entertainments, and on the romantic use of the supernatural in poetry, and in works of fiction not poetical. On the conditions and regulations under which such books may be employed advantageously in the earlier periods of education.

XII. March 6.—On tales of witches, apparitions, &c. as distinguished from the magic and magicians of Asiatic origin. The probable sources of the former, and of the belief in them in certain ages and classes of men. Criteria by which mistaken and exaggerated facts may be distinguished from absolute falsehood and imposture. Lastly, the causes of the terror and interest which stories of ghosts and witches inspire, in early life at least, whether believed or not.

XIII. March 10.—On colour, sound, and form in Nature, as connected with poesy: the word " Poesy" used as the generic or class term, including poetry, music, painting, statuary, and ideal architecture, as its species. The reciprocal relations of poetry and philosophy to each other; and of both to religion, and the moral sense.

XIV. March 13.—On the corruptions of the English language since the reign of Queen Anne in our style of writing prose. A few easy rules for the attainment of a manly, unaffected, and pure language, in our genuine mother tongue, whether for the purpose of writing, oratory, or conversation.

LECTURE I.*

General Character of the Gothic Mind in
the Middle Ages.

MR. COLERIDGE began by treating of the races of mankind as descended from Shem, Ham, and Japhet, and therein of the early condition of man in his antique form. He then dwelt on the pre-eminence of the Greeks in Art and Philosophy, and noticed the suitableness of polytheism to small insulated states, in which patriotism acted as a substitute for religion, in destroying or suspending self. Afterwards, in consequence of the extension of the Roman empire, some universal or common spirit became necessary for the conservation of the vast body, and this common spirit was, in fact, produced in Christianity. The causes of the decline of the Roman empire were in operation long before the time of the actual overthrow; that overthrow had been foreseen by many eminent Romans, especially by Seneca. In fact, there was under the empire an Italian and a German party in Rome, and in the end the latter prevailed.

He then proceeded to describe the generic character of the Northern nations, and defined it as

---

* From Mr. Green's note taken at the delivery. *Ed.*

an independence of the whole in the freedom of
the individual, noticing their respect for women,
and their consequent chivalrous spirit in war; and
how evidently the participation in the general coun-
cil laid the foundation of the representative form of
government, the only rational mode of preserving
individual liberty in opposition to the licentious democracy of the ancient republics.

He called our attention to the peculiarity of
their art, and showed how it entirely depended on
a symbolical expression of the infinite,—which is
not vastness, nor immensity, nor perfection, but
whatever cannot be circumscribed within the limits
of actual, sensuous being. In the ancient art,
on the contrary, every thing was finite and material.—Accordingly, sculpture was not attempted
by the Gothic races till the ancient specimens were
discovered, whilst painting and architecture were
of native growth amongst them. In the earliest
specimens of the paintings of modern ages, as in
those of Giotto and his associates in the cemetery
at Pisa, this complexity, variety, and symbolical
character are evident, and are more fully developed
in the mightier works of Michel Angelo and Raf-
fael. The contemplation of the works of antique
art excites a feeling of elevated beauty, and exalted
notions of the human self; but the Gothic architecture impresses the beholder with a sense of self-
annihilation ; he becomes, as it were, a part of the
work contemplated. An endless complexity and

variety are united into one whole, the plan of which is not distinct from the execution. A Gothic cathedral is the petrefaction of our religion. The only work of truly modern sculpture is the Moses of Michel Angelo.

The Northern nations were prepared by their own previous religion for Christianity; they, for the most part received it gladly, and it took root as in a native soil. The deference to woman, characteristic of the Gothic races, combined itself with devotion in the idea of the Virgin Mother, and gave rise to many beautiful associations.*

Mr. C. remarked how Gothic an instrument in origin and character the organ was.

He also enlarged on the influence of female character on our education, the first impressions of our childhood being derived from women. Amongst oriental nations, he said, the only distinction was between lord and slave. With the antique Greeks, the will of every one conflicting with the will of all, produced licentiousness; with the modern descendants from the northern stocks, both these extremes were shut out, to reappear mixed and condensed into this principle or temper;—submission, but with

* The reader may compare the last two paragraphs with the first of Schlegel's Prelections on Dramatic Art and Literature—*Vol.* i. *pp.* 10—16. 2nd. edit.—and with Schelling *Ueber das Verhältniss der bildenden Künste, p.* 377; though the resemblance in thought is but general.

free choice, illustrated in chivalrous devotion to women as such, in attachment to the sovereign, &c.

LECTURE II.[*]

General Character of the Gothic Literature and Art.

IN my last lecture I stated that the descendants
of Japhet and Shem peopled Europe and Asia,
fulfilling in their distribution the prophecies of
Scripture, while the descendants of Ham passed
into Africa, there also actually verifying the inter-
diction pronounced against them. The Keltic and
Teutonic nations occupied that part of Europe,
which is now France, Britain, Germany, Sweden,
Denmark, &c. They were in general a hardy race,
possessing great fortitude, and capable of great endurance. The Romans slowly conquered the more
southerly portion of their tribes, and succeeded only
by their superior arts, their policy, and better discipline. After a time, when the Goths,—to use the
name of the noblest and most historical of the Teutonic tribes,—had acquired some knowledge of these
arts from mixing with their conquerors, they invaded
the Roman territories. The hardy habits, the steady
perseverance, the better faith of the enduring Goth

---

[*] From Mr. William Hammond's note taken at the delivery. *Ed.*

rendered him too formidable an enemy for the corrupt Roman, who was more inclined to purchase the subjection of his enemy, than to go through the suffering necessary to secure it. The conquest of the Romans gave to the Goths the Christian religion as it was then existing in Italy; and the light and graceful building of Grecian, or Roman-Greek order, became singularly combined with the massy architecture of the Goths, as wild and varied as the forest vegetation which it resembled. The Greek art is beautiful. When I enter a Greek Church, my eye is charmed, and my mind elated; I feel exalted, and proud that I am a man. But the Gothic art is sublime. On entering a cathedral, I am filled with devotion and with awe; I am lost to the actualities that surround me, and my whole being expands into the infinite; earth and air, nature and art, all swell up into eternity, and the only sensible impression left, is ' that I am nothing!' This religion, while it tended to soften the manners of the Northern tribes, was at the same time highly congenial to their nature. The Goths are free from the stain of hero worship. Gazing on their rugged mountains, surrounded by impassable forests, accustomed to gloomy seasons, they lived in the bosom of nature, and worshipped an invisible and unknown deity. Firm in his faith, domestic in his habits, the life of the Goth was simple and dignified, yet tender and affectionate.

The Greeks were remarkable for complacency

and completion; they delighted in whatever pleased
the eye; to them it was not enough to have merely
the idea of a divinity, they must have it placed
before them, shaped in the most perfect symmetry,
and presented with the nicest judgment: and if we
look upon any Greek production of art, the beauty
of its parts, and the harmony of their union, the
complete and complacent effect of the whole, are
the striking characteristics.   It is the same in their
poetry.   In Homer you have a poem perfect in its
form, whether originally so, or from the labour of
after critics, I know not; his descriptions are pictures brought vividly before you, and as far as the
eye and understanding are concerned, I am indeed
gratified.   But if I wish my feelings to be affected,
if I wish my heart to be touched, if I wish to melt
into sentiment and tenderness, I must turn to the
heroic songs of the Goths, to the poetry of the
middle ages.   The worship of statues in Greece
had, in a civil sense, its advantage, and disadvantage; advantage, in promoting statuary and the
arts; disadvantage, in bringing their gods too much
on a level with human beings, and thence depriving
them of their dignity, and gradually giving rise to
scepticism and ridicule.   But no statue, no artificial emblem, could satisfy the Northman's mind;
the dark wild imagery of nature which surrounded
him, and the freedom of his life, gave his mind a
tendency to the infinite, so that he found rest in
that which presented no end, and derived satisfaction from that which was indistinct.

We have few and uncertain vestiges of Gothic literature till the time of Theodoric, who encouraged his subjects to write, and who made a collection of their poems. These consisted chiefly of heroic songs, sung at the Court; for at that time this was the custom. Charlemagne, in the beginning of the ninth century, greatly encouraged letters, and made a further collection of the poems of his time, among which were several epic poems of great merit; or rather in strictness there was a vast cycle of heroic poems, or minstrelsies, from and out of which separate poems were composed. The form of poetry was, however, for the most part, the metrical romance and heroic tale. Charlemagne's army, or a large division of it, was utterly destroyed in the Pyrenees, when returning from a successful attack on the Arabs of Navarre and Arragon; yet the name of Roncesvalles became famous in the songs of the Gothic poets. The Greeks and Romans would not have done this; they would not have recorded in heroic verse the death and defeat of their fellow-countrymen. But the Goths, firm in their faith, with a constancy not to be shaken, celebrated those brave men who died for their religion and their country! What, though they had been defeated, they died without fear, as they had lived without reproach; they left no stain on their names, for they fell fighting for their God, their liberty, and their rights; and the song that sang that day's reverse animated them to future victory and certain vengeance.

I must now turn to our great monarch, Alfred, one of the most august characters that any age has ever produced; and when I picture him after the toils of government and the dangers of battle, seated by a solitary lamp, translating the holy scriptures into the Saxon tongue,—when I reflect on his moderation in success, on his fortitude and perseverance in difficulty and defeat, and on the wisdom and extensive nature of his legislation, I am really at a loss which part of this great man's character most to admire.   Yet above all, I see the grandeur, the freedom, the mildness, the domestic unity, the universal character of the middle ages condensed into Alfred's glorious institution of the trial by jury.   I gaze upon it as the immortal symbol of that age;—an age called indeed dark;—but how could that age be considered dark, which solved the difficult problem of universal liberty, freed man from the shackles of tyranny, and subjected his actions to the decision of twelve of his fellow countrymen?   The liberty of the Greeks was a phenomenon, a meteor, which blazed for a short time, and then sank into eternal darkness.   It was a combination of most opposite materials, slavery and liberty.   Such can neither be happy nor lasting.   The Goths on the other hand said, You shall be our Emperor; but we must be Princes on our own estates, and over them you shall have no power!   The Vassals said to their Prince, We will serve you in your wars, and defend your castle; but we must have liberty in our own circle, our cottage, our cattle, our proportion of land. The Cities said, We acknowledge you for our Emperor; but we must have our walls and our strong holds, and be governed by our own laws. Thus all combined, yet all were separate; all served, yet all were free. Such a government could not exist in a dark age. Our ancestors may not indeed have been deep in the metaphysics of the schools; they may not have shone in the fine arts; but much knowledge of human nature, much practical wisdom must have existed amongst them, when this admirable constitution was formed; and I believe it is a decided truth, though certainly an awful lesson, that nations are not the most happy at the time when literature and the arts flourish the most among them.

The translations I had promised in my syllabus I shall defer to the end of the course, when I shall give a single lecture of recitations illustrative of the different ages of poetry. There is one Northern tale I will relate, as it is one from which Shakspeare derived that strongly marked and extraordinary scene between Richard III. and the Lady Anne. It may not be equal to that in strength and genius, but it is, undoubtedly, superior in decorum and delicacy.

A Knight had slain a Prince, the lord of a strong castle, in combat. He afterwards contrived to get into the castle, where he obtained an interview with the Princess's attendant, whose life he had saved

in some encounter; he told her of his love for her
mistress, and won her to his interest. She then
slowly and gradually worked on her mistress's
mind, spoke of the beauty of his person, the fire of
his eyes, the sweetness of his voice, his valour in
the field, his gentleness in the court; in short, by
watching her opportunities, she at last filled the
Princess's soul with this one image; she became
restless; sleep forsook her; her curiosity to see
this Knight became strong; but her maid still de-
ferred the interview, till at length she confessed she
was in love with him;—the Knight is then introduced, and the nuptials are quickly celebrated.

In this age there was a tendency in writers to
the droll and the grotesque, and in the little dramas
which at that time existed, there were singular instances of these. It was the disease of the age. It
is a remarkable fact that Luther and Melancthon,
the great religious reformers of that day, should
have strongly recommended, for the education of
children, dramas, which at present would be considered highly indecorous, if not bordering on a
deeper sin. From one which they particularly recommended, I will give a few extracts; more I
should not think it right to do. The play opens
with Adam and Eve washing and dressing their
children to appear before the Lord, who is coming
from heaven to hear them repeat the Lord's Prayer,
Belief, &c. In the next scene the Lord appears
seated like a schoolmaster, with the children stand-

ing round, when Cain, who is behind hand, and a sad pickle, comes running in with a bloody nose and his hat on. Adam says, "What, with your hat on!" Cain then goes up to shake hands with the Almighty, when Adam says (giving him a cuff), "Ah, would you give your left hand to the Lord?" At length Cain takes his place in the class, and it becomes his turn to say the Lord's Prayer. At this time the Devil (a constant attendant at that time) makes his appearance, and getting behind Cain, whispers in his ear; instead of the Lord's Prayer, Cain gives it so changed by the transposition of the words, that the meaning is reversed; yet this is so artfully done by the author, that it is exactly as an obstinate child would answer, who knows his lesson, yet does not choose to say it. In the last scene, horses in rich trappings and carriages covered with gold are introduced, and the good children are to ride in them and be Lord Mayors, Lords, &c.; Cain and the bad ones are to be made cobblers and tinkers, and only to associate with such.

This, with numberless others, was written by Hans Sachs. Our simple ancestors, firm in their faith, and pure in their morals, were only amused by these pleasantries, as they seemed to them, and neither they nor the reformers feared their having any influence hostile to religion. When I was many years back in the north of Germany, there were several innocent superstitions in practice.

Among others at Christmas, presents used to be given to the children by the parents, and they were delivered on Christmas day by a person who personated, and was supposed by the children to be, Christ: early on Christmas morning he called, knocking loudly at the door, and (having received his instructions) left presents for the good and a rod for the bad. Those who have since been in Germany have found this custom relinquished; it was considered profane and irrational. Yet they have not found the children better, nor the mothers more careful of their offspring; they have not found their devotion more fervent, their faith more strong, nor their morality more pure.*

LECTURE III.

The Troubadours—Boccaccio—Petrarch— .Pulci—Chaucer—Spenser.

THE last Lecture was allotted to an investigation into the origin and character of a species of poetry, the least influenced of any by the literature of Greece and Rome,—that in which the portion contributed by the Gothic conquerors, the pre-

---

* See this custom of Knecht Rupert more minutely described in Mr. Coleridge's own letter from Germany, published in the 2nd vol. of the Friend, p. 320. *Ed.*

dilections and general tone or habit of thought and feeling, brought by our remote ancestors with them from the forests of Germany, or the deep dells and rocky mountains of Norway, are the most prominent. In the present Lecture I must introduce you to a species of poetry, which had its birth-place near the centre of Roman glory, and in which, as might be anticipated, the influences of the Greek and Roman muse are far more conspicuous,—as great, indeed, as the efforts of intentional imitation on the part of the poets themselves could render them. But happily for us and for their own fame, the intention of the writers as men is often at complete variance with the genius of the same men as poets. To the force of their intention we owe their mythological ornaments, and the greater definiteness of their imagery; and their passion for the beautiful, the voluptuous, and the artificial, we must in part attribute to the same intention, but in part likewise to their natural dispositions and tastes. For the same climate and many of the same circumstances were acting on them, which had acted on the great classics, whom they were endeavouring to imitate. But the love of the marvellous, the deeper sensibility, the higher reverence for womanhood, the characteristic spirit of sentiment and courtesy, — these were the heir-looms of nature, which still regained the ascendant, whenever the use of the living mother-language enabled the inspired poet to appear instead of the toilsome scholar.

From this same union, in which the soul (if I may dare so express myself) was Gothic, while the outward forms and a majority of the words themselves, were the reliques of the Roman, arose the Romance, or romantic language, in which the Troubadours or Love-singers of Provence sang and wrote, and the different dialects of which have been modified into the modern Italian, Spanish, and Portuguese; while the language of the Trouveurs, Trouveres, or Norman-French poets, forms the intermediate link between the Romance or modified Roman, and the Teutonic, including the Dutch, Danish, Swedish, and the upper and lower German, as being the modified Gothic. And as the northernmost extreme of the Norman-French, or that part of the link in which it formed on the Teutonic, we must take the Norman-English minstrels and metrical romances, from the greater predominance of the Anglo-Saxon Gothic in the derivation of the words. I mean, that the language of the English metrical romance is less romanized, and has fewer words, not originally of a northern origin, than the same romances in the Norman-French; which is the more striking, because the former were for the most part translated from the latter; the authors of which seem to have eminently merited their name of Trouveres, or inventors. Thus then we have a chain with two rings or staples: — at the southern end there is the Roman, or Latin; at the northern end the Keltic, Teutonic, or Gothic; and the links beginning with the southern end, are the Romance, including the Provençal, the Italian, Spanish, and Portuguese, with their different dialects, then the Norman-French, and lastly the English.

My object in adverting to the Italian poets, is not so much for their own sakes, in which point of view Dante and Ariosto alone would have acquired separate Lectures, but for the elucidation of the merits of our countrymen, as to what extent we must consider them as fortunate imitators of their Italian predecessors, and in what points they have the higher claims of original genius. Of Dante, I am to speak elsewhere. Of Boccaccio, who has little interest as a metrical poet in any respect, and none for my present purpose, except, perhaps, as the reputed inventor or introducer of the octave stanza in his Teseide, it will be sufficient to say, that we owe to him the subjects of numerous poems taken from his famous tales, the happy art of narration, and the still greater merit of a depth and fineness in the workings of the passions, in which last excellence, as likewise in the wild and imaginative character of the situations, his almost neglected romances appear to me greatly to excel his far famed Decameron. To him, too, we owe the more doubtful merit of having introduced into the Italian prose, and by the authority of his name and the influence of his example, more or less throughout Europe, the long interwoven periods, and archi-

tectural structure which arose from the very nature
of their language in the Greek writers, but which
already in the Latin orators and historians, had betrayed a species of effort, a foreign something,
which had been superinduced on the language, instead of growing out of it ; and which was far too
alien from that individualizing and confederating,
yet not blending, character of the North, to become
permanent, although its magnificence and stateliness
were objects of admiration and occasional imitation.
This style diminished the control of the writer over
the inner feelings of men, and created too great a
chasm between the body and the life ; and hence
especially it was abandoned by Luther.

But lastly, to Boccaccio's sanction we must trace
a large portion of the mythological pedantry and
incongruous paganisms, which for so long a period
deformed the poetry, even of the truest poets.   To
such an extravagance did Boccaccio himself carry
this folly, that in a romance of chivalry he has uni-
formly styled God the Father Jupiter, our Saviour Apollo, and the Evil Being Pluto.   But for
this there might be some excuse pleaded.   I dare
make none for the gross and disgusting licentiousness, the daring profaneness, which rendered the
Decameron of Boccaccio the parent of a hundred
worse children, fit to be classed among the enemies
of the human race ; which poisons Ariosto—(for
that I may not speak oftener than necessary of so
odious a subject, I mention it here once for all)—

which interposes a painful mixture in the humour of Chaucer, and which has once or twice seduced even our pure-minded Spenser into a grossness, as heterogeneous from the spirit of his great poem, as it was alien to the delicacy of his morals.

PETRARCH.

Born at Arezzo, 1304.—Died 1374.

Petrarch was the final blossom and perfection of the Troubadours. See Biog. Lit. vol. ii. p. 27, &c.

NOTES ON PETRARCH'S * SONNETS, CANZONES, &c.

VOL. I.

Good.

SONNET. 1. Voi, ch' ascoltate, &c.
7. La gola, e 'l sonno, &c.
11. Se la mia vita, &c.
12. Quando fra l'altre, &c.
18. Vergognando talor, &c.
25. Quanto più m' avvicino, &c.
28. Solo e pensoso, &c.
29. S' io credessi, &c.
CANZ. 14. Sì è debile il filo, &c.

---

* These notes, by Mr. C., are written in a Petrarch in my possession, and are of some date before 1812. It is hoped that they will not seem ill placed here. *Ed.*

Pleasing.

BALL. 1. Lassare il velo, &c.
CANZ. 1. Nel dolce tempo, &c.

This poem was imitated by our old Herbert;* it is
ridiculous in the thoughts, but simple and sweet in
diction.

Dignified.

CANZ. 2. O aspettata in ciel, &c.
9. Gentil mia Donna, &c.

The first half of this ninth canzone is exquisite;
and in canzone 8, the nine lines beginning

O poggi, o valli, &c.

to *cura*, are expressed with vigour and chastity.

CANZ. 9. Daquel dì innanzi a me medesmo piacqui,
Empiendo d'un pensier' alto, e soave
Quel core, ond' hanno i begli occhi la chiave.

Note. O that the Pope would take these eternal
keys, which so for ever turn the bolts on the finest
passages of true passion !

VOL. II.

CANZ. 1. Che debb' io far? &c.

Very good; but not equal, I think, to Canzone 2,

Amor, se vuoi ch' i' torni, &c.

---

* If George Herbert is meant, I can find nothing like an
imitation of this canzone in his poems. *Ed.*

though less faulty. With the omission of half-a-dozen conceits and Petrarchisms of *hooks*, *baits*, *flames*, and *torches*, this second canzone is a bold and impassioned lyric, and leaves no doubt in my mind of Petrarch's having possessed a true poetic genius. *Utinam deleri possint sequentia :—*

L. 17—19. ———— e la soave fiamma
Ch' ancor, lasso ! m' infiamma
Essendo spenta, or che fea dunque ardendo?

L. 54—56. ———— ov' erano a tutt' ore
Disposti gli ami ov' io fui preso, e l'esca
Ch' i' bramo sempre.

L. 76—79. ———— onde l' accese
Saette uscivan d' invisibil foco,
E ragion temean poco;
Chè contra 'l ciel non val difesa umana.

And the lines 86, 87.
Poser' in dubbio, a cui
Devesse il pregio di più laude darsi—

are rather flatly worded.

LUIGI PULCI.

Born at Florence, 1431.—Died about 1487.

Pulci was of one of the noblest families in Florence, reported to be one of the Frankish stocks which remained in that city after the departure of Charlemagne:—

Pulcia Gallorum soboles descendit in urbem,
Clara quidem bello, sacris nec inhospita Musis.
Verino de illustrat. Cort. Flor. III. v. 118.

Members of this family were five times elected to
the Priorate, one of the highest honours of the republic. Pulci had two brothers, and one of their
wives, Antonia, who were all poets :—

> Carminibus patriis notissima Pulcia proles;
> Quis non hanc urbem Musarum dicat amicam,
> Si tres producat fratres domus una poetas?
>
>   Ib. II. v. 241.

Luigi married Lucrezia di Uberto, of the Albizzi
family, and was intimate with the great men of his
time, but more especially with Angelo Politian, and
Lorenzo the Magnificent. His Morgante has been
attributed, in part at least,* to the assistance of
Marsilius Ficinus, and by others the whole has been
attributed to Politian. The first conjecture is utterly
improbable ; the last is possible, indeed, on account
of the licentiousness of the poem ; but there are no
direct grounds for believing it. The Morgante
Maggiore is the first proper romance; although,
perhaps, Pulci had the Teseide before him. The
story is taken from the fabulous history of Turpin ;
and if the author had any distinct object, it seems to
have been that of making himself merry with the absurdities of the old romancers. The Morgante sometimes makes you think of Rabelais. It contains the
most remarkable guess or allusion upon the subject
of America that can be found in any book published

---

* Meaning the 25th canto. *Ed.*

before the discovery.* The well known passage in
the tragic Seneca is not to be compared with it.
The *copia verborum* of the mother Florentine
tongue, and the easiness of his style, afterwards
brought to perfection by Berni, are the chief merits
of Pulci; his chief demerit is his heartless spirit of
jest and buffoonery, by which sovereigns and their
courtiers were flattered by the degradation of nature, and the *impossibilification* of a pretended virtue.

---

* The reference is, of course, to the following stanzas:—

    Disse Astarotte: un error lungo e fioco
    Per molti secol non ben conosciuto,
    Fa che si dice d' Ercol le colonne,
    E che più là molti periti sonne.
Sappi che questa opinione è vana;
    Perchè più oltre navicar si puote,
    Però che l' acqua in ogni parte è piana,
    Benchè la terra abbi forma di ruote:
    Era più grossa allor la gente humana;
    Talche potrebbe arrosirne le gote
    Ercule ancor d' aver posti que' segni,
    Perchè più oltre passeranno i legni.
E puossi andar giù ne l' altro emisperio,
    Però che al centro ogni cosa reprime;
    Sì che la terra per divin misterio
    Sospesa sta fra le stelle sublime,
    E là giù son città, castella, e imperio;
    Ma nol cognobbon quelle genti prime:
    Vedi che il sol di camminar s' affretta,
    Dove io ti dico che là giù s' aspetta.
E come un segno surge in Oriente,
    Un altro cade con mirabil arte,

CHAUCER.

Born in London, 1328.—Died 1400.*

Chaucer must be read with an eye to the Norman-French Trouveres, of whom he is the best representative in English. He had great powers of invention. As in Shakspeare, his characters represent classes, but in a different manner; Shakspeare's characters are the representatives of the interior nature of humanity, in which some element has become so predominant as to destroy the health of the mind; whereas Chaucer's are rather representatives of classes of manners. He is therefore more led to individualize in a mere personal sense. Observe Chaucer's love of nature; and how hap-

---

Come si vede qua ne l' Occidente,
Però che il ciel giustamente comparte;
Antipodi appellata è quella gente;
Adora il sole e Jupiterre e Marte,
E piante e animal come voi hanno,
E spesso insieme gran battaglie fanno.

C. XXV. st. 228, &c.

The Morgante was printed in 1488. *Ed.* Another very curious anticipation, said to have been first noticed by Amerigo Vespucci, occurs in Dante's *Purgatorio:*

I mi volsi a man destra e posi mente
All 'altro polo: e vidi quattro stelle
Non viste mai, fuor ch' alla prima gente.

C. I. l. 22-4.

* From Mr. Green's note. *Ed.*

pily the subject of his main work is chosen. When you reflect that the company in the Decameron have retired to a place of safety, from the raging of a pestilence, their mirth provokes a sense of their unfeelingness; whereas in Chaucer nothing of this sort occurs, and the scheme of a party on a pilgrimage, with different ends and occupations, aptly allows of the greatest variety of expression in the tales.

SPENSER.

Born in London, 1553.—Died 1599.

There is this difference, among many others, between Shakspeare and Spenser:—Shakspeare is never coloured by the customs of his age; what appears of contemporary character in him is merely negative; it is just not something else. He has none of the fictitious realities of the classics, none of the grotesquenesses of chivalry, none of the allegory of the middle ages; there is no sectarianism either of politics or religion, no miser, no witch, — no common witch,—no astrology—nothing impermanent of however long duration; but he stands like the yew tree in Lorton vale, which has known so many ages that it belongs to none in particular; a living image of endless self-reproduction, like the immortal tree of Malabar. In Spenser the spirit of chivalry is entirely predominant, although with a much greater infusion of the poet's own individual self

into it than is found in any other writer. He has
the wit of the southern with the deeper inwardness
of the northern genius.

No one can appreciate Spenser without some reflection on the nature 'of allegorical writing. The
mere etymological meaning of the word, allegory,—
to talk of one thing and thereby convey another,—
is too wide. The true sense is this,—the employment of one set of agents and images to convey in
disguise a moral meaning, with a likeness to the
imagination, but with a difference to the understanding,—those agents and images being so combined
as to form a homogeneous whole. This distinguishes
it from metaphor, which is part of an allegory.
But allegory is not properly distinguishable from
fable, otherwise than as the first includes the second, as a genus its species; for in a fable there
must be nothing but what is universally known and
acknowledged, but in an allegory there may be that
which is new and not previously admitted. The
pictures of the great masters, especially of the
Italian schools, are genuine allegories. Amongst
the classics, the multitude of their gods either precluded allegory altogether, or else made every thing
allegory, as in the Hesiodic Theogonia; for you
can scarcely distinguish between power and the personification of power. The Cupid and Psyche of,
or found in, Apuleius, is a phænomenon. It is the
Platonic mode of accounting for the fall of man.

The Battle of the Soul* by Prudentius is an early instance of Christian allegory.

Narrative allegory is distinguished from mythology as reality from symbol; it is, in short, the proper intermedium between person and personification. Where it is too strongly individualized, it ceases to be allegory; this is often felt in the Pilgrim's Progress, where the characters are real persons with nick names. Perhaps one of the most curious warnings against another attempt at narrative allegory on a great scale, may be found in Tasso's account of what he himself intended in and by his Jerusalem Delivered.

As characteristic of Spenser, I would call your particular attention in the first place to the indescribable sweetness and fluent projection of his verse, very clearly distinguishable from the deeper and more inwoven harmonies of Shakspeare and Milton. This stanza is a good instance of what I mean :—

> Yet she, most faithfull ladie, all this while
> Forsaken, wofull, solitarie mayd,
> Far from all peoples preace, as in exile,
> In wildernesse and wastfull deserts strayd
> To seeke her knight; who, subtily betrayd
> Through that late vision which th' enchaunter wrought,
> Had her abandond; she, of nought affrayd,
> Through woods and wastnes wide him daily sought,
> Yet wished tydinges none of him unto her brought.
>   F. Qu. B. I. c. 3. st. 3.

---

* Psychomachia. *Ed.*

2. Combined with this sweetness and fluency, the scientific construction of the metre of the Faery Queene is very noticeable.. One of Spenser's arts is that of alliteration, and he uses it with great effect in doubling the impression of an image :—

> In wildernesse and wastful deserts,—
> Through woods and wastnes wilde,—
> They passe the bitter waves of Acheron,
> Where many soules sit wailing woefully,
> And come to fiery flood of Phlegeton,
> Whereas the damned ghosts in torments fry,
> And with sharp shrilling shrieks doth bootlesse cry,—&c.

He is particularly given to an alternate alliteration, which is, perhaps, when well used, a great secret in melody :—

> A ramping lyon rushed suddenly,—
> And sad to see her sorrowful constraint,—
> And on the grasse her daintie limbes did lay,—&c.

You cannot read a page of the Faery Queene, if you read for that purpose, without perceiving the intentional alliterativeness of the words; and yet so skilfully is this managed, that it never strikes any unwarned ear as artificial, or other than the result of the necessary movement of the verse.

3. Spenser displays great skill in harmonizing his descriptions of external nature and actual incidents with the allegorical character and epic activity of the poem. Take these two beautiful passages as illustrations of what I mean :—

> By this the northerne wagoner had set
> His sevenfol teme behind the stedfast starre

That was in ocean waves yet never wet,
But firme is fixt, and sendeth light from farre
To all that in the wide deepe wandring arre;
And chearefull chaunticlere with his note shrill
Had warned once, that Phœbus' fiery carre
In hast was climbing up the easterne hill,
Full envious that Night so long his roome did fill;

When those accursed messengers of hell,
That feigning dreame, and that faire-forged spright
Came, &c. B. I. c. 2. st. 1.

　　*　　　　*　　　　*

At last, the golden orientall gate
Of greatest Heaven gan to open fayre;
And Phœbus, fresh as brydegrome to his mate,
Came dauncing forth, shaking his deawie hayre;
And hurld his glistring beams through gloomy ayre.
Which when the wakeful Elfe perceiv'd, streightway
He started up, and did him selfe prepayre
In sunbright armes and battailons array;
For with that Pagan proud he combat will that day.

Ib. c. 5. st. 2.

Observe also the exceeding vividness of Spenser's descriptions. They are not, in the true sense of the word, picturesque; but are composed of a wondrous series of images, as in our dreams. Compare the following passage with any thing you may remember *in pari materia* in Milton or Shakspeare:—

His haughtie helmet, horrid all with gold,
Both glorious brightnesse and great terrour bredd;
For all the crest a dragon did enfold
With greedie pawes, and over all did spredd
His golden winges; his dreadfull hideous hedd,
Close couched on the bever, seemd to throw
From flaming mouth bright sparkles fiery redd,

2　　　　　　　D

That suddeine horrour to faint hartes did show;
And scaly tayle was stretcht adowne his back full low.

Upon the top of all his loftie crest
A bounch of haires discolourd diversly,
With sprinkled pearle and gold full richly drest,
Did shake, and seemd to daunce for jollitie; .
Like to an almond tree ymounted hye
On top of greene Selinis all alone,
With blossoms brave bedecked daintily,
Whose tender locks do tremble every one
At everie little breath that under heaven is blowne.

Ib. c. 7. st. 31-2.

4. You will take especial note of the marvellous
independence and true imaginative absence of all
particular space or time in the Faery Queene.   It
is in the domains neither of history or geography ;
it is ignorant of all artificial boundary, all material
obstacles ; it is truly in land of Faery, that is, of
mental space. The poet has placed you in a dream,
a charmed sleep, and you neither wish, nor have
the power, to inquire where you are, or how you
got there. It reminds me of some lines of my own :—

Oh ! would to Alla !
The raven or the sea-mew were appointed
To bring me food !—or rather that my soul
Might draw in life from the universal air !
It were a lot divine in some small skiff
Along some ocean's boundless solitude
To float for ever with a careless course
And think myself the only being alive !

Remorse, Act iv. sc. 3.

Indeed Spenser himself, in the conduct of his great

poem, may be represented under the same image,
his symbolizing purpose being his mariner's compass :—

> As pilot well expert in perilous wave,
> That to a stedfast starre his course hath bent,
> When foggy mistes or cloudy tempests have
> The faithfull light of that faire lampe yblent,
> And coverd Heaven with hideous dreriment;
> Upon his card and compas firmes his eye,
> The maysters of his long experiment,
> And to them does the steddy helme apply,
> Bidding his winged vessell fairely forward fly.
>
> B. II. c. 7. st. 1.

So the poet through the realms of allegory.

5. You should note the quintessential character
of Christian chivalry in all his characters, but more
especially in his women. The Greeks, except, perhaps, in Homer, seem to have had no way of making their women interesting, but by unsexing them,
as in the instances of the tragic Medea, Electra,
&c. Contrast such characters with Spenser's Una,
who exhibits no prominent feature, has no particu-
larization, but produces the same feeling that a
statue does, when contemplated at a distance :—

> From her fayre head her fillet she undight,
> And layd her stole aside: her angels face,
> As the great eye of Heaven, shyned bright,
> And made a sunshine in the shady place;
> Did never mortal eye behold such heavenly grace.
>
> B. I. c. 3. st. 4.

6. In Spenser we see the brightest and purest
form of that nationality which was so common a

characteristic of our elder poets. There is nothing unamiable, nothing contemptuous of others, in it. To glorify their country—to elevate England into a queen, an empress of the heart—this was their passion and object; and how dear and important an object it was or may be, let Spain, in the recollection of her Cid, declare! There is a great magic in national names. What a damper to all interest is a list of native East Indian merchants! Unknown names are non-conductors; they stop all sympathy. No one of our poets has touched this string more exquisitely than Spenser; especially in his chronicle of the British Kings (B. II. c. 10.), and the marriage of the Thames with the Medway (B. IV. c. 11.), in both which passages the mere names constitute half the pleasure we receive. To the same feeling we must in particular attribute Spenser's sweet reference to Ireland:—

> Ne thence the Irishe rivers absent were;
> Sith no lesse famous than the rest they be, &c. Ib.
>
> *   *   *   *
>
> And Mulla mine, whose waves I whilom taught to weep.
> Ib.

And there is a beautiful passage of the same sort in the Colin Clout's Come Home Again:—

> "One day," quoth he, "I sat, as was my trade,
> Under the foot of Mole," &c.

Lastly, the great and prevailing character of Spenser's mind is fancy under the conditions of

imagination, as an ever present but not always active power. He has an imaginative fancy, but he
has not imagination, in kind or degree, as Shakspeare and Milton have; the boldest effort of his
powers in this way is the character of Talus.[*]
Add .to this a feminine tenderness and almost
maidenly purity of feeling, and above all, a deep
moral earnestness which produces a believing sympathy and acquiescence in the reader, and you have
a tolerably adequate view of Spenser's intellectual
being.

LECTURE VII.

Ben Jonson, Beaumont and Fletcher, and Massinger.

A CONTEMPORARY is rather an ambigu-
ous term, when applied to authors. It may
simply mean that one man lived and wrote while
another was yet alive, however deeply the former
may have been indebted to the latter as his model.
There have been instances in the literary world
that might remind a botanist of a singular sort of
parasite plant, which rises above ground, independent and unsupported, an apparent original; but
trace its roots, and you will find the fibres all ter-

---

[*] B. 5. Legend of Artegall. *Ed.*

minating in the root of another plant at an unsuspected distance, which, perhaps, from want of sun and genial soil, and the loss of sap, has scarcely been able to peep above the ground.—Or the word may mean those whose compositions were contemporaneous in such a sense as to preclude all likelihood of the one having borrowed from the other. In the latter sense I should call Ben Jonson a contemporary of Shakspeare, though he long survived him; while I should prefer the phrase of immediate successors for Beaumont and Fletcher, and Massinger, though they too were Shakspeare's contemporaries in the former sense.

BEN JONSON.*

Born, 1574.—Died, 1637.

Ben Jonson is original; he is, indeed, the only one of the great dramatists of that day who was not either directly produced, or very greatly modified, by Shakspeare. In truth, he differs from our great master in every thing—in form and in substance—and betrays no tokens of his proximity. He is not original in the same way as Shakspeare is original; but after a fashion of his own, Ben Jonson is most truly original.

The characters in his plays are, in the strictest sense of the term, abstractions. Some very pro-

---

* From Mr. Green's note. *Ed.*

minent feature is taken from the whole man, and that single feature or humour is made the basis upon which the entire character is built up. Ben Jonson's *dramatis personæ* are almost as fixed as the masks of the ancient actors; you know from the first scene — sometimes from the list of names —exactly what every one of them is to be. He was a very accurately observing man; but he cared only to observe what was external or open to, and likely to impress, the senses. He individualizes, not so much, if at all, by the exhibition of moral or intellectual differences, as by the varieties and contrasts of manners, modes of speech and tricks of temper; as in such characters as Puntarvolo, Bobadill, &c.

I believe there is not one whim or affectation in common life noted in any memoir of that age which may not be found drawn and framed in some corner or other of Ben Jonson's dramas; and they have this merit, in common with Hogarth's prints, that not a single circumstance is introduced in them which does not play upon, and help to bring out, the dominant humour or humours of the piece. Indeed I ought very particularly to call your attention to the extraordinary skill shown by Ben Jonson in contriving situations for the display of his characters.† In fact, his care and anxiety in this matter

---

† "In Jonson's comic inventions," says Schlegel, "a spirit of observation is manifested more than fancy." Vol. 4. p. 93.

led him to do what scarcely any of the dramatists
of that age did—that is, invent his plots. It is not
a first perusal that suffices for the full perception
of the elaborate artifice of the plots of the Alche-
mist and the Silent Woman;—that of the former
is absolute perfection for a necessary entanglement,
and an unexpected, yet natural, evolution.

Ben Jonson exhibits a sterling English diction,
and he has with great skill contrived varieties of
construction; but his style is rarely sweet or harmonious, in consequence of his labour at point and
strength being so evident. In all his works, in
verse or prose, there is an extraordinary opulence
of thought; but it is the produce of an amassing
power in the author, and not of a growth from within. Indeed a large proportion of Ben Jonson's
thoughts may be traced to classic or obscure modern writers, by those who are learned and curious
enough to follow the steps of this robust, surly, and
observing dramatist.

BEAUMONT. Born. 1586.*—Died, 1615-16.
FLETCHER. Born, 1579.—Died, 1625.

Mr. Weber, to whose taste, industry, and appropriate erudition, we owe, I will not say the best,
(for that would be saying little,) but a good, edition

---

* Mr. Dyce thinks that " Beaumont's birth ought to be
fixed at a somewhat earlier date," because, in the Funeral
Certificate on the decease of his father, dated 22nd April,

of Beaumont and Fletcher, has complimented the Philaster, which he himself describes as inferior to the Maid's Tragedy by the same writers, as but little below the noblest of Shakspeare's plays, Lear, Macbeth, Othello, &c. and consequently implying the equality, at least, of the Maid's Tragedy ;—and an eminent living critic,—who in the manly wit, strong sterling sense, and robust style of his original works, had presented the best possible credentials of office, as *chargé d'affaires* of literature in general,—and who by his edition of Massinger— a work in which there was more for an editor to do, and in which more was actually well done, than in any similar work within my knowledge—has proved an especial right of authority in the appreciation of dramatic poetry, and hath potentially a double voice with the public in his own right and in that of the critical synod, where, as *princeps senatus*, he possesses it by his prerogative,—has affirmed that Shakspeare's superiority to his contemporaries rests on his superior wit alone, while in all the other, and, as I should deem, higher excellencies of the drama, character, pathos, depth of thought, &c. he is equalled by Beaumont and Fletcher, Ben Jonson, and Massinger ! *

1598, he is said to be *of the age of thirteen years or more ;* and because "at the age of twelve, 4th February, 1596-7," according to Wood's Ath. Oxon, " he was admitted a gentleman-commoner of Broadgates Hall."

* See Mr. Gifford's introduction to his edition of Massinger. *Ed.*

Of wit I am engaged to treat in another Lecture. It is a genus of many species; and at present I shall only say, that the species which is predominant in Shakspeare, is so completely Shakspearian, and in its essence so interwoven with all his other characteristic excellencies, that I am equally incapable of comprehending, both how it can be detached from his other powers, and how, being disparate in kind from the wit of contemporary dramatists, it can be compared with theirs in degree. And again —the detachment and the practicability of the comparison being granted—I should, I confess, be rather inclined to concede the contrary;—and in the most common species of wit, and in the ordinary application of the term, to yield this particular palm to Beaumont and Fletcher, whom here and hereafter I take as one poet with two names,—leaving undivided what a rare love and still rarer congeniality have united. At least, I have never been able to distinguish the presence of Fletcher during the life of Beaumont, nor the absence of Beaumont during the survival of Fletcher.

But waiving, or rather deferring this question, I protest against the remainder of the position *in toto*. And indeed, whilst I can never, I trust, show myself blind to the various merits of Jonson, Beaumont and Fletcher, and Massinger, or insensible to the greatness of the merits which they possess in common, or to the specific excellencies which give to each of the three a worth of his own,—I confess,

that one main object of this Lecture was to prove
that Shakspeare's eminence is his own, and not that
of his age;—even as the pine-apple, the melon, and
the gourd may grow on the same bed;—yea, the
same circumstances of warmth and soil may be necessary to their full development, yet do not account
for the golden hue, the ambrosial flavour, the perfect shape of the pine-apple, or the tufted crown on
its head. Would that those, who seek to twist it
off, could but promise us in this instance to make
it the germ of an equal successor!

What had a grammatical and logical consistency
for the ear,—what could be put together and represented to the eye—these poets took from the
ear and eye, unchecked by any intuition of an inward impossibility;—just as a man might put together a quarter of an orange, a quarter of an apple,
and the like of a lemon and a pomegranate, and
make it look like one round diverse-coloured fruit.
But nature, which works from within by evolution
and assimilation according to a law, cannot do so,
nor could Shakspeare; for he too worked in the
spirit of nature, by evolving the germ from within
by the imaginative power according to an idea.
For as the power of seeing is to light, so is an idea
in mind to a law in nature. They are correlatives,
which suppose each other.

The plays of Beaumont and Fletcher are mere
aggregations without unity; in the Shakspearian
drama there is a vitality which grows and evolves

itself from within,— a key note which guides and controls the harmonies throughout. What is Lear? —It is storm and tempest—the thunder at first grumbling in the far horizon, then gathering around us, and at length bursting in fury over our heads, —succeeded by a breaking of the clouds for a while, a last flash of lightning, the closing in of night, and the single hope of darkness! And Romeo and Juliet?—It is a spring day, gusty and beautiful in the morn, and closing like an April evening with the song of the nightingale ;*—whilst Macbeth is deep and earthy,—composed to the subterranean music of a troubled conscience, which converts every thing into the wild and fearful!

Doubtless from mere observation, or from the occasional similarity of the writer's own character more or less in Beaumont and Fletcher, and other such writers will happen to be in correspondence with nature, and still more in apparent compatibility with it. But yet the false source is always discoverable, first by the gross contradictions to nature in so many other parts, and secondly, by the want of the impression which Shakspeare makes, that the thing said not only might have been said, but that nothing else could be substituted, so as to excite the same sense of its exquisite propriety. I have

---

* Was der Duft eines südlichen Frühlings berauschendes, der Gesang der Nachtigall sehnsüchtiges, das erste Aufblühung der Rose wollüstiges hat, das athmet aus diesem Gedicht. Schlegel's *Dram. Vorlesungen.* Vol. III. p. 107.

always thought the conduct and expressions of Othello and Iago in the last scene, when Iago is brought in prisoner, a wonderful instance of Shakspeare's consummate judgment :—

> *Oth.* I look down towards his feet ;—but that's a fable.
>   If that thou be'st a devil, I cannot kill thee.
> *Iago.* I bleed, Sir ; but not kill'd.
> *Oth.* I am not sorry neither.

Think what a volley of execrations and defiances Beaumont and Fletcher would have poured forth here !

Indeed Massinger and Ben Jonson are both more perfect in their kind than Beaumont and Fletcher ; the former in the story and affecting incidents ; the latter in the exhibition of manners and peculiarities, whims in language, and vanities of appearance.

There is, however, a diversity of the most dangerous kind here. Shakspeare shaped his characters out of the nature within ; but we cannot so safely say, out of his own nature as an individual person. No ! this latter is itself but a *natura naturata*,—an effect, a product, not a power. It was Shakspeare's prerogative to have the universal, which is potentially in each particular, opened out to him, the *homo generalis*, not as an abstraction from observation of a variety of men, but as the substance capable of endless modifications, of which his own personal existence was but one, and to use this one as the eye that beheld the other, and as the tongue that could convey the discovery. There is

no greater or more common vice in dramatic writers than to draw out of themselves. How I—alone
and in the self sufficiency of my study, as all men
are apt to be proud in their dreams—should like to
be talking *king!* Shakspeare, in composing, had
no *I*, but the *I* representative. In Beaumont and
Fletcher you have descriptions of characters by the
poet rather than the characters themselves: we are
told, and impressively told, of their being; but we
rarely or never feel that they actually are.

Beaumont and Fletcher are the most lyrical of
our dramatists. I think their comedies the best
part of their works, although there are scenes of
very deep tragic interest in some of their plays. I
particularly recommend Monsieur Thomas for good
pure comic humour.

There is, occasionally, considerable license in
their dramas; and this opens a subject much need-
ing vindication and sound exposition, but which is
beset with such difficulties for a Lecturer, that I
must pass it by. Only as far as Shakspeare is
concerned, I own, I can with less pain admit a
fault in him than beg an excuse for it. I will not,
therefore, attempt to palliate the grossness that actually exists in his plays by the customs of his age,
or by the far greater coarseness of all his contemporaries, excepting Spenser, who is himself not
wholly blameless, though nearly so;—for I place
Shakspeare's merit on being of no age. But I would
clear away what is, in my judgment, not his, as that

scene of the Porter* in Macbeth, and many other such passages, and abstract what is coarse in manners only, and all that which from the frequency of our own vices, we associate with his words. If this were truly done, little that could be justly reprehensible would remain. Compare the vile comments, offensive and defensive, on Pope's

Lust thro' some gentle strainers, &c.

with the worst thing in Shakspeare, or even in Beaumont and Fletcher; and then consider how unfair the attack is on our old dramatists; especially because it is an attack that cannot be properly answered in that presence in which an answer would be most desirable, from the painful nature of one part of the position; but this very pain is almost a demonstration of its falsehood!

MASSINGER.
Born at Salisbury, 1584.—Died, 1640.

With regard to Massinger, observe,

1. The vein of satire on the times; but this is not as in Shakspeare, where the natures evolve themselves according to their incidental disproportions, from excess, deficiency, or mislocation, of one or more of the component elements; but is merely satire on what is attributed to them by others.

---

* Act ii. sc. 3.

2. His excellent metre—a better model for dramatists in general to imitate than Shakspeare's,—even if a dramatic taste existed in the frequenters of the stage, and could be gratified in the present size and management, or rather mismanagement, of the two patent theatres. I do not mean that Massinger's verse is superior to Shakspeare's or equal to it. Far from it; but it is much more easily constructed, and may be more successfully adopted by writers in the present day. It is the nearest approach to the language of real life at all compatible with a fixed metre. In Massinger, as in all our poets before Dryden, in order to make harmonious verse in the reading, it is absolutely necessary that the meaning should be understood; —when the meaning is once seen, then the harmony is perfect. Whereas in Pope and in most of the writers who followed in his school, it is the mechanical metre which determines the sense.

3. The impropriety, and indecorum of demeanour in his favourite characters, as in Bertoldo in the Maid of Honour, who is a swaggerer, talking to his sovereign what no sovereign could endure, and to gentlemen what no gentlemen would answer without pulling his nose.

4. Shakspeare's Ague-cheek, Osric, &c. are displayed through others, in the course of social intercourse, by the mode of their performing some office in which they are employed; but Massinger's *Sylli* come forward to declare themselves fools *ad arbi-*

trium auctoris, and so the diction always needs the *subintelligitur* (' the man looks as if he thought so and so,') expressed in the language of the satirist, and not in that of the man himself:—

> *Sylli.* You may, madam,
> Perhaps, believe that I in this use art
> To make you dote upon me, by exposing
> My more than most rare features to your view;
> But I, as I have ever done, deal simply,
> A mark of sweet simplicity, ever noted
> In the family of the Syllis. Therefore, lady,
> Look not with too much contemplation on me;
> If you do, you are in the suds.
>
> Maid of Honour, Act i. sc. 2.

The author mixes his own feelings and judgments concerning the presumed fool; but the man himself, till mad, fights up against them, and betrays, by his attempts to modify them, that he is no fool at all, but one gifted with activity and copiousness of thought, image and expression, which belong not to a fool, but to a man of wit making himself merry with his own character.

5. There is an utter want of preparation in the decisive acts of Massinger's characters, as in Camiola and Aurelia in the Maid of Honour. Why? Because the *dramatis personæ* were all planned each by itself. Whereas in Shakspeare, the play is *syngenesia*; each character has, indeed, a life of its own, and is an *individuum* of itself, but yet an organ of the whole, as the heart in the human

2   E

B. d.
Bed does
h 87,
629
619

body. Shakspeare was a great comparative anato-
mist.

Hence Massinger and all, indeed, but Shakspeare, take a dislike to their own characters, and
spite themselves upon them by making them talk
like fools or monsters; as Fulgentio in his visit to
Camiola, (Act ii. sc. 2.)   Hence too, in Massinger,
the continued flings at kings, courtiers, and all the
favourites of fortune, like one who had enough of
intellect to see injustice in his own inferiority in the
share of the good things of life, but not genius
enough to rise above it, and forget himself. Beaumont and Fletcher have the same vice in the opposite pole, a servility of sentiment and a spirit of
partizanship with the monarchical faction.

6. From the want of a guiding point in Massinger's characters, you never know what they are
about.   In fact they have no character.

7. Note the faultiness of his soliloquies, with
connectives and arrangements that have no other
motive but the fear lest the audience should not
understand him.

8. A play of Massinger's produces no one single
effect, whether arising from the spirit of the whole,
as in the As You Like It; or from any one indis-
putably prominent character, as Hamlet.   It is just
" which you like best, gentlemen !"

9. The unnaturally irrational passions and strange
whims of feeling which Massinger delights to draw,
deprive the reader of all sound interest in the cha-

racters;—as in Mathias in the Picture, and in other
instances.

10. The comic scenes in Massinger not only do
not harmonize with the tragic, not only interrupt
the feeling, but degrade the characters that are to
form any part in the action of the piece, so as to
render them unfit for any tragic interest. At least,
they do not concern, or act upon, or modify, the
principal characters. As when a gentleman is in-
sulted by a mere blackguard,—it is the same as if
any other accident of nature had occurred, a pig
run under his legs, or his horse thrown him. There
is no dramatic interest in it.

I like Massinger's comedies better than his tragedies, although where the situation requires it, he
often rises into the truly tragic and pathetic. He
excels in narration, and for the most part displays
his mere story with skill. But he is not a poet of
high imagination; he is like a Flemish painter, in
whose delineations objects appear as they do in nature, have the same force and truth, and produce
the same effect upon the spectator. But Shakspeare
is beyond this; he always by metaphors and figures
involves in the thing considered a universe of past
and possible experiences; he mingles earth, sea and
air, gives a soul to every thing, and at the same
time that he inspires human feelings, adds a dignity
in his images to human nature itself:—

> Full many a glorious morning have I seen
> Flatter the mountain tops with sovereign eye;

Kissing with golden face the meadows green,
Gilding pale streams with heavenly alchymy, &c.
33rd Sonnet.

NOTES ON MASSINGER.

Have I not over-rated Gifford's edition of Massinger?—Not,—if I have, as but just is, main reference to the restitution of the text; but yes, perhaps, if I were talking of the notes. These are more often wrong than right. In the Maid of Honour, Act i. sc. 5. Astutio describes Fulgentio as " A gentleman, yet no lord." Gifford supposes a transposition of the press for " No gentleman, yet a lord." But this would have no connection with what follows; and we have only to recollect that " lord" means a lord of lands, to see that the after lines are explanatory. He is a man of high birth, but no landed property; —as to the former, he is a distant branch of the blood royal;—as to the latter, his whole rent lies in a narrow compass, the king's ear! In the same scene the text stands :

> *Bert.* No! they are useful
> For your *imitation;*—I remember you, &c.;—

and Gifford condemns Mason's conjecture of ' initiation' as void of meaning and harmony. Now my ear deceives me if ' initiation' be not the right word. In fact, ' imitation' is utterly impertinent to all that follows. Bertoldo tells Antonio that he had been initiated in the manners suited to the court by two or three sacred beauties, and that a similar experience would be equally useful for his

initiation into the camp. Not a word of his imitation. Besides, I say the rhythm requires ' initiation,' and is lame as the verse now stands.

* Two or three tales, each in itself independent of
the others, and united only by making the persons
that are the agents in the story the *relations* of
those in the other, as when a bind-weed or thread
is twined round a bunch of flowers, each having its
own root — and this novel narrative in *dialogue* —
such is the *character* of Massinger's plays — That
the juxta-position and the tying together by a common thread, which goes round this and round that,
and then round them all, twine and intertwine, are
contrived ingeniously — that the component tales
are well chosen, and the whole well and conspicu-
ously told; so as to excite and sustain the mind
by kindling and keeping alive the curiosity of the
reader — that the language is most pure, equally
free from bookishness and from vulgarism, from
the peculiarities of the School, and the transiencies
of fashion, whether fine or coarse; that the rhythm
and metre are incomparably good, and form the
very model of dramatic versification, flexible and
seeming to rise out of the passions, so that whenever a line sounds immetrical, the speaker may
be certain he has recited it amiss, either that he
has misplaced or misproportioned the emphasis, or

---

* The notes on Massinger which follow were transcribed
from a copy of that dramatist's works, belonging to Mr. Gillman. I do not know whence the first was taken by the
original editor.

neglected the acceleration or retardation of the voice in the pauses (all which the mood or passion would have produced in the real Agent, and therefore demand from the Actor or {translator emulator}) and that read aright the blank verse is not less smooth than varied, a rich harmony, puzzling the fingers, but satisfying the ear — these are Massinger's characteristic merits. .

Among the varieties of blank verse Massinger is fond of the anapæst in the first and third foot, as :

" Tŏ yoŭr mōre | thăn m̄a | scŭlinĕ reā | sŏn
    thāt | commānds 'ĕm‖ —" *

                    The Guardian, Act i. sc. 2. .

Likewise of the second Pæon (ᴗ — ᴗᴗ) in the first foot followed by four trochees (— ᴗ) as :

" Sŏ greēdĭlȳ | lōng fŏr, | knōw thĕir |
        tītĭll | ātiŏns."   Ib. ib.

The emphasis too has a decided influence on the metre, and, contrary to the metres of the Greek and Roman classics, at least to all their more common sorts of verse, as the hexameter and hex and pentameter, Alchaic, Sapphic, &c. has an es-

---

* Gifford divides the lines in question thus:

" Command my sensual appetites.
   Calip.   As vassals to
Your more than masculine reason, that commands them."

But it is obviously better to make the first line end with " vassals," so as to give it only the one over-running syllable, which is so common in the last foot.

sential agency on the character of the feet and power of the verse. One instance only of this I recollect in Theocritus :

τα μῆ κᾰλᾰ κᾱλᾰ πῐφᾱντᾱι,

unless Homer's Ἄρες, Ἄρες, may (as I believe) be deemed another—For I cannot bring my ear to believe that Homer would have perpetrated such a cacophony as Ὦρες, Ἄρες.

" In feār | my chaasteetee | may be | sus-
       pected." | Ib. ib.

In short, musical notes are required to explain Massinger—metres in addition to prosody. When a speech is interrupted, or one of the characters speaks aside, the last syllable of the former speech and first of the succeeding Massinger counts but for one, because both are supposed to be spoken at the same moment.

" And felt the sweetness of't."
           " *How* her mouth runs over"
                Ib. ib.

Emphasis itself is twofold, the *rap* and the *drawl*, or the emphasis by quality of sound, and that by quantity — the hammer, and the spatula — the latter over 2, 3, 4 syllables or even a whole line. It is in this that the actors and speakers are generally speaking defective, they cannot equilibrate an emphasis, or spread it over a number of syllables, all emphasized, sometimes equally, sometimes unequally.

LECTURE VIII.

Don Quixote.

CERVANTES.

BORN at Madrid, 1547 ;—Shakspeare, 1564 ; both put off mortality on the same day, the 23rd of April, 1616,—the one in the sixty-ninth, the other in the fifty-second, year of his life. The resemblance in their physiognomies is striking, but with a predominance of acuteness in Cervantes, and of reflection in Shakspeare, which is the specific difference between the Spanish and English characters of mind.

I. The nature and eminence of Symbolical writing ;—

II. Madness, and its different sorts, (considered without pretension to medical science);—

To each of these, or at least to my own notions respecting them, I must devote a few words of explanation, in order to render the after critique on Don Quixote, the master work of Cervantes' and his country's genius, easily and throughout intelligible. This is not the least valuable, though it may most often be felt by us both as the heaviest and least entertaining portion of these critical disquisitions : for without it, I must have foregone one at

least of the two appropriate objects of a Lecture,
that of interesting you during its delivery, and of
leaving behind in your minds the germs of after-
thought, and the materials for future enjoyment.
To have been assured by several of my intelligent
auditors that they have reperused Hamlet or Othello ·
with increased satisfaction in consequence of the
new points of view in which I had placed those
characters—is the highest compliment I could receive or desire ; and should the address of this evening open out a new source of pleasure, or enlarge
the former in your perusal of Don Quixote, it will
compensate for the failure of any personal or temporary object.

I. The Symbolical cannot, perhaps, be better defined in distinction from the Allegorical, than that
it is always itself a part of that, of the whole of
which it is the representative.—" Here comes a
sail,"—(that is, a ship) is a symbolical expression.
" Behold our lion !" when we speak of some gallant
soldier, is allegorical.   Of most importance to our
present subject is this point, that the latter (the
allegory) cannot be other than spoken consciously ;
—whereas in the former (the symbol) it is very
possible that the general truth represented may be
working unconsciously in the writer's mind during
the construction of the symbol ;—and it proves itself by being produced out of his own mind, — as
the Don Quixote out of the perfectly sane mind of
Cervantes ; and not by outward observation, or his-

torically. The advantage of symbolical writing
over allegory is, that it presumes no disjunction of
faculties, but simple predominance.

II. Madness may be divided as—

    1. hypochondriasis; or, the man is out of his
       senses.

    2. derangement of the understanding; or, the
       man is out of his wits.

    3. loss of reason.

    4. frenzy, or derangement of the sensations.

Cervantes's own preface to Don Quixote is a perfect model of the gentle, every where intelligible,
irony in the best essays of the Tatler and the
Spectator. Equally natural and easy, Cervantes
is more spirited than Addison; whilst he blends
with the terseness of Swift, an exquisite flow and
music of style, and above all, contrasts with the
latter by the sweet temper of a superior mind, which
saw the follies of mankind, and was even at the
moment suffering severely under hard mistreat-
ment;* and yet seems every where to have but
one thought as the undersong — "Brethren! with
all your faults I love you still!"—or as a mother
that chides the child she loves, with one hand holds

---

* *Bien como quien se engendrò en una carcel, donde toda in-
comodidad tiene su assiento, y todo triste ruido hace su habita-
cion.* Like one you may suppose born in a prison, where
every inconvenience keeps its residence, and every dismal
sound its habitation. Pref. Jarvis's Tr. *Ed.*

up the rod, and with the other wipes off each tear
as it drops!

Don Quixote was neither fettered to the earth
by want, nor holden in its embraces by wealth;—
of which, with the temperance natural to his country,
as a Spaniard, he had both far too little, and somewhat too much, to be under any necessity of thinking about it. His age too, fifty, may be well supposed to prevent his mind from being tempted out
of itself by any of the lower passions;—while his
habits, as a very early riser and a keen sportsman,
were such as kept his spare body in serviceable
subjection to his will, and yet by the play of hope
that accompanies pursuit, not only permitted, but
assisted, his fancy in shaping what it would. Nor
must we omit his meagerness and entire featureliness, face and frame, which Cervantes gives us at
once: " It is said that his surname was *Quixada*
or *Quesada*," &c. — even in this trifle showing an
exquisite judgment;—just once insinuating the association of *lantern-jaws* into the reader's mind,
yet not retaining it obtrusively like the names in
old farces and in the Pilgrim's Progress,—but taking for the regular appellative one which had the
no meaning of a proper name in real life, and which
yet was capable of recalling a number of very different, but all pertinent, recollections, as old ar-
mour, the precious metals hidden in the ore, &c.
Don Quixote's leanness and featureliness are happy
exponents of the excess of the formative or imagi-

native in him, contrasted with Sancho's plump ro-
tundity, and recipiency of external impression.

He has no knowledge of the sciences or scientific arts which give to the meanest portions of
matter an intellectual interest, and which enable
the mind to decypher in the world of the senses the
invisible agency—that alone, of which the world's
phenomena are the effects and manifestations,—
and thus, as in a mirror, to contemplate its own reflex, its life in the powers, its imagination in the
symbolic forms, its moral instincts in /the final
causes, and its reason in the laws of material nature : but—estranged from all the motives to observation from self-interest—the persons that surround him too few and too familiar to enter into
any connection with his thoughts, or to require any
adaptation of his conduct to their particular characters or relations to himself— his judgment lies fal-
low, with nothing to excite, nothing to employ it.
Yet,—and here is the point, where genius even of
the most perfect kind, allotted but to few in the
course of many ages, does not preclude the necessity in part, and in part counterbalance the craving
by sanity of judgment, without which genius either
cannot be, or cannot at least manifest itself,—the
dependency of our nature asks for some confirma-
tion from without, though it be only from the shadows of other men's fictions.

Too uninformed, and with too narrow a sphere of
power and opportunity to rise into the scientific

artist, or to be himself a patron of art, and with too
deep a principle and too much innocence to become
a mere projector, Don Quixote has recourse to romances :—

His curiosity and extravagant fondness herein arrived at
that pitch, that he sold many acres of arable land to purchase
books of knight-errantry, and carried home all he could lay
hands on of that kind!   C. 1.

The more remote these romances were from the
language of common life, the more akin on that
very account were they to the shapeless dreams
and strivings of his own mind;—a mind, which
possessed not the highest order of genius which
lives in an atmosphere of power over mankind, but
that minor kind which, in its restlessness, seeks for
a vivid representative of its own wishes, and substitutes the movements of that objective puppet for
an exercise of actual power in and by itself.   The
more wild and improbable these romances were, the
more were they akin to his will, which had been in
the habit of acting as an unlimited monarch over
the creations of his fancy! Hence observe how the
startling of the remaining common sense, like a
glimmering before its death, in the notice of the
impossible-improbable of Don Belianis, is dismissed
by Don Quixote as impertinent —

He had some doubt* as to the dreadful wounds which Don
Belianis gave and received : for he imagined, that notwith-

---

* No estaba muy bien con.   Ed.

standing the most expert surgeons had cured him, his face
and whole body must still be full of seams and scars. *Ne-*
vertheless † he commended in his author the concluding his
book with a promise of that unfinishable adventure! C. 1.

Hence also his first intention to turn author; but
who, with such a restless struggle within him, would
content himself with writing in a remote village
among apathists and ignorants? During his collo-
quies with the village priest and the barber surgeon,
in which the fervour of critical controversy feeds
the passion and gives reality to its object—what
more natural than that the mental striving should become an eddy?—madness may perhaps be defined
as the circling in a stream which should be progressive and adaptive; Don Quixote grows at length
to be a man out of his wits; his understanding is
deranged; and hence without the least deviation
from the truth of nature, without losing the least
trait of personal individuality, he becomes a substantial living allegory, or personification of the
reason and the moral sense, divested of the judgment and the understanding. Sancho is the converse. He is the common sense without reason or
imagination; and Cervantes not only shows the excellence and power of reason in Don Quixote, but
in both him and Sancho the mischiefs resulting from
a severance of the two main constituents of sound
intellectual and moral action. Put him and his

---

† *Pero con todo.* Ed.

master together, and they form a perfect intellect; but they are separated and without cement; and hence each having a need of the other for its own completeness, each has at times a mastery over the other. For the common sense, although it may see the practical inapplicability of the dictates of the imagination or abstract reason, yet cannot help submitting to them. These two characters possess the world, alternately and interchangeably the cheater and the cheated. To impersonate them, and to combine the permanent with the individual, is one of the highest creations of genius, and has been achieved by Cervantes and Shakspeare, almost alone.

Observations on particular passages,

B. I. c. 1. But not altogether approving of his having broken it to pieces with so much ease, to secure himself from the like danger for the future, he made it over again, fencing it with small bars of iron within, in such a manner, *that he rested satisfied of its strength; and without caring to make a fresh experiment on it, he approved and looked upon it as a most excellent helmet.*

His not trying his improved scull-cap is an exquisite trait of human character, founded on the oppugnancy of the soul in such a state to any disturbance by doubt of its own broodings. Even the long deliberation about his horse's name is full of meaning;—for in these day-dreams the greater part of the history passes and is carried on in words, which look forward to other words as what will be said of them.

> Ib. Near the place where he lived, there dwelt a very comely country lass, with whom he had formerly been in love ; though, as it is supposed, she never knew it, nor troubled herself about it.

The nascent love for the country lass, but without any attempt at utterance, or an opportunity of knowing her, except as the hint — the ὅτι ἔστι — of the inward imagination, is happily conceived in both parts;—first, as confirmative of the shrinking back of the mind on itself, and its dread of having a cherished image destroyed by its own judgment; and secondly, as showing how necessarily love is the passion of novels.   Novels are to love as fairy tales to dreams.   I never knew but two men of taste and feeling who could not understand why I was delighted with the Arabian Nights' Tales, and they were likewise the only persons in my knowledge who scarcely remembered having ever dreamed. Magic and war—itself a magic—are the day-dreams of childhood; love is the day-dream of youth, and early manhood.

> C. 2. " Scarcely had ruddy Phœbus spread the golden tresses of his beauteous hair over the face of the wide and spacious earth; and scarcely had the little painted birds, with the sweet and mellifluous harmony of their forked tongues, saluted the approach of rosy Aurora, who, quitting the soft couch of her jealous husband, disclosed herself to

mortals through the gates of the Manchegan horizon; when the renowned Don Quixote," &c.

How happily already is the abstraction from the senses, from observation, and the consequent confusion of the judgment, marked in this description! The knight is describing objects immediate to his senses and sensations without borrowing a single trait from either. Would it be difficult to find parallel descriptions in Dryden's plays and in those of his successors?

C. 3. The host is here happily conceived as one who from his past life as a sharper, was capable of entering into and humouring the knight, and so perfectly in character, that he precludes a considerable source of improbability in the future narrative, by enforcing upon Don Quixote the necessity of taking money with him.

C. 3. "Ho, there, whoever thou art, rash knight, that approachest to touch the arms of the most valorous adventurer that ever girded sword," &c.

Don Quixote's high eulogiums on himself—"the most valorous adventurer!"—but it is not himself that he has before him, but the idol of his imagination, the imaginary being whom he is acting. And this, that it is entirely a third person, excuses his heart from the otherwise inevitable charge of selfish vanity; and so by madness itself he preserves our esteem, and renders those actions natural by which he, the first person, deserves it.

2   F

C. 4. Andres and his master.

The manner in which Don Quixote redressed this wrong, is a picture of the true revolutionary passion in its first honest state, while it is yet only a bewilderment of the understanding. You have a benevolence limitless in its prayers, which are in fact aspirations towards omnipotence; but between it and beneficence, the bridge of judgment—that is, of measurement of personal power—intervenes, and must be passed. Otherwise you will be bruised by the leap into the chasm, or be drowned in the revolutionary river, and drag others with you to the same fate.

C. 4. Merchants of Toledo.

When they were come so near as to be seen and heard, Don Quixote raised his voice, and with arrogant air cried out: " Let the whole world stand; if the whole world does not confess that there is not in the whole world a damsel more beautiful than," &c.

Now mark the presumption which follows the self-complacency of the last act! That was an honest attempt to redress a real wrong; this is an arbitrary determination to enforce a Brissotine or Rousseau's ideal on all his fellow creatures.

Let the whole world stand!

' If there had been any experience in proof of the excellence of our code, where would be our superiority in this enlightened age ? '

" No ? the business is that without seeing her, you believe, confess, affirm, swear, and maintain it; *and if not, I challenge you all to battle."* *

Next see the persecution and fury excited by opposition however moderate! The only words listened to are those, that without their context and their conditionals, and transformed into positive assertions, might give some shadow of excuse for the violence shown! This rich story ends, to the compassion of the men in their senses, in a sound rib-roasting of the idealist by the muleteer, the mob. And happy for thee, poor knight! that the mob were against thee! For had they been with thee, by the change of the moon and of them, thy head would have been off.

C. 5. first part—The idealist recollects the causes that had been necessary to the reverse and attempts to remove them—too late. He is beaten and disgraced.

C. 6. This chapter on Don Quixote's library proves that the author did not wish to destroy the romances, but to cause them to be read as romances—that is, for their merits as poetry.

C. 7. Among other things, Don Quixote told him, he should dispose himself to go with him willingly;—for some time or other such an adventure might present, that an island might be won, in the turn of a hand, and he be left governor thereof.

---

* *Donde no, conmigo sois en buttalla, gente descomunal!* Ed.

At length the promises of the imaginative reason
begin to act on the plump, sensual, honest common
sense accomplice,—but unhappily not in the same
person, and without the *copula* of the judgment,—
in hopes of the substantial good things, of which
the former contemplated only the glory and the colours.

C. 7. Sancho Panza went riding upon his ass, like any
patriarch, with his wallet and leathern bottle, and with a
vehement desire to find himself governor of the island which
his master had promised him.

The first relief from regular labour is so pleasant
to poor Sancho!

C. 8. " I no gentleman! I swear by the great God, thou
liest, as I am a Christian. Biscainer by land, gentleman by
sea, gentleman for the devil, and thou liest: look then if
thou hast any thing else to say."

This Biscainer is an excellent image of the prejudices and bigotry provoked by the idealism of a
speculator. This story happily detects the trick
which our imagination plays in the description of
single combats: only change the preconception of
the magnificence of the combatants, and all is gone.

B. II. c. 2. " Be pleased, my lord Don Quixote, to bestow
upon me the government of that island," &c.

Sancho's eagerness for his government, the nascent lust of actual democracy, or isocracy!

C. 2. " But tell me, on your life, have you ever seen a
more valorous knight than I, upon the whole face of the

known earth? Have you read in story of any other, who has, or ever had, more bravery in assailing, more breath in holding out, more dexterity in wounding, or more address in giving a fall?"—"The truth is," answered Sancho, "that I never read any history at all; for I can neither read nor write; but what I dare affirm is, that I never served a bolder master," &c.

This appeal to Sancho, and Sancho's answer are exquisitely humorous. It is impossible not to think of the French bulletins and proclamations. Remark the necessity under which we are of being sympathized with, fly as high into abstraction as we may, and how constantly the imagination is recalled to the ground of our common humanity! And note a little further on, the knight's easy vaunting of his balsam, and his quietly deferring the making and application of it.

C. 3. The speech before the goatherds:

" Happy times and happy ages," &c.*

Note the rhythm of this, and the admirable beauty and wisdom of the thoughts in themselves, but the total want of judgment in Don Quixote's addressing them to such an audience.

B. III. c. 3. Don Quixote's balsam, and the vomiting and consequent relief; an excellent hit at *panacea nostrums*, which cure the patient by his being himself cured of the medicine by revolting nature.

---

* *Dichosa edad y siglos dichosos aquellos, &c.* Ed.

C. 4. " Peace! and have patience; the day will come," &c.

The perpetual promises of the imagination !

Ib. " Your Worship," said Sancho, " would make a better preacher than knight errant !"

Exactly so.   This is the true moral.

C. 6. The uncommon beauty of the description
in the commencement of this chapter.   In truth,
the whole of it seems to put all nature in its heights
and its humiliations, before us.

Ib. Sancho's story of the goats :

" Make account, he carried them all over," said Don
Quixote, " and do not be going and coming in this manner;
for at this rate, you will not have done carrying them over
in a twelvemonth."   " How many are passed already ?"
said Sancho, &c.

Observe the happy contrast between the all-ge-
neralizing mind of the mad knight, and Sancho's
all-particularizing memory. How admirable a symbol of the dependance of all *copula* on the higher
powers of the mind, with the single exception of the
succession in time and the accidental relations of
space.   Men of mere common sense have no theory or means of making one fact more important or
prominent than the rest; if they lose one link, all
is lost.   Compare Mrs. Quickly and the Tapster.*
And note also Sancho's good heart, when his mas-

---

* See the Friend, vol. iii. p. 138   *Ed.*

ter is about to leave him. Don Quixote's conduct upon discovering the fulling-hammers, proves he was meant to be in his senses. Nothing can be better conceived than his fit of passion at Sancho's laughing, and his sophism of self-justification by the courage he had shown.

Sancho is by this time cured, through experience, as far as his own errors are concerned; yet still is he lured on by the unconquerable awe of his master's superiority, even when he is cheating him.

C. 8. The adventure of the Galley-slaves. I think this is the only passage of moment in which Cervantes slips the mask of his hero, and speaks for himself.

C. 9. Don Quixote desired to have it, and bade him take the money, and keep it for himself. Sancho kissed his hands for the favour, &c.

Observe Sancho's eagerness to avail himself of the permission of his master, who, in the war sports of knight-errantry, had, without any selfish dishonesty, overlooked the *meum* and *tuum*. Sancho's selfishness is modified by his involuntary goodness of heart, and Don Quixote's flighty goodness is debased by the involuntary or unconscious selfishness of his vanity and self-applause.

C. 10. Cardenio is the madman of passion, who meets and easily overthrows for the moment the madman of imagination. And note the contagion of madness of any kind, upon Don Quixote's interruption of Cardenio's story.

C. 11. Perhaps the best specimen of Sancho's proverbializing is this:

" And I (Don Q.) say again, they lie, and will lie two hundred times more, all who say, or think her so." " I neither say, nor think so," answered Sancho; " let those who say it, eat the lie, and swallow it with their bread: whether they were guilty or no, they have given an account to God before now : I come from my vineyard, I know nothing; I am no friend to inquiring into other men's lives; *for* he that buys and lies shall find the lie left in his purse behind; *besides*, naked was I born, and naked I remain; I neither win nor lose; if they were guilty, what is that to me ? Many think to find bacon, where there is not so much as a pin to hang it on : *but* who can hedge in the cuckoo ? *Especially*, do they spare God himself ?"

Ib. " And it is no great matter, if it be in another hand ; for by what I remember, Dulcinea can neither write nor read," &c.

The wonderful twilight of the mind ! and mark Cervantes's courage in daring to present it, and trust to a distant posterity for an appreciation of its truth to nature.

P. II. B. III. c. 9. Sancho's account of what he had seen on Clavileno is a counterpart in his style to Don Quixote's adventures in the cave of Montesinos. This last is the only impeachment of the knight's moral character; Cervantes just gives one instance of the veracity failing before the strong cravings of the imagination for something real and external; the picture would not have been complete without this; and yet it is so well managed, that the reader has no unpleasant sense of Don Quixote having told a lie. It is evident that he hardly knows whether it was a dream or not; and goes to the enchanter to inquire the real nature of the adventure.

Summary of Cervantes.

A Castilian of refined manners; a gentleman, true to religion, and true to honour.

A scholar and a soldier, and fought under the banners of Don John of Austria, at Lepanto, lost his arm and was captured.

Endured slavery not only with fortitude, but with mirth; and by the superiority of nature, mastered and overawed his barbarian owner.

Finally ransomed, he resumed his native destiny, the awful task of achieving fame; and for that reason died poor and a prisoner, while nobles and kings over their goblets of gold gave relish to their pleasures by the charms of his divine genius. He was the inventor of novels for the Spaniards, and in his Persilis and Sigismunda, the English may find the germ of their Robinson Crusoe.

The world was a drama to him. His own thoughts, in spite of poverty and sickness, perpetuated for him the feelings of youth. He painted only what he knew and had looked into, but he knew and had looked into much indeed; and his imagination was ever at hand to adapt and modify the world of his experience. Of delicious love he fabled, yet with stainless virtue.

LECTURE IX.

On the Distinctions of the Witty, the Droll, the Odd, and the Humourous; the Nature and Constituents of Humour; — Rabelais — Swift — Sterne.

I.

PERHAPS the most important of our intellectual operations are those of detecting the difference in similar, and the identity in dissimilar, things. Out of the latter operation it is that wit arises; and it, generically regarded, consists in presenting thoughts or images in an unusual connection with each other, for the purpose of exciting pleasure by the surprise. This connection may be real; and there is in fact a scientific wit; though where the object, consciously entertained, is truth, and not amusement, we commonly give it some higher name. But in wit popularly understood, the connection may be, and for the most part is, apparent only, and transitory; and this connection may be by thoughts, or by words, or by images. The first is our Butler's especial eminence; the second, Voltaire's; the third, which we oftener call fancy, consitutes the larger and more peculiar part of the wit of Shakspeare. You can scarcely turn to a single speech of Falstaff's without finding instances of it.

Nor does wit always cease to deserve the name by being transient, or incapable of analysis. I may add that the wit of thoughts belongs eminently to the Italians, that of words to the French, and that of images to the English.

II. Where the laughable is its own end, and neither inference, nor moral is intended, or where at least the writer would wish it so to appear, there arises what we call drollery. The pure, unmixed, ludicrous or laughable belongs exclusively to the understanding, and must be presented under the form of the senses; it lies within the spheres of the eye and the ear, and hence is allied to the fancy. It does not appertain to the reason or the moral sense, and accordingly is alien to the imagination. I think Aristotle has already excellently defined * the laughable, τὸ γελοῖον, as consisting of, or de-

---

* He elsewhere commends this Def: "To resolve laughter into an expression of contempt is contrary to fact, and laughable enough. Laughter is a convulsion of the nerves, and it seems as if nature cut short the rapid thrill of pleasure on the nerves by a sudden convulsion of them to prevent the sensation becoming painful—*Aristotle's Def.* is as good as can be. Surprise at perceiving anything out of its usual place when the unusualness is not accompanied by a sense of serious danger. Such surprise is always pleasurable, and it is observable that surprise accompanied with circumstances of danger becomes Tragic. Hence *Farce may* often *border on Tragedy;* indeed *Farce* is *nearer Tragedy* in its *Essence* than *Comedy is.*"

                                        Table Talk.

pending on, what is out of its proper time and place, yet without danger or pain. Here the *impropriety*—τὸ ἄτοπον—is the positive qualification; the *dangerlessness*—τὸ ἀκίνδυνον—the negative. Neither the understanding without an object of the senses, as for example, a mere notional error, or idiocy;— nor any external object, unless attributed to the understanding, can produce the poetically laughable. Nay, even in ridiculous positions of the body laughed at by the vulgar, there is a subtle personification always going on, which acts on the, perhaps, unconscious mind of the spectator as a symbol of intellectual character. And hence arises the imperfect and awkward effect of comic stories of animals; because although the understanding is satisfied in them, the senses are not. Hence too, it is, that the true ludicrous is its own end. When serious satire commences, or satire that is felt as serious, however comically drest, free and genuine laugher ceases; it becomes sardonic. This you experience in reading Young, and also not unfrequently in Butler. The true comic is the blossom of the nettle.

III. When words or images are placed in unusual juxta-position rather than connection, and are so placed merely because the juxta-position is unusual—we have the odd or the grotesque; the occasional use of which in the minor ornaments of architecture, is an interesting problem for a student in the psychology of the Fine Arts.

IV. In the simply laughable there is a mere disproportion between a definite act and a definite purpose or end, or a disproportion of the end itself to the rank or circumstances of the definite person; but humour is of more difficult description. I must try to define it in the first place by its points of diversity from the former species. Humour does not, like the different kinds of wit, which is impersonal, consist wholly in the understanding and the senses. No combination of thoughts, words, or images will of itself constitute humour, unless some peculiarity of individual temperament and character be indicated thereby, as the cause of the same. Compare the comedies of Congreve with the Falstaff in Henry IV. or with Sterne's Corporal Trim, Uncle Toby, and Mr. Shandy, or with some of Steele's charming papers in the Tatler, and you will feel the difference better than I can express it. Thus again, (to take an instance from the different works of the same writer), in Smollett's Strap, his Lieutenant Bowling, his Morgan the honest Welshman, and his Matthew Bramble, we have exquisite humour,—while in his Peregrine Pickle we find an abundance of drollery, which too often degenerates into mere oddity; in short, we feel that a number of things are put together to counterfeit humour, but that there is no growth from within. And this indeed is the origin of the word, derived from the humoral pathology, and excellently described by Ben Jonson:

>   So in every human body,
> The choler, melancholy, phlegm, and blood,
> By reason that they flow continually
> In some one part, and are not continent,
> Receive the name of humours. Now thus far
> It may, by metaphor, apply itself
> Unto the general disposition :
> As when some one peculiar quality
> Doth so possess a man, that it doth draw
> All his effects, his spirits, and his powers,
> In their confluctions, all to run one way,
> This may be truly said to be a humour.*

Hence we may explain the congeniality of humour with pathos, so exquisite in Sterne and Smollett, and hence also the tender feeling which we always have for, and associate with, the humours or hobby-horses of a man. First, we respect a humourist, because absence of interested motive is the ground-work of the character, although the imagination of an interest may exist in the individual himself, as if a remarkably simple-hearted man should pride him-self on his knowledge of the world, and how well he can manage it : — and secondly, there always is in a genuine humour an acknowledgment of the hollowness and farce of the world, and its dispro-portion to the godlike within us. And it follows immediately from this, that whenever particular acts have reference to particular selfish motives, the humourous bursts into the indignant and ab-

---

* Every Man Out Of His Humour. Prologue.

horring; whilst all follies not selfish are pardoned or palliated. The danger of this habit, in respect of pure morality, is strongly exemplified in Sterne.

This would be enough, and indeed less than this has passed, for a sufficient account of humour, if we did not recollect that not every predominance of character, even where not precluded by the moral sense, as in criminal dispositions, constitutes what we mean by a humourist, or the presentation of its produce, humour. What then is it? Is it manifold? Or is there some one humorific point common to all that can be called humourous?—I am not prepared to answer this fully, even if my time permitted; but I think there is;—and that it consists in a certain reference to the general and the universal, by which the finite great is brought into identity with the little, or the little with the finite great, so as to make both nothing in comparison with the infinite. The little is made great, and the great little, in order to destroy both; because all is equal in contrast with the infinite. "It is not without reason, brother Toby, that learned men write dialogues on long noses."* I would suggest, therefore, that whenever a finite is contemplated in reference to the infinite, whether consciously or unconsciously, humour essentially arises. In the highest humour, at least, there is always a reference to, and a connection with, some general power

* Trist. Sh. Vol. iii. c. 37.

not finite, in the form of some finite ridiculously disproportionate in our feelings to that of which it is, nevertheless, the representative, or by which it is to be displayed. Humourous writers, therefore, as Sterne in particular, delight, after much preparation, to end in nothing, or in a direct contradiction.

That there is some truth in this definition, or origination of humour, is evident; for you cannot conceive a humorous man who does not give some disproportionate generality, or even a universality to his hobby-horse, as is the case with Mr. Shandy; or at least there is an absence of any interest but what arises from the humour itself, as in my Uncle Toby, and it is the idea of the soul, of its undefined capacity and dignity, that gives the sting to any absorption of it by any one pursuit, and this not in respect of the humourist as a mere member of society for a particular, however mistaken, interest, but as a man.

The English humour is the most thoughtful, the Spanish the most etherial—the most ideal—of modern literature. Amongst the classic ancients there was little or no humour in the foregoing sense of the term. Socrates, or Plato under his name, gives some notion of humour in the Banquet, when he argues that tragedy and comedy rest upon the same ground. But humour properly took its rise in the middle ages; and the Devil, the Vice of the mysteries, incorporates the modern humour in its ele-

ments. It is a spirit measured by disproportionate
finites. The Devil is not, indeed, perfectly humorous; but that is only because he is the extreme of
all humour.

RABELAIS.*

Born at Chinon, 1483-4.—Died 1553.

One cannot help regretting that no friend of
Rabelais, (and surely friends he must have had),
has left an authentic account of him. His buffoonery was not merely Brutus' rough stick, which
contained a rod of gold; it was necessary as an
amulet against the monks and bigots. Beyond a
doubt, he was among the deepest as well as boldest
thinkers of his age. Never was a more plausible,
and seldom, I am persuaded, a less appropriate line
than the thousand times quoted,

> Rabelais laughing in his easy chair—

of Mr. Pope. The caricature of his filth and zany-
ism proves how fully he both knew and felt the
danger in which he stood. I could write a treatise
in proof and praise of the morality and moral elevation of Rabelais' work which would make the

---

* No note remains of that part of this Lecture which
treated of Rabelais. This seems, therefore, a convenient
place for the reception of some remarks written by Mr. C.
in Mr. Gillman's copy of Rabelais, about the year 1825,
See Table Talk, vol. i. p. 177. *Ed.*

church stare, and the conventicle groan, and yet should be the truth and nothing but the truth. I class Rabelais with the creative minds of the world, Shakspeare, Dante, Cervantes, &c.

All Rabelais' personages are phantasmagoric allegories, but Panurge above all. He is throughout the πανουργία,—the wisdom, that is, the cunning of the human animal,—the understanding, as the faculty of means to purposes without ultimate ends, in the most comprehensive sense, and including art, sensuous fancy, and all the passions of the understanding. It is impossible to read Rabelais without an admiration mixed with wonder at the depth and extent of his learning, his multifarious knowledge, and original observation beyond what books could in that age have supplied him with.

B. III. c. 9. How Panurge asketh counsel of Pantagruel, whether he should marry, yea or no.

Note this incomparable chapter. Pantagruel stands for the reason as contradistinguished from the understanding and choice, that is, from Panurge; and the humour consists in the latter asking advice of the former on a subject in which the reason can only give the inevitable conclusion, the syllogistic *ergo*, from the premisses provided by the understanding itself, which puts each case so as of necessity to predetermine the verdict thereon. This chapter, independently of the allegory, is an exquisite satire on the spirit in which people commonly ask advice.

SWIFT.*

Born in Dublin, 1667.—Died 1745.

In Swift's writings there is a false misanthropy grounded upon an exclusive contemplation of the vices and follies of mankind, and this misanthropic tone is also disfigured or brutalized by his obtrusion of physical dirt and coarseness. I think Gulliver's Travels the great work of Swift. In the voyages to Lilliput and Brobdingnag he displays the little-ness and moral contemptibility of human nature; in that to the Houyhnhnms he represents the dis-gusting spectacle of man with the understanding only, without the reason or the moral feeling, and in his horse he gives the misanthropic ideal of man —that is, a being virtuous from rule and duty, but untouched by the principle of love.

STERNE.

Born at Clonmel, 1713.—Died 1768.

With regard to Sterne, and the charge of licen-tiousness which presses so seriously upon his cha-racter as a writer, I would remark that there is a sort of knowingness, the wit of which depends— 1st, on the modesty it gives pain to; or, 2dly, on

---

From Mr. Green's note. *Ed.*

the innocence and innocent ignorance over which it
triumphs ; or, 3dly, on a certain oscillation in the
individual's own mind between the remaining good
and the encroaching evil of his nature—a sort of
dallying with the devil—a fluxionary act of combining courage and cowardice, as when a man snuffs
a candle with his fingers for the first time, or better
still, perhaps, like that trembling daring with which
a child touches a hot tea urn, because it has been
forbidden ; so that the mind has in its own white
and black angel the same or similar amusement, as
may be supposed to take place between an old de-
bauchee and a prude,—she feeling resentment, on
the one hand, from a prudential anxiety to preserve
appearances and have a character, and, on the other,
an inward sympathy with the enemy. We have
only to suppose society innocent, and then nine-
tenths of this sort of wit would be like a stone that
falls in snow, making no sound because exciting no
resistance ; the remainder rests on its being an offence against the good manners of human nature
itself.

This source, unworthy as it is, may doubtless be
combined with wit, drollery, fancy, and even humour, and we have only to regret the misalliance ;
but that the latter are quite distinct from the former, may be made evident by abstracting in our
imagination the morality of the characters of Mr.
Shandy, my Uncle Toby, and Trim, which are all
antagonists to this spurious sort of wit, from the

rest of Tristram Shandy. And by supposing, instead of them, the presence of two or three callous debauchees. The result will be pure disgust. Sterne cannot be too severely censured for thus using the best dispositions of our nature as the panders and condiments for the basest.

The excellencies of Sterne consist—

1. In bringing forward into distinct consciousness those minutiæ of thought and feeling which appear trifles, yet have an importance for the moment, and which almost every man feels in one way or other. Thus is produced the novelty of an individual peculiarity, together with the interest of a something that belongs to our common nature. In short, Sterne seizes happily on those points, in which every man is more or less a humourist. And, indeed, to be a little more subtle, the propensity to notice these things does itself constitute the humourist, and the superadded power of so presenting them to men in general gives us the man of humour. Hence the difference of the man of humour, the effect of whose portraits does not depend on the felt presence of himself, as a humourist, as in the instances of Cervantes and Shakspeare—nay, of Rabelais too; and of the humourist, the effect of whose works does very much depend on the sense of his own oddity, as in Sterne's case, and perhaps Swift's; though Swift again would require a separate classification.

2. In the traits of human nature, which so easily assume a particular cast and colour from individual

character.   Hence this excellence and the pathos connected with it quickly pass into humour, and form the ground of it.   See particularly the beautiful passage, so well known, of Uncle Toby's catching and liberating the fly :

" Go,"—says he, one day at dinner, to an overgrown one which had buzzed about his nose, and tormented him cruelly all dinner-time, and which, after infinite attempts, he had caught at last, as it flew by him ;—" I'll not hurt thee," says my Uncle Toby, rising from his chair, and going across the room, with the fly in his hand,—" I'll not hurt a hair of thy head :—" Go," says he, lifting up the sash, and opening his hand as he spoke, to let it escape ;—" go, poor devil, get thee gone, why should I hurt thee ? This world is surely wide enough to hold both thee and me."   Vol. ii. ch. 12.

Observe in this incident how individual character may be given by the mere delicacy of presentation and elevation in degree of a common good quality, humanity, which in itself would not be characteristic at all.

3. In Mr. Shandy's character,—the essence of which is a craving for sympathy in exact proportion to the oddity and unsympathizability of what he proposes ;—this coupled with an instinctive desire to be at least disputed with, or rather both in one, to dispute and yet to agree—and holding as worst of all—to acquiesce without either resistance or sympathy.   This is charmingly, indeed, profoundly conceived, and is psychologically and ethically true of all Mr. Shandies.   Note, too, how the contrasts of character, which are always either balanced or remedied, increase the love between the brothers.

No writer is so happy as Sterne in the unexag-gerated and truly natural representation of that species of slander, which consists in gossiping about our neighbours, as whetstones of our moral discrimination ; as if they were conscience-blocks which we used in our apprenticeship, in order not to waste such precious materials as our own con-sciences in the trimming and shaping of ourselves by self-examination :—

Alas o'day !—had Mrs. Shandy, (poor gentlewoman !) had but her wish in going up to town just to lie in and come down again ; which, they say, she begged and prayed for upon her bare knees, and which, in my opinion, considering the fortune which Mr. Shandy got with her, was no such mighty matter to have complied with, the lady and her babe might both of them have been alive at this hour.   Vol. i. c. 18.

5. When you have secured a man's likings and prejudices in your favour, you may then safely ap-peal to his impartial judgment.   In the following passage not only is acute sense shrouded in wit, but a life and a character are added which exalt the whole into the dramatic :—

" I see plainly, Sir, by your looks" (or as the case hap-pened) my father would say—" that you do not heartily sub-scribe to this opinion of mine — which, to those," he would add, " who have not carefully sifted it to the bottom,—I own has an air more of fancy than of solid reasoning in it ; and yet, my dear Sir, if I may presume to know your character, I am morally assured I should hazard little in stating a case to you, not as a party in the dispute, but as a judge, and trusting my appeal upon it to your good sense and candid disquisition in this matter ; you are a person free from a

many narrow prejudices of education as most men ; and, if
I may presume to penetrate farther into you, of a liberality
of genius above bearing down an opinion, merely because it
wants friends. Your son,—your dear son,—from whose sweet
and open temper you have so much to expect,—your Billy,
Sir!—would you, for the world, have called him JUDAS?
Would you, my dear Sir," he would say, laying his hand
upon your breast, with the genteelest address,—and in that
soft and irresistible *piano* of voice, which the nature of the
argumentum ad hominem absolutely requires,—" Would you,
Sir, if a *Jew* of a godfather had proposed the name for your
child, and offered you his purse along with it, would you have
consented to such a desecration of him? O my God!" he would
say, looking up, " if I know your temper rightly, Sir, you are
incapable of it;—you would have trampled upon the offer;
—you would have thrown the temptation at the tempter's
head with abhorrence. Your greatness of mind in this action, which I admire, with that generous contempt of money,
which you show me in the whole transaction, is really noble ;—and what renders it more so, is the principle of it ;—
the workings of a parent's love upon the truth and conviction of this very hypothesis, namely, that were your son
called Judas,—the sordid and treacherous idea, so insepa-
rable from the name, would have accompanied him through
life like his shadow, and in the end made a miser and a ras-
cal of him, in spite, Sir, of your example." Vol. i. c. 19.

6. There is great physiognomic tact in Sterne.
See it particularly displayed in his description of
Dr. Slop, accompanied with all that happiest use of
drapery and attitude, which at once give reality by
individualizing and vividness by unusual, yet probable, combinations :—

Imagine to yourself a little squat uncourtly figure of a
Doctor Slop, of about four feet and a half perpendicular

height, with a breadth of back, and a sesquipedality of belly, which might have done honour to a serjeant in the horse-guards.

    *   *   *   *   *

Imagine such a one ;—for such, I say, were the outlines of Doctor Slop's figure, coming slowly along, foot by foot, waddling through the dirt upon the *vertebræ* of a little diminutive pony, of a pretty colour—but of strength,—alack ! scarce able to have made an amble of it, under such a fardel, had the roads been in an ambling condition ;—they were not. Imagine to yourself Obadiah mounted upon a strong monster of a coach-horse, pricked into a full gallop, and making all practicable speed the adverse way. Vol. ii. c. 9.

7. I think there is more humour in the single remark, which I have quoted before — " Learned men, brother Toby, don't write dialogues upon long noses for nothing !"—than in the whole Slawkenburghian tale that follows, which is mere oddity interspersed with drollery.

8. Note Sterne's assertion of, and faith in a moral good in the characters of Trim, Toby, &c. as contrasted with the cold scepticism of motives which is the stamp of the Jacobin spirit. Vol. v. c. 9.

9. You must bear in mind, in order to do justice to Rabelais and Sterne, that by right of humoristic universality each part is essentially a whole in itself. Hence the digressive spirit is not mere wantonness, but in fact the very form and vehicle of their genius. The connection, such as was needed, is given by the continuity of the characters.

Instances of different forms of wit, taken largely:

1. " Why are you reading romances at your age?"—"Why, I used to be fond of history, but I have given it up,—it was so grossly improbable."

2. " Pray, sir, do it!—although you have promised me."

3. The Spartan mother's—

" Return with, or on, thy shield."

" My sword is too short!"—" Take a step forwarder."

4. The Gasconade:—

" I believe you, Sir! but you will excuse my repeating it on account of my provincial accent."

5. Pasquil on Pope Urban, who had employed a committee to rip up the old errors of his predecessors.

Some one placed a pair of spurs on the heels of the statue of St. Peter, and a label from the opposite statue of St. Paul, on the same bridge ;—

St. Paul. " Whither then are you bound ?"
St. Peter. " I apprehend danger here ;—they'll soon call me in question for denying my Master."
St. Paul. " Nay, then, I had better be off too ; for they'll question me for having persecuted the Christians, before my conversion."

6. Speaking of the small German potentates, I dictated the phrase, — *officious for equivalents*. This my amanuensis wrote,—*fishing for elephants;* —which, as I observed at the time, was a sort of Noah's angling, that could hardly have occurred, except at the commencement of the Deluge.

LECTURE X.

Donne — Dante — Milton — Paradise Lost.

DONNE.*

Born in London, 1573.—Died, 1631.

I.

With Donne, whose muse on dromedary trots,
Wreathe iron pokers into true-love knots;
Rhyme's sturdy cripple, fancy's maze and clue,
Wit's forge and fire-blast, meaning's press and screw.

II.

See lewdness and theology combin'd,—
A cynic and a sycophantic mind;
A fancy shar'd party per pale between
Death's heads and skeletons, and Aretine!—
Not his peculiar defect or crime,
But the true current mintage of the time.
Such were the establish'd signs and tokens given
To mark a loyal churchman, sound and even,
Free from papistic and fanatic leaven.

THE wit of Donne, the wit of Butler, the wit of Pope, the wit of Congreve, the wit of Sheridan—how many disparate things are here expressed by one and the same word, Wit!—Won-

---

* Nothing remains of what was said on Donne in this Lecture. Here, therefore, as in previous like instances, the gap is filled up with some notes written by Mr. Coleridge in a volume of Chalmer's Poets, belonging to Mr. Gillman. The verses were added in pencil to the collection of com-

der-exciting vigour, intenseness and peculiarity of
thought, using at will the almost boundless stores
of a capacious memory, and exercised on subjects,
where we have no right to expect it — this is the
wit of Donne! The four others I am just in the
mood to describe and inter-distinguish; — what a
pity that the marginal space will not let me!

> My face in thine eye, thine in mine appears,
> And true plain hearts do in the faces rest;
> Where can we find two fitter hemispheres
> Without sharp north, without declining west?
>   Good-Morrow, v. 15, &c.

The sense is; — Our mutual loves may in many
respects be fitly compared to corresponding hemispheres; but as no simile squares (*nihil simile est
idem*), so here the simile fails, for there is nothing
in our loves that corresponds to the cold north, or
the declining west, which in two hemispheres must
necessarily be supposed. But an ellipse of such
length will scarcely rescue the line from the charge
of nonsense or a bull. *January*, 1829.

> Woman's constancy.

A misnomer.   The title ought to be—

> Mutual Inconstancy.

---

mendatory lines; No. I. is Mr. C.'s; the publication of No.
II. I trust the all-accomplished author will, under the circumstances, pardon. Numerous and elaborate notes by Mr.
Coleridge on Donne's Sermons are in existence, and will be
published hereafter. *Ed.*

Whether both th' Indias of spice and *mine*, &c.
Sun Rising, v. 17.

And see at night thy western land of *mine*, &c.
Progress of the Soul, 1 Song, 2. st.

This use of the word *mine* specifically for mines of gold, silver, or precious stones, is, I believe, peculiar to Donne.

DANTE.

Born at Florence, 1265.—Died, 1321.

As I remarked in a former Lecture on a different subject (for subjects the most diverse in literature have still their tangents), the Gothic character, and its good and evil fruits, appeared less in Italy than in any other part of European Christendom. There was accordingly much less romance, as that word is commonly understood; or, perhaps, more truly stated, there was romance instead of chivalry. In Italy, an earlier imitation of, and a more evident and intentional blending with, the Latin literature took place than elsewhere. The operation of the feudal system, too, was incalculably weaker, of that singular chain of independent interdependents, the principle of which was a confederacy for the preservation of individual, consistently with general, freedom. In short, Italy, in the time of Dante, was an after-birth of eldest Greece, a renewal or a reflex of the old Italy under its kings and first Roman consuls, a net-work of free little republics, with

the same domestic feuds, civil wars, and party spirit,
—the same vices and virtues produced on a similarly
narrow theatre,—the existing state of things being,
as in all small democracies, under the working and
direction of certain individuals, to whose will even
the laws were swayed;—whilst at the same time the
singular spectacle was exhibited amidst all this confusion of the flourishing of commerce, and the protection and encouragement of letters and arts.
Never was the commercial spirit so well reconciled
to the nobler principles of social polity as in Florence.   It tended there to union and permanence
and elevation,—not as the overbalance of it in England is now doing, to dislocation, change and moral
degradation.   The intensest patriotism reigned in
these communities, but confined and attached exclusively to the small locality of the patriot's birth
and residence; whereas in the true Gothic feudal-
ism, country was nothing but the preservation of
personal independence.   But then, on the other
hand, as a counterbalance to these disuniting elements, there was in Dante's Italy, as in Greece, a
much greater uniformity of religion common to all
than amongst the northern nations.

Upon these hints the history of the republican
æras of ancient Greece and modern Italy ought to
be written.   There are three kinds or stages of
historic narrative; — 1. that of the annalist or chronicler, who deals merely in facts and events arranged in order of time, having no principle of se-

lection, no plan of arrangement, and whose work
properly constitutes a supplement to the poetical
writings of romance or heroic legends :—2. that of
the writer who takes his stand on some moral point,
and selects a series of events for the express purpose of illustrating it, and in whose hands the narrative of the selected events is modified by the
principle of selection ;—as Thucydides, whose object was to describe the evils of democratic and
aristocratic partizanships ;—or Polybius, whose design was to show the social benefits resulting from
the triumph and grandeur of Rome, in public institutions and military discipline ;—or Tacitus, whose
secret aim was to exhibit the pressure and corruptions of despotism ;—in all which writers and others
like them, the ground-object of the historian colours
with artificial lights the facts which he relates:—3.
and which in idea is the grandest—the most truly
founded in philosophy — there is the Herodotean
history, which is not composed with reference to
any particular causes, but attempts to describe human nature itself on a great scale as a portion of
the drama of providence, the free will of man re-
sisting the destiny of events,—for the individuals
often succeeding against it, but for the race always
yielding to it, and in the resistance itself invariably
affording means towards the completion of the ultimate result. Mitford's history is a good and useful
work; but in his zeal against democratic government, Mitford forgot, or never saw, that ancient

Greece was not, nor ought ever to be considered, a permanent thing, but that it existed, in the disposition of providence, as a proclaimer of ideal truths, and that everlasting proclamation being made, that its functions were naturally at an end.

However, in the height of such a state of society in Italy, Dante was born and flourished; and was himself eminently a picture of the age in which he lived. But of more importance even than this, to a right understanding of Dante, is the consideration that the scholastic philosophy was then at its acme even in itself; but more especially in Italy, where it never prevailed so exclusively as northward of the Alps. It is impossible to understand the genius of Dante, and difficult to understand his poem, without some knowledge of the characters, studies, and writings of the schoolmen of the twelfth, thirteenth, and fourteenth centuries. For Dante was the living link between religion and philosophy; he philosophized the religion and christianized the philosophy of Italy; and, in this poetic union of religion and philosophy, he became the ground of transition into the mixed Platonism and Aristotelianism of the Schools, under which, by numerous minute articles of faith and ceremony, Christianity became a craft of hair-splitting, and was ultimately degraded into a complete *fetisch* worship, divorced from philosophy, and made up of a faith without thought, and a credulity directed by passion. Afterwards, indeed, philosophy revived under condi-

tion of defending this very superstition; and, in so
doing, it necessarily led the way to its subversion,
and that in exact proportion to the influence of the
philosophic schools. Hence it did its work most
completely in Germany, then in England, next in
France, then in Spain, least of all in Italy. We
must, therefore, take the poetry of Dante as christianized, but without the further Gothic accession
of proper chivalry. It was at a somewhat later period, that the importations from the East, through
the Venetian commerce and the crusading armaments, exercised a peculiarly strong influence on
Italy.

In studying Dante, therefore, we must consider
carefully the differences produced, first, by allegory
being substituted for polytheism; and secondly and
mainly, by the opposition of Christianity to the spirit of pagan Greece, which receiving the very names
of its gods from Egypt, soon deprived them of all
that was universal. The Greeks changed the ideas
into finites, and these finites into *anthropomor-
phi*, or forms of men. Hence their religion, their
poetry, nay, their very pictures, became statuesque.
With them the form was the end. The reverse of
this was the natural effect of Christianity; in which
finites, even the human form, must, in order to satisfy the mind, be brought into connexion with, and
be in fact symbolical of, the infinite; and must be
considered in some enduring, however shadowy and

H

indistinct, point of view, as the vehicle or representative of moral truth.

Hence resulted two great effects; a combination
of poetry with doctrine, and, by turning the mind
inward on its own essence instead of letting it act
only on its outward circumstances and communities,
a combination of poetry with sentiment.   And it is
this inwardness or subjectivity, which principally
and most fundamentally distinguishes all the classic
from all the modern poetry.   Compare the passage
in the Iliad (Z'. vi. 119—236.) in which Diomed
and Glaucus change arms,—

Χεῖράς τ' ἀλλήλων λαβέτην καὶ πιστώσαντο—
They took each other by the hand, and pledged friendship—

with the scene in Ariosto (Orlando Furioso, c. 1.
st. 20-22.), where Rinaldo and Ferrauto fight and
afterwards make it up :—

Al Pagan la proposta non dispiacque :
Così fu differita la tenzone ;
E tal tregua tra lor subito nacque,
Sì l' odio e l' ira va in oblivione,
Che 'l Pagano al partir dalle fresche acque
Non lasciò a piede il buon figliuol d' Amone ;
Con preghi invita, e al fin lo toglie in groppa,
E per l' orme d' Angelica galoppa.

Here Homer would have left it. But the Christian
poet has his own feelings to express, and goes on :—

Oh gran bontà de' cavalieri antiqui !
Eran rivali, eran di fè diversi,
E si sentian degli aspri colpi iniqui
Per tutta la persona anco dolersi ;

E pur per selve oscure e calli obbliqui
Insieme van senza sospetto aversi !

And here you will observe, that the reaction of
Ariosto's own feelings on the image or act is more
fore-grounded (to use a painter's phrase) than the
image or act itself.

The two different modes in which the imagination is acted-on-by the ancient and modern poetry,
may be illustrated by the parallel effects caused by
the contemplation of the Greek or Roman-Greek
architecture, compared with the Gothic.   In the
Pantheon, the whole is perceived in a perceived
harmony with the parts which compose it; and generally you will remember that where the parts preserve any distinct individuality, there simple beauty,
or beauty simply, arises; but where the parts melt
undistinguished into the whole, there majestic
beauty, or majesty, is the result. In York Minster,
the parts, the grotesques, are in themselves very
sharply distinct and separate, and this distinction
and separation of the parts is counterbalanced only
by the multitude and variety of those parts, by
which the attention is bewildered;—whilst the whole,
or that there is a whole produced, is altogether a
feeling in which the several thousand distinct impressions lose themselves as in a universal solvent.
Hence in a Gothic cathedral, as in a prospect from
a mountain's top, there is, indeed, a unity, an awful
oneness;—but it is, because all distinction evades
the eye. And just such is the distinction between

the Antigone of Sophocles and the Hamlet of Shakspeare.*

The Divina Commedia is a system of moral, political, and theological truths, with arbitrary personal exemplifications, which are not, in my opinion, allegorical. I do not even feel convinced that the punishments in the Inferno are strictly allegorical. I rather take them to have been in Dante's mind *quasi*-allegorical, or conceived in analogy to pure allegory.

I have said, that a combination of poetry with doctrines, is one of the characteristics of the Christian muse; but I think Dante has not succeeded in effecting this combination nearly so well as Milton.

This comparative failure of Dante, as also some other peculiarities of his mind, *in malam partem*, must be immediately attributed to the state of North Italy in his time, which is vividly represented in Dante's life; a state of intense democratical partizanship, in which an exaggerated importance was attached to individuals, and which whilst it afforded a vast field for the intellect, opened also a boundless arena for the passions, and in which envy, jealousy, hatred, and other malignant feelings, could and did assume the form of patriotism, even to the individual's own conscience.

All this common, and, as it were, natural partizanship, was aggravated and coloured by the Guelf

---

* See Lect. I. p. 9, and note: and compare with Schlegel's *Dram. Vorlesung.* Lect. I. vol. i. p. 10.

and Ghibelline factions; and, in part explanation of Dante's adherence to the latter, you must particularly remark, that the Pope had recently territorialized his authority to a great extent, and that this increase of territorial power in the church, was by no means the same beneficial movement for the citizens of free republics, as the parallel advance in other countries was for those who groaned as vassals under the oppression of the circumjacent baronial castles.*

By way of preparation to a satisfactory perusal of the Divina Commedia, I will now proceed to state what I consider to be Dante's chief excellences as a poet. And I begin with

1. Style — the vividness, logical connexion, strength and energy of which cannot be surpassed. In this I think Dante superior to Milton; and his style is accordingly more imitable than Milton's, and does to this day exercise a greater influence on the literature of his country. You cannot read Dante without feeling a gush of manliness of thought within you. Dante was very sensible of his own excellence in this particular, and speaks of poets as guardians of the vast armory of language, which is the intermediate something between matter and spirit :—

Or se' tu quel Virgilio, e quella fonte,
Che spande di parlar sì largo fiume ?

---

* Mr. Coleridge here notes: " I will, If I can, here make an historical movement, and pay a proper compliment to Mr. Hallam." *Ed.*

Risposi lui con vergognosa fronte.
  O degli altri poeti onore e lume,
Vagliami 'l lungo studio e 'l grande amore,
Che m' han fatto cercar lo tuo volume.
  Tu se' lo mio maestro, e 'l mio autore :
Tu se' solo colui, da cu' io tolsi
Lo bello stile, che m' ha fatto onore.

Inf c. 1. v. 79.

" And art thou then that Virgil, that well-spring,
From which such copious floods of eloquence
Have issued ?" I, with front abash'd, replied :
  " Glory and light of all the tuneful train !
May it avail me, that I long with zeal
Have sought thy volume, and with love immense
Have conn'd it o'er. My master, thou, and guide !
Thou he from whom I have alone deriv'd
That style, which for its beauty into fame
Exalts me." CARY.

Indeed there was a passion and a miracle of words in the twelfth and thirteenth centuries, after the long slumber of language in barbarism, which gave an almost romantic character, a virtuous quality and power, to what was read in a book, independently of the thoughts or images contained in it. This feeling is very often perceptible in Dante.

II. The Images in Dante are not only taken from obvious nature, and are all intelligible to all, but are ever conjoined with the universal feeling received from nature, and therefore affect the general feelings of all men. And in this respect, Dante's excellence is very great, and may be contrasted with the idiosyncracies of some meritorious modern poets, who attempt an eruditeness, the result of particular feelings. Consider the simplicity, I may say plainness, of the following simile, and how differently we should in all probability deal with it at the present day :

Quale i fioretti dal notturno gelo
Chinati e chiusi, poi che 'l sol gl' imbianca,
Si drizzan tutti aperti in loro stelo,—
    Fal mi fec' io di mia virtute stanca:

                                  Inf. c. 2. v. 127.

As florets, by the frosty air of night
Bent down and clos'd, when day has blanch'd their leaves,
Rise all unfolded on their spiry stems,—
So was my fainting vigour new restor'd.

                                  CARY.*

III. Consider the wonderful profoundness of the whole third canto of the Inferno ; and especially of the inscription over Hell gate :

                Per me si va, &c.—

which can only be explained by a meditation on the true nature of religion ; that is,—reason *plus* the understanding. I say profoundness rather than sublimity ; for Dante does not so much elevate your thoughts as send them down deeper. In this canto all the images are distinct, and even vividly distinct; but there is a total impression of infinity ; the wholeness is not in vision or conception, but in an inner feeling of totality, and absolute being.

_____

* Mr. Coleridge here notes: " Here to speak of Mr. Cary's translation."—*Ed.*

IV. In picturesqueness, Dante is beyond all other poets, modern, or ancient, and more in the stern style of Pindar, than of any other. Michael Angelo is said to have made a design for every page of the Divina Commedia. As superexcellent in this respect, I would note the conclusion of the third canto of the Inferno:

> Ed ecco verso noi venir per nave
> Un vecchio bianco per antico pelo
> Gridando: guai a voi anime prave : &c.
>
> Ver. 82. &c.

> *   *   *   *   *   *
>
>   And lo ! toward us in a bark
> Comes on an old man, hoary white with eld,
> Crying, " Woe to you, wicked spirits !
>
> *   *   *   *   *   *
>
> Cary.

> Caron dimonio con occhi di bragia
> Loro accennando, tutte le raccoglie :
> Batte col remo qualunque s' adagia.
>   Come d' autunno si levan le foglie
> L' una appresso dell' altra, infin che 'l ramo
> Rende alla terra tutte le sue spoglie ;
>   Similemente il mal seme d' Adamo,
> Gittansi di quel lito ad una ad una
> Per cenni, com' augel per suo richiamo.
>
> Ver. 100, &c.

> ————Charon, demoniac form,
> With eyes of burning coal, collects them all,
> Beck'ning, and each that lingers, with his oar
> Strikes. As fall off the light autumnal leaves,
> One still another following, till the bough
> Strews all its honours on the earth beneath ;—
> E'en in like manner Adam's evil brood

Cast themselves one by one down from the shore
Each at a beck, as falcon at his call.   CARY.

And this passage, which I think admirably picturesque:

Ma poco valse, che l' ale al sospetto
Non·potero avanzar : quegli andò sotto,
E quei drizzò, volando, suso il petto :
   Non altrimenti l' anitra di botto,
Quando 'l falcon s' appressa, giù s' attuffa,
Ed ei ritorna su crucciato e rotto.
   Irato Calcabrina della buffa,
Volando dietro gli tenne, invaghito,
Che quei campasse, per aver la zuffa:
   E come 'l barattier fu disparito,
Così volse gli artigli al suo compagno,
E fu con lui sovra 'l fosso ghermito.
   Ma l' altro fu bene sparvier grifagno
Ad artigliar ben lui, e amedue
Cadder nel mezzo del bollente stagno.
   Lo caldo sghermidor subito fue:
Ma però di levarsi era niente,
Sì aveano inviscate l' ale sue.

                    Infer. c. xxii. ver. 127, &c.

But little it avail'd : terror outstripp'd
His following flight : the other plung'd beneath,
And he with upward pinion rais'd his breast:
E'en thus the water-fowl, when she perceives
The falcon near, dives instant down, while he
Enrag'd and spent retires.   That mockery
In Calcabrina fury stirr'd, who flew
After him, with desire of strife inflam'd ;
And, for the barterer had 'scap'd, so turn'd
His talons on his comrade.   O'er the dyke
In grapple close they join'd ; but th' other prov'd
A goshawk, able to rend well his foe ;

And in the boiling lake both fell.   The heat·
Was umpire soon between them, but in vain
To lift themselves they strove, so fast were glued
Their pennons.   CARY.

V. Very closely connected with this picturesqueness, is the topographic reality of Dante's journey
through Hell.   You should note and dwell on this
as one of his great charms, and which gives a striking peculiarity to his poetic power.   He thus takes
the thousand delusive forms of a nature worse than
chaos, having no reality but from the passions which
they excite, and compels them into the service of
the permanent.   Observe the exceeding truth of
these lines :

Noi ricidemmo 'l cerchio all' altra riva,
Sovr' una fonte che bolle, e riversa,
Per un fossato che da lei diriva.
   L' acqua era buja molto più che persa :
E noi in compagnia dell' onde bige
Entrammo giù per una via diversa.
   Una palude fa, ch' ha nome Stige,
Questo tristo ruscel, quando è disceso
Al piè delle maligne piagge grige.
   Ed io che di mirar mi stava inteso,—
Vidi genti fangose in quel pantano
Ignude tutte, e con sembiante offeso.
   Questi si percotean non pur con mano,
Ma con la testa, e col petto, e co' piedi,
Troncandosi co' denti a brano a brano.
         *   *   *   *   *   *
   Così girammo della lorda pozza
Grand' arco tra la ripa secca e 'l mezzo,
Con gli occhi volti a chi del fango ingozza :
   Venimmo appiè d' una torre al dassezzo.
                              C. vii. ver. 100 and 127.

——We the circle cross'd
To the next steep, arriving at a well,
That boiling pours itself down to a foss
Sluic'd from its source. Far murkier was the wave
Than sablest grain : and we in company
Of th' inky waters, journeying by their side,
Enter'd, though by a different track, beneath.
Into a lake, the Stygian nam'd, expands
The dismal stream, when it hath reach'd the foot
Of the grey wither'd cliffs. Intent I stood
To gaze, and in the marsh sunk, descried
A miry tribe, all naked, and with looks
Betok'ning rage. They with their hands alone
Struck not, but with the head, the breast, the feet,
Cutting each other piecemeal with their fangs.

*   *   *   *   *   *

————Our route
Thus compass'd, we a segment widely stretch'd
Between the dry embankment and the cove
Of the loath'd pool, turning meanwhile our eyes
Downward on those who gulp'd its muddy lees ;
Nor stopp'd, till to a tower's low base we came.

CARY.

VI. For Dante's power,—his absolute mastery
over, although rare exhibition of, the pathetic, I can
do no more than refer to the passages on Francesca
di Rimini (Infer. C. v. ver. 73 to the end) and on
Ugolino, (Infer. C. xxxiii. ver. 1 to 75.) They are
so well known, and rightly so admired, that it would
be pedantry to analyze their composition ; but you
will note that the first is the pathos of passion, the
second that of affection ; and yet even in the first,
you seem to perceive that the lovers have sacrificed

their passion to the cherishing of a deep and re-
memberable impression.

VII. As to going into the endless subtle beauties of Dante, that is impossible; but I cannot help
citing the first triplet of the 29th canto of the Inferno :

> La molta gente e le diverse piaghe
> Avean le luci mie sì inebriate,
> Che dello stare a piangere eran vaghe.

> So were mine eyes inebriate with the view
> Of the vast multitude, whom various wounds
> Disfigur'd, that they long'd to stay and weep.
>
> CARY.

Nor have I now room for any specific comparison
of Dante with Milton. But if I had, I would insti-
tute it upon the ground of the last canto of the Inferno from the 1st to the 69th line, and from the
106th to the end. And in this comparison I should
notice Dante's occasional fault of becoming grotesque from being too graphic without imagination;
as in his Lucifer compared with Milton's Satan.
Indeed he is sometimes horrible rather than terri-
ble,—falling into the μισητὸν instead of the δεινὸν
of Longinus;* in other words, many of his images
excite bodily disgust, and not moral fear. But
here, as in other cases, you may perceive that the
faults of great authors are generally excellencies
carried to an excess.

---

* De Subl. l. ix.

MILTON.

Born in London, 1608.—Died, 1674.

If we divide the period from the accession of Elizabeth to the Protectorate of Cromwell into two unequal portions, the first ending with the death of James I. the other comprehending the reign of Charles and the brief glories of the Republic, we are forcibly struck with a difference in the character of the illustrious actors, by whom each period is rendered severally memorable. Or rather, the difference in the characters of the great men in each period, leads us to make this division. Eminent as the intellectual powers were that were displayed in both; yet in the number of great men, in the various sorts of excellence, and not merely in the variety but almost diversity of talents united in the same individual, the age of Charles falls short of its predecessor; and the stars of the Parliament, keen as their radiance was, in fulness and richness of lustre, yield to the constellation at the court of Elizabeth;—which can only be paralleled by Greece in her brightest moment, when the titles of the poet, the philosopher, the historian, the statesman and the general not seldom formed a garland round the same head, as in the instances of our Sidneys and Raleighs. But then, on the other hand, there was a vehemence of will, an enthusiasm of principle, a depth and an earnestness of spirit, which the charms of individual fame and personal aggrandisement could not pacify,—an aspiration after reality, permanence, and general good, —in short, a moral grandeur in the latter period, with which the low intrigues, Machiavellic maxims, and selfish and servile ambition of the former, stand in painful contrast.

The causes of this it belongs not to the present occasion to detail at length; but a mere allusion to the quick succession of revolutions in religion, breeding a political indifference in the mass of men to religion itself, the enormous increase of the royal power in consequence of the humiliation of the nobility and the clergy—the transference of the papal authority to the crown,—the unfixed state of Elizabeth's own opinions, whose inclinations were as popish as her interests were protestant—the controversial extravagance and practical imbecility of her successor—will help to explain the former period ; and the persecutions that had given a life-and-soul-interest to the disputes so imprudently fostered by James,—the ardour of a conscious increase of power in the commons, and the greater austerity of manners and maxims, the natural product and most formidable weapon of religious disputation, not merely in conjunction, but in closest combination, with newly awakened political and republican zeal, these perhaps account for the character of the latter æra.

In the close of the former period, and during the

bloom of the latter, the poet Milton was educated and formed; and he survived the latter, and all the fond hopes and aspirations which had been its life; and so in evil days, standing as the representative of the combined excellence of both periods, he produced the Paradise Lost as by an after-throe of nature. "There are some persons," (observes a divine, a contemporary of Milton's) " of whom the grace of God takes early hold, and the good spirit inhabiting them, carries them on in an even constancy through innocence into virtue, their Christianity bearing equal date with their manhood, and reason and religion, like warp and woof, running together, make up one web of a wise and exemplary life. This (he adds) is a most happy case, wherever it happens; for, besides that there is no sweeter or more lovely thing on earth than the early buds of piety, which drew from our Saviour signal affection to the beloved disciple, it is better to have no wound than to experience the most sovereign balsam, which, if it work a cure, yet usually leaves a scar behind." Although it was and is my intention to defer the consideration of Milton's own character to the conclusion of this Lecture, yet I could not prevail on myself to approach the Paradise Lost without impressing on your minds the conditions under which such a work was in fact producible at all, the original genius having been assumed as the immediate agent and efficient cause; and these conditions I find in the character of the

times and in his own character.   The age in which
the foundations of his mind were laid, was congenial to it as one golden æra of profound erudition
and individual genius;—that in which the super-
structure was carried up, was no less favourable to
it by a sternness of discipline and a show of self-
control, highly flattering to the imaginative dignity
of an heir of fame, and which won Milton over from
the dear-loved delights of academic groves and cathedral aisles to the anti-prelatic party.   It acted
on him, too, no doubt, and modified his studies by
a characteristic controversial spirit, (his presentation of God is tinted with it)—a spirit not less busy
indeed in political than in theological and ecclesiastical dispute, but carrying on the former almost
always, more or less, in the guise of the latter.
And so far as Pope's censure* of our poet, —that
he makes God the Father a school divine—is just,
we must attribute it to the character of his age, from
which the men of genius, who escaped, escaped by
a worse disease, the licentious indifference of a
Frenchified court.

Such was the *nidus* or soil, which constituted, in
the strict sense of the word, the circumstances of
Milton's mind.   In his mind itself there were purity and piety absolute; an imagination to which
neither the past nor the present were interesting,
except as far as they called forth and enlivened the

---

* Table Talk, vol. ii. p. 264.

great ideal, in which and for which he lived; a keen
love of truth, which, after many weary pursuits,
found a harbour in a sublime listening to the still
voice in his own spirit, and as keen a love of his
country, which, after a disappointment still more
depressive, expanded and soared into a love of man
as a probationer of immortality. These were, these
alone could be, the conditions under which such a
work as the Paradise Lost could be conceived and
accomplished. By a life-long study Milton had
known—

> What was of use to know,
> What best to say could say, to do had done.
> His actions to his words agreed, his words
> To his large heart gave utterance due, his heart
> Contain'd of good, wise, fair, the perfect shape;

and he left the imperishable total, as a bequest to
the ages coming, in the PARADISE LOST.*

Difficult as I shall find it to turn over these leaves
without catching some passage, which would tempt
me to stop, I propose to consider, 1st, the general
plan and arrangement of the work;—2ndly, the subject with its difficulties and advantages;—3rdly, the
poet's object, the spirit in the letter, the ἐνθύμιον ἐν

---

* Here Mr. C. notes: " Not perhaps here, but towards,
or as, the conclusion, to chastise the fashionable notion that
poetry is a relaxation or amusement, one of the superfluous
toys and luxuries of the intellect! To contrast the permanence of poems with the transiency and fleeting moral effects
of empires, and what are called, great events." *Ed.*

2   I

μύθῳ, the true school-divinity; and lastly, the characteristic excellencies of the poem, in what they
consist, and by what means they were produced.

1. As to the plan and ordonnance of the Poem.

Compare it with the Iliad, many of the books of
which might change places without any injury to
the thread of the story. Indeed, I doubt the original existence of the Iliad as one poem; it seems
more probable that it was put together about the
time of the Pisistratidæ. The Iliad—and, more
or less, all epic poems, the subjects of which are
taken from history—have no rounded conclusion;
they remain, after all, but single chapters from the
volume of history, although they are ornamental
chapters. Consider the exquisite simplicity of the
Paradise Lost. It and it alone really possesses a
beginning, a middle, and an end; it has the totality of the poem as distinguished from the *ab ovo*
birth and parentage, or straight line, of history.

2. As to the subject.

In Homer, the supposed importance of the subject, as the first effort of confederated Greece, is an
after-thought of the critics; and the interest, such
as it is, derived from the events themselves, as distinguished from the manner of representing them,
is very languid to all but Greeks. It is a Greek
poem. The superiority of the Paradise Lost is obvious in this respect, that the interest transcends
the limits of a nation. But we do not generally
dwell on this excellence of the Paradise Lost, be-

cause it seems attributable to Christianity itself;—
yet in fact the interest is wider than Christendom,
and comprehends the Jewish and Mohammedan
worlds;—nay, still further, inasmuch as it represents the origin of evil, and the combat of evil and
good, it contains matter of deep interest to all mankind, as forming the basis of all religion, and the
true occasion of all philosophy whatsoever.

The FALL of man is the subject; Satan is the
cause; man's blissful state the immediate object of
his enmity and attack; man is warned by an angel
who gives him an account of all that was requisite to
be known, to make the warning at once intelligible
and awful, then the temptation ensues, and the Fall;
then the immediate sensible consequence; then the
consolation, wherein an angel presents a vision of
the history of men with the ultimate triumph of the
Redeemer.   Nothing is touched in this vision but
what is of general interest in religion; any thing
else would have been improper.

The inferiority of Klopstock's Messiah is inex-
pressible. I admit the prerogative of poetic feeling,
and poetic faith; but I cannot suspend the judgment even for a moment.   A poem may in one
sense be a dream, but it must be a waking dream.
In Milton you have a religious faith combined with
the moral nature; it is an efflux; you go along with
it.   In Klopstock there is a wilfulness; he makes
things so and so. The feigned speeches and events
in the Messiah shock us like falsehoods; but no-

thing of that sort is felt in the Paradise Lost, in which no particulars, at least very few indeed, are touched which can come into collision or juxta-position with recorded matter.

But notwithstanding the advantages in Milton's subject, there were concomitant insuperable difficulties, and Milton has exhibited marvellous skill in keeping most of them out of sight. High poetry is the translation of reality into the ideal under the predicament of succession of time only.   The poet is an historian, upon condition of moral power being the only force in the universe. The very grandeur of his subject ministered a difficulty to Milton. The statement of a being of high intellect, warring against the supreme Being, seems to contradict the idea of a supreme Being.   Milton precludes our feeling this, as much as possible, by keeping the peculiar attributes of divinity less in sight, making them to a certain extent allegorical only.   Again poetry implies the language of excitement; yet how to reconcile such language with God ! Hence Milton confines the poetic passion in God's speeches to the language of scripture ; and once only allows the *passio vera,* or *quasi humana* to appear, in the passage, where the Father contemplates his own likeness in the Son before the battle :—

Go then, thou Mightiest, in thy Father's might,
Ascend my chariot, guide the rapid wheels
That shake Heaven's basis, bring forth all my war,
My bow and thunder; my almighty arms

Gird on, and sword upon thy puissant thigh ;
Pursue these sons of darkness, drive them out
From all Heaven's bounds into the utter deep :
There let them learn, as likes them, to despise
God and Messiah his anointed king.

B. VI. v. 710.

3. As to Milton's object :

It was to justify the ways of God to man! The controversial spirit observable in many parts of the poem, especially in God's speeches, is immediately attributable to the great controversy of that age, the origination of evil. The Arminians considered it a mere calamity. The Calvinists took away all human will. Milton asserted the will, but declared for the enslavement of the will out of an act of the will itself. There are three powers in us, which distinguish us from the beasts that perish ;—1, reason ; 2, the power of viewing universal truth ; and 3, the power of contracting universal truth into particulars. Religion is the will in the reason, and love in the will.

The character of Satan is pride and sensual indulgence, finding in self the sole motive of action. It is the character so often seen *in little* on the political stage. It exhibits all the restlessness, temerity, and cunning which have marked the mighty hunters of mankind from Nimrod to Napoleon. The common fascination of men is, that these great men, as they are called, must act from some great motive. Milton has carefully marked in his Satan the intense selfishness, the alcohol of egotism, which

would rather reign in hell than serve in heaven.
To place this lust of self in opposition to denial of
self or duty, and to show what exertions it would
make, and what pains endure to accomplish its end,
is Milton's particular object in the character of Satan.   But around this character he has thrown a
singularity of daring, a grandeur of sufferance, and
a ruined splendour, which constitute the very height
of poetic sublimity.

Lastly, as to the execution :—

The language and versification of the Paradise
Lost are peculiar in being so much more necessarily correspondent to each than those in any other
poem or poet. /The connexion of the sentences
and the position of the words are exquisitely artificial; but the position is rather according to the
logic of passion or universal logic, than to the logic
of grammar.   Milton attempted to make the English language obey the logic of passion, as perfectly
as the Greek and Latin.   Hence the occasional
harshness in the construction.

Sublimity is the pre-eminent characteristic of the
Paradise Lost.   It is not an arithmetical sublime
like Klopstock's, whose rule always is to treat what
we might think large as contemptibly small. Klopstock mistakes bigness for greatness.   There is a
greatness arising from images of effort and daring,
and also from those of moral endurance ; in Milton
both are united. The fallen angels are human passions, invested with a dramatic reality.

The apostrophe to light at the commencement of

the third book is particularly beautiful as an intermediate link between Hell and Heaven; and observe, how the second and third book support the
subjective character of the poem. In all modern
poetry in Christendom there is an under consciousness of a sinful nature, a fleeting away of external
things, the mind or subject greater than the object,
the reflective character predominant. In the Paradise Lost the sublimest parts are the revelations
of Milton's own mind, producing itself and evolving
its own greatness; and this is so truly so, that when
that which is merely entertaining for its objective
beauty is introduced, it at first seems a discord.

In the description of Paradise itself, you have
Milton's sunny side as a man; here his descriptive
powers are exercised to the utmost, and he draws
deep upon his Italian resources. In the description
of Eve, and throughout this part of the poem, the
poet is predominant over the theologian. Dress is
the symbol of the Fall, but the mark of intellect;
and the metaphysics of dress are, the hiding what is
not symbolic and displaying by discrimination what
is. The love of Adam and Eve in Paradise is of
the highest merit — not phantomatic, and yet removed from every thing degrading. It is the sentiment of one rational being towards another made
tender by a specific difference in that which is essentially the same in both; it is a union of opposites,
a giving and receiving mutually of the permanent
in either, a completion of each in the other.

Milton is not a picturesque, but a musical, poet;

although he has this merit, that the object chosen
by him for any particular foreground always re-.
mains prominent to the end, enriched, but not in-
cumbered, by the opulence of descriptive details
furnished by an exhaustless imagination. I wish
the Paradise Lost were more carefully read and
studied than I can see any ground for believing it
is, especially those parts which, from the habit of
always looking for a story in poetry, are scarcely
read at all, — as for example, Adam's vision of future events in the 11th and 12th books. No one
can rise from the perusal of this immortal poem
without a deep sense of the grandeur and the purity
of Milton's soul, or without feeling how susceptible
of domestic enjoyments he really was, notwithstanding the discomforts which actually resulted from an
apparently unhappy choice in marriage. He was,
as every truly great poet has ever been, a good man ;
but finding it impossible to realize his own aspirations, either in religion or politics, or society, he
gave up his heart to the living spirit and light
within him, and avenged himself on the world by en-
riching it with this record of his own transcendant
ideal.

!

Notes on Milton. 1807.*

(Hayley quotes the following passage :—)

" Time serves not now, and, perhaps, I might seem too profuse to give any certain account of what the mind at home, in the spacious circuit of her musing, hath liberty to propose to herself, though of highest hope and hardest attempting; whether that epic form, whereof the two poems of Homer, and those other two of Virgil and Tasso, are a diffuse, and *the book of Job a brief, model.*" p. 69.

These latter words deserve particular notice. I do not doubt that Milton intended his Paradise Lost as an epic of the first class, and that the poetic dialogue of the Book of Job was his model for the general scheme of his Paradise Regained. Readers would not be disappointed in this latter poem, if they proceeded to a perusal of it with a proper preconception of the kind of interest intended to be excited in that admirable work. In its kind it is the most perfect poem extant, though its kind may be inferior in interest—being in its essence didactic —to that other sort, in which instruction is conveyed more effectively, because less directly, in connection with stronger and more pleasurable emotions, and thereby in a closer affinity with action. But might we not as rationally object to an accom-

---

* These notes were written by Mr. Coleridge in a copy of Hayley's Life of Milton, (4to. 1796), belonging to Mr. Poole. By him they were communicated, and this seems the fittest place for their publication. *Ed.*

plished woman's conversing, however agreeably, because it has happened that we have received a
keener pleasure from her singing to the harp? *Si
genus sit probo et sapienti viro haud indignum,
et si poema sit in suo genere perfectum, satis est.
Quod si hoc auctor idem altioribus numeris et
carmini diviniori ipsum per se divinum superad-
diderit, mehercule satis est, et plusquam satis.* I
cannot, however, but wish that the answer of Jesus
to Satan in the 4th book, (v. 285.)—

> Think not but that I know these things; or think
> I know them not, not therefore am I short
> Of knowing what I ought, &c.

had breathed the spirit of Hayley's noble quotation
rather than the narrow bigotry of Gregory the
Great. The passage is, indeed, excellent, and is
partially true; but partial truth is the worst mode
of conveying falsehood.

> Hayley, p. 75. " The sincerest friends of Milton may
> here agree with Johnson, who speaks of *his controversial
> merriment as disgusting.*"

The man who reads a work meant for immediate
effect on one age with the notions and feelings of
another, may be a refined gentleman, but must be
a sorry critic. He who possesses imagination
enough to live with his forefathers, and, leaving
comparative reflection for an after moment, to give
himself up during the first perusal to the feelings
of a contemporary, if not a partizan, will, I dare

aver, rarely find any part of Milton's prose works disgusting.

(Hayley, p. 104. Hayley is speaking of the passage in Milton's Answer to Icon Basilice, in which he accuses Charles of taking his Prayer in captivity from Pamela's prayer in the 3rd book of Sidney's Arcadia. The passage begins,—

" But this king, not content with that which, although in a thing holy, is no holy theft, to attribute to his own making other men's whole prayers," &c. Symmons' ed. 1806 p. 407.)

Assuredly, I regret that Milton should have written this passage; and yet the adoption of a prayer from a romance on such an occasion does not evince a delicate or deeply sincere mind. We are the creatures of association. There are some excellent moral and even serious lines in Hudibras; but what if a clergyman should adorn his sermon with a quotation from that poem! Would the abstract propriety of the verses leave him " honourably acquitted?" The Christian baptism of a line in Virgil is so far from being a parallel, that it is ridiculously inappropriate,—an absurdity as glaring as that of the bigoted Puritans, who objected to some of the noblest and most scriptural prayers ever dictated by wisdom and piety, simply because the Roman Catholics had used them.

Hayley, p. 107. " The ambition of Milton," &c.

I do not approve the so frequent use of this word relatively to Milton. Indeed the fondness for ingrafting a good sense on the word " ambition," is not a Christian impulse in general.

Hayley, p. 110. " Milton himself seems to have thought it allowable in literary contention to vilify, &c. the character of an opponent; but surely this doctrine is unworthy," &c.

If ever it were allowable, in this case it was especially so. But these general observations, without meditation on the particular times and the genius of the times, are most often as unjust as they are always superficial.

(Hayley, p. 133. Hayley is speaking of Milton's panegyric on Cromwell's government :—)

Besides, however Milton might and did regret the immediate necessity, yet what alternative was there? Was it not better that Cromwell should usurp power, to protect religious freedom at least, than that the Presbyterians should usurp it to introduce a religious persecution,— extending the notion of spiritual concerns so far as to leave no freedom even to a man's bedchamber?

(Hayley, p. 250. Hayley's conjectures on the origin of the Paradise Lost :—)

If Milton borrowed a hint from any writer, it was more probably from Strada's Prolusions, in which the Fall of the Angels is pointed out as the noblest subject for a Christian poet.* The more dissimilar

---

* The reference seems generally to be to the 5th Prolusion of the 1st Book. *Hic arcus hac tela, quibus olim in magno illo Superum tumultu princeps armorum Michael confixit auctorem proditionis; hic fulmina humanæ mentis terror.*

the detailed images are, the more likely it is that a great genius should catch the general idea.

(Hayl. p. 294. Extracts from the Adamo of Andreini:)

" Lucifero. Che dal mio centro oscuro
    Mi chiama a rimirar cotanta luce?

    Who from my dark abyss
    Calls me to gaze on this *excess of light ?*"

The words in italics are an unfair translation. They may suggest that Milton really had read and did imitate this drama. The original is ' in so great light.' Indeed the whole version is affectedly and inaccurately Miltonic.

Ib. v. 11.   Che di fango opre festi—
    Forming thy works of *dust* (no, dirt.—)

Ib. v. 17.   Tessa pur stella a stella,
    V' aggiunga e luna, e sole.—

    Let him unite above
    Star upon star, moon, sun.

    Let him weave star to star,
    Then join both moon and sun !

Ib. v. 21.   Ch 'al fin con biasmo e scorno
    Vana l'opra sarà, vano il sudore!

    Since in the end division
    Shall prove his works and all his efforts vain.

---

*   *   *   *. *In"nubibus armatas bello legiones instruam, atque inde pro re nata auxiliares ad terram copias evocabo.* *
*   *   *   *. *Hic mihi Cælites, quos esse ferunt elemento- rum tutelares, prima illa corpora miscebunt. sect. 4.* Ed.

Since finally with censure and disdain
Vain shall the work be, and his toil be vain!

1796.*

The reader of Milton must be always on his duty : he is surrounded with sense ; it rises in every line ; every word is to the purpose. There are no lazy intervals ; all has been considered, and demands and merits observation. If this be called obscurity, let it be remembered that it is such an obscurity as is a compliment to the reader ; not that vicious obscurity, which proceeds from a muddled head.

LECTURE XI.†

Asiatic and Greek Mythologies—Robinson Crusoe —Use of works of Imagination in Education.

A CONFOUNDING of God with Nature, and an incapacity of finding unity in the manifold and infinity in the individual,—these are the origin of polytheism. The most perfect instance of this kind of theism is that of early Greece ; other nations seem to have either transcended, or come short of, the old Hellenic standard,—a mythology in itself fundamentally allegorical, and typical of the

---

* From a common-place book of Mr. C.'s, communicated by Mr. J. M. Gutch. *Ed.*

† Partly from Mr. Green's note. *Ed.*

powers and functions of nature, but subsequently mixed up with a deification of great men and hero-worship, — so that finally the original idea became inextricably combined with the form and attributes of some legendary individual. In Asia, probably from the greater unity of the government and the still surviving influence of patriarchal tradition, the idea of the unity of God, in a distorted reflection of the Mosaic scheme, was much more generally preserved; and accordingly all other super or ultra-human beings could only be represented as ministers of, or rebels against, his will. The Asiatic genii and fairies are, therefore, always endowed with moral qualities, and distinguishable as malignant or benevolent to man. It is this uniform attribution of fixed moral qualities to the supernatural agents of eastern mythology that particularly separates them from the divinities of old Greece.

Yet it is not altogether improbable that in the Samothracian or Cabeiric mysteries the link between the Asiatic and Greek popular schemes of mythology lay concealed. Of these mysteries there are conflicting accounts, and, perhaps, there were variations of doctrine in the lapse of ages and intercourse with other systems. But, upon a review of all that is left to us on this subject in the writings of the ancients, we may, I think, make out thus much of an interesting fact,—that *Cabiri*, impliedly at least, meant *socii*, *complices*, having a hypostatic or fundamental union with, or relation to, each

other; that these mysterious divinities were, ultimately at least, divided into a higher and lower
triad; that the lower triad, *primi quia infimi*, consisted of the old Titanic deities or powers of nature,
under the obscure names of *Axieros, Axiokersos,*
and *Axiokersa*, representing symbolically different
modifications of animal desire or material action,
such as hunger, thirst, and fire, without consciousness; that the higher triad, *ultimi quia superiores,*
consisted of Jupiter, (Pallas, or Apollo, or Bacchus,
or Mercury, mystically called *Cadmilos*) and Venus,
representing, as before, the νοῦς or reason, the
λόγος or word or communicative power, and the
ἔρως or love;—that the *Cadmilos* or Mercury, the
manifested, communicated, or sent, appeared not
only in his proper person as second of the higher
triad, but also as a mediator between the higher
and lower triad, and so there were seven divinities;
and, indeed, according to some authorities, it might
seem that the *Cadmilos* acted once as a mediator
of the higher, and once of the lower, triad, and that
so there were eight Cabeiric divinities. The lower
or Titanic powers being subdued, chaos ceased,
and creation began in the reign of the divinities of
mind and love; but the chaotic gods still existed in
the abyss, and the notion of evoking them was the
origin, the idea, of the Greek necromancy.

These mysteries, like all the others, were certainly in connection with either the Phœnician or
Egyptian systems, perhaps with both. Hence the

old Cabeiric powers were soon made to answer to the corresponding popular divinities; and the lower triad was called by the uninitiated, Ceres, Vulcan or Pluto, and Proserpine, and the *Cadmilos* became Mercury. It is not without ground that I direct your attention, under these circumstances, to the probable derivation of some portion of this most remarkable system from patriarchal tradition, and to the connection of the Cabeiri with the Kabbala.

The Samothracian mysteries continued in celebrity till some time after the commencement of the Christian era.* But they gradually sank with the rest of the ancient system of mythology, to which, in fact, they did not properly belong. The peculiar doctrines, however, were preserved in the memories of the initiated, and handed down by individuals. No doubt they were propagated in Europe, and it is not improbable that Paracelsus received many of his opinions from such persons, and I think a connection may be traced between him and Jacob Behmen.

The Asiatic supernatural beings are all produced by imagining an excessive magnitude, or an excessive smallness combined with great power; and the broken associations, which must have given rise to such conceptions, are the sources of the interest

---

* In the reign of Tiberius, A.D. 18, Germanicus attempted to visit Samothrace;—*illum in regressu sacra Samothracum visere nitentem obvii aquilones depulere.* Tacit. Ann. II. c. 54. *Ed.*

which they inspire, as exhibiting, through the working of the imagination, the idea of power in the will.
This is delightfully exemplified in the Arabian
Nights' Entertainments, and indeed, more or less,
in other works of the same kind. In all these there
is the same activity of mind as in dreaming, that is—
an exertion of the fancy in the combination and recom-
bination of familiar objects so as to produce novel
and wonderful imagery. To this must be added
that these tales cause no deep feeling of a moral
kind—whether of religion or love; but an impulse
of motion is communicated to the mind without
excitement, and this is the reason of their being so
generally read and admired.

I think it not unlikely that the Milesian Tales
contained the germs of many of those now in the
Arabian Nights; indeed it is scarcely possible to
doubt that the Greek Empire must have left deep
impression on the Persian intellect. So also many
of the Roman Catholic legends are taken from
Apuleius.   In that exquisite story of Cupid and
Psyche, the allegory is of no injury to the dramatic
vividness of the tale.   It is evidently a philosophic
attempt to parry Christianity with a *quasi*-Platonic
account of the fall and redemption of the soul.

The charm of De Foe's works, especially of Robinson Crusoe, is founded on the same principle. It
always interests, never agitates. Crusoe himself is
merely a representative of humanity in general; neither his intellectual or his moral qualities set him

above the middle degree of mankind; his only prominent characteristic is the spirit of enterprise and wandering, which is, nevertheless, a very common disposition. You will observe that all that is wonderful in
this tale is the result of external circumstances—
of things which fortune brings to Crusoe's hand.

NOTES ON ROBINSON CRUSOE.*

Vol. i. p. 17. But my ill fate pushed me on now with an
obstinacy that nothing could resist; and though I had several times loud calls from my reason, and my more composed
judgment to go home, yet I had no power to do it. I know
not what to call this, nor will I urge that it is a secret overruling decree that hurries us on to be the instruments of our
own destruction, even though it be before us, and that we
rush upon it with our eyes open.

The wise only possess ideas; the greater part
of mankind are possessed by them. Robinson
Crusoe was not conscious of the master impulse,
even because it was his master, and had taken, as
he says, full possession of him. When once the
mind, in despite of the remonstrating conscience,
has abandoned its free power to a haunting impulse
or idea, then whatever tends to give depth and
vividness to this idea or indefinite imagination,
increases its despotism, and in the same proportion
renders the reason and free will ineffectual. Now,
fearful calamities, sufferings, horrors, and hair-

---

* These notes were written by Mr. C. in Mr. Gillman's
copy of Robinson Crusoe, in the summer of 1830. The references in the text are to Major's edition, 1831. *Ed.*

breadth escapes will have this effect, far more than even sensual pleasure and prosperous incidents. Hence the evil consequences of sin in such cases, instead of retracting or deterring the sinner, goad him on to his destruction. This is the moral of Shakspeare's Macbeth, and the true solution of this paragraph,—not any overruling decree of divine wrath, but the tyranny of the sinner's own evil imagination, which he has voluntarily chosen as his master.

Compare the contemptuous Swift with the contemned De Foe, and how superior will the latter be found! But by what test?—Even by this; that the writer who makes me sympathize with his presentations with the whole of my being, is more estimable than he who calls forth, and appeals but to, a part of my being—my sense of the ludicrous, for instance. De Foe's excellence it is, to make me forget my specific class, character, and circumstances, and to raise me while I read him, into the universal man.

P. 80. I smiled to myself at the sight of this money: " O drug !" said I aloud, &c. *However upon second thoughts, I took it away ;* and wrapping all this in a piece of canvass, &c.

Worthy of Shakspeare!—and yet the simple semicolon after it, the instant passing on without the least pause of reflex consciousness, is more exquisite and masterlike than the touch itself. A meaner writer, a Marmontel, would have put an (!) after ' *away*,' and have commenced a fresh paragraph. 30th July, 1830.

P. 111. And I must confess, my religious thankfulness
to God's providence began to abate too, upon the discovering that all this was nothing but what was common; though
I ought to have been as thankful for so strange and unfore-
seen a providence, as if it had been miraculous.

To make men feel the truth of this is one characteristic object of the miracles worked by Moses;
—in them the providence is miraculous, the miracles providential.

P. 126. The growing up of the corn, as is hinted in my
Journal, had, at first, some little influence upon me, and
began to affect me with seriousness, as long as I thought it
had something miraculous in it, &c.

By far the ablest vindication of miracles which I
have met with. It is indeed the true ground, the
proper purpose and intention of a miracle.

P. 141. To think that this was all my own, that I was
king and lord of all this country indefeasibly, &c.

By the by, what is the law of England respecting
this? Suppose I had discovered, or been wrecked
on an uninhabited island, would it be mine or the
king's?

P. 223. I considered—that as I could not foresee what
the ends of divine wisdom might be in all this, so I was not
to dispute his sovereignty, who, as I was his creature, had
an undoubted right, by creation, to govern and dispose of
me absolutely as he thought fit, &c.

I could never understand this reasoning, grounded
on a complete misapprehension of St. Paul's image
of the potter, Rom. ix., or rather I do fully understand the absurdity of it. The susceptibility of

pain and pleasure, of good and evil, constitutes a
right in every creature endowed therewith in relation to every rational and moral being,—*a fortiori*
therefore, to the Supreme Reason, to the absolutely
good Being.   Remember Davenant's verses ;—

> Doth it our reason's mutinies appease
> To say, the potter may his own clay mould
> To every use, or in what shape he please,
> At first not counsell'd, nor at last controll'd ?
>
> Power's hand can neither easy be, nor strict
> To lifeless clay, which ease nor torment knows,
> And where it cannot favour or afflict,
> It neither justice or injustice shows.
>
> But souls have life, and life eternal too:
> Therefore if doom'd before they can offend,
> It seems to show what heavenly power can do,
> But does not in that deed that power commend.
>
> Death of Astragon. st. 88, &c.

P. 232-3.   And this I must observe with grief too, that
the discomposure of my mind had too great impressions also
upon the religious parts of my thoughts,—praying to God
being properly an act of the mind, not of the body.

As justly conceived as it is beautifully expressed.
And a mighty motive for habitual prayer; for this
cannot but greatly facilitate the performance of rational prayer even in moments of urgent distress.

P. 244.   That this would justify the conduct of the Spaniards in all their barbarities practised in America.

De Foe was a true philanthropist, who had risen
above the antipathies of nationality; but he was
evidently partial to the Spanish character, which,

however, it is not, I fear, possible to acquit of cruelty. Witness the Netherlands, the Inquisition, the late Guerilla warfare, &c.

P. 249. That I shall not discuss, and perhaps cannot account for ; but certainly they are a proof of the converse of spirits, &c.

This reminds me of a conversation I once overheard. " How a statement so injurious to Mr A. and so contrary to the truth, should have been made to you by Mr. B. I do not pretend to account for ; —only I know of my own knowledge that B. is an inveterate liar, and has long borne malice against Mr. A.; and I can prove that he has repeatedly declared that in some way or other he would do Mr. A. a mischief."

P. 254. The place I was in was a most delightful cavity or grotto of its kind, as could be expected, though perfectly dark ; the floor was dry and level, and had a sort of small loose gravel on it, &c.

How accurate an observer of nature De Foe was! The reader will at once recognise Professor Buckland's caves and the diluvial gravel.

P. 308. I entered into a long discourse with him about the devil, the original of him, his rebellion against God, his enmity to man, the reason of it, his setting himself up in the dark parts of the world to be worshipped instead of God, &c.

I presume that Milton's Paradise Lost must have been bound up with one of Crusoe's Bibles; otherwise I should be puzzled to know where he found all this history of the Old Gentleman. Not a word of it in the Bible itself, I am quite sure. But to be serious. De Foe did not reflect that all these difficulties are attached to a mere fiction, or, at the best, an allegory, supported by a few popular phrases and figures of speech used incidentally or dramatically by the Evangelists, — and that the existence of a personal, intelligent, evil being, the counterpart and antagonist of God, is in direct contradiction to the most express declarations of Holy Writ. *" Shall there be evil in a city, and the Lord hath not done it ?"* Amos, iii. 6. *" I make peace and create evil."* Isa. xlv. 7. This is the deep mystery of the abyss of God.

Vol ii. p. 3. I have often heard persons of good judgment say, * * * that there is no such thing as a spirit appearing, a ghost walking, and the like, &c.

I cannot conceive a better definition of Body than " spirit appearing," or of a flesh-and-blood man than a rational spirit apparent. But a spirit *per se* appearing is tantamount to a spirit appearing without its appearances. And as for ghosts, it is enough for a man of common sense to observe, that a ghost and a shadow are concluded in the same definition, that is, visibility without tangibility.

P. 9. She was, in a few words, the stay of all my affairs, the centre of all my enterprises, &c.

The stay of his affairs, the centre of his interests, the regulator of his schemes and movements, whom it soothed his pride to submit to, and in complying with whose wishes the conscious sensation of his acting will increased the impulse, while it disguised the coercion, of duty!—the clinging dependent, yet the strong supporter—the comforter, the comfort, and the soul's living home! This is De Foe's comprehensive character of the wife, as she should be; and, to the honour of womanhood be it spoken, there are few neighbourhoods in which one name at least might not be found for the portrait.

The exquisite paragraphs in this and the next page, in addition to others scattered, though with a sparing hand, through his novels, afford sufficient proof that De Foe was a first-rate master of periodic style; but with sound judgment, and the fine tact of genius, he has avoided it as adverse to, nay, incompatible with, the every-day matter of fact realness, which forms the charm and the character of all his romances. The Robinsoe Crusoe is like the vision of a happy night-mair, such as a denizen of Elysium might be supposed to have from a little excess in his nectar and ambrosia supper. Our imagination is kept in full play, excited to the highest; yet all the while we are touching, or touched by, common flesh and blood.

P. 67. The ungrateful creatures began to be as insolent and troublesome as before, &c.

How should it be otherwise? They were idle; and when we will not sow corn, the devil will be sure to sow weeds, night-shade, henbane, and devil's bit.

P. 82. That hardened villain was so far from denying it,

that he said it was true, and ———— him they would do
it still before they had done with them.

Observe when a man has once abandoned himself to wickedness, he cannot stop, and does not
join the devils till he has become a devil himself.
Rebelling against his conscience he becomes the
slave of his own furious will.

One excellence of De Foe, amongst many, is his
sacrifice of lesser interest to the greater because
more universal.   Had he (as without any improbability he might have done) given his Robinson
Crusoe any of the turn for natural history, which
forms so striking and delightful a feature in the
equally uneducated Dampier;—had he made him
find out qualities and uses in the before (to him)
unknown plants of the island, discover, for instance
a substitute for hops, or describe birds, &c.—many
delightful pages and incidents might have enriched
the book;—but then Crusoe would have ceased to
be the universal representative, the person for
whom every reader could substitute himself.   But
now nothing is done, thought, suffered, or desired,
but what every man can imagine himself doing,
thinking, feeling, or wishing for.   Even so very
easy a problem as that of finding a substitute for
ink, is with exquisite judgment made to baffle Crusoe's inventive faculties.   And in what he does, he
arrives at no excellence; he does not make basket
work like Will Atkins; the carpentering, tailoring,
pottery, &c. are all just what will answer his pur-

poses, and those are confined to needs that all men
have, and comforts that all men desire.   Crusoe
rises only to the point to which all men may be
made to feel that they might, and that they ought
to, rise in religion,—to resignation, dependence on,
and thankful acknowledgment of, the divine mercy
and goodness.

In the education of children, love is first to be
instilled, and out of love obedience is to be educed.
Then impulse and power should be given to the intellect, and the ends of a moral being be exhibited.
For this object thus much is effected by works of
imagination ;—that they carry the mind out of self,
and show the possible of the good and the great in
the human character. The height, whatever it may
be, of the imaginative standard will do no harm ;
we are commanded to imitate one who is inimitable.
We should address ourselves to those faculties in a
child's mind, which are first awakened by nature,
and consequently first admit of cultivation, that is
to say, the memory and the imagination.* The com-
paring power, the judgment, is not at that age ac-

---

* He (Sir W. Scott) " detested and despised the whole
generation of modern children's books in which the attempt
is made to convey accurate notions of scientific minutiæ, de-
lighting cordially on the other hand in those of the preceding
age, which addressing themselves chiefly to the *imagination*
obtain *through it,* as he believed, the best chance of stirring
our graver faculties also."—*Life of Scott.*

tive, and ought not to be forcibly excited, as is too
frequently and mistakenly done in the modern systems of education, which can only lead to selfish
views, debtor and creditor principles of virtue, and
an inflated sense of merit.   In the imagination of
man exist the seeds of all moral and scientific improvement; chemistry was first alchemy, and out
of astrology sprang astronomy.   In the childhood
of those sciences the imagination opened a way, and
furnished materials, on which the ratiocinative powers in a maturer state operated with success.   The
imagination is the distinguishing characteristic of
man as a progressive being; and I repeat that it
ought to be carefully guided and strengthened as
the indispensable means and instrument of continued amelioration and refinement. Men of genius
and goodness are generally restless in their minds
in the present, and this, because they are by a law
of their nature unremittingly regarding themselves
in the future, and contemplating the possible of
moral and intellectual advance towards perfection.
Thus we live by hope and faith; thus we are for
the most part able to realize what we will, and thus
we accomplish the end of our being.   The contemplation of futurity inspires humility of soul in our
judgment of the present.

I think the memory of children cannot, in reason,
be too much stored with the objects and facts of
natural history.   God opens the images of nature,
like the leaves of a book, before the eyes of his

creature, Man—and teaches him all that is grand
and beautiful in the foaming cataract, the glassy
lake, and the floating mist.

The common/modern novel, in which there is no
imagination, but a miserable struggle to excite and
gratify mere curiosity, ought, in my judgment, to
be wholly forbidden to children. Novel-reading of
this sort is especially injurious to the growth of the
imagination, the judgment, and the morals, especially to the latter, because it excites mere feelings
without at the same time ministering an impulse to
action. Women are good novelists, but indifferent
poets; and this because they rarely or never thoroughly distinguish between fact and fiction. In
the jumble of the two lies the secret of the modern
novel, which is the *medium aliquid* between them,
having just so much of fiction as to obscure the
fact, and so much of fact as to render the fiction
insipid. The perusal of a fashionable lady's novel,
is to me very much like looking at the scenery and
decorations of a theatre by broad daylight. The
source of the common fondness for novels of this
sort rests in that dislike of vacancy, and that love
of sloth, which are inherent in the human mind;
they afford excitement without producing reaction.
By reaction I mean an activity of the intellectual
faculties, which shows itself in consequent reasoning and observation, and originates action and conduct according to a principle. Thus, the act of
thinking presents two sides for contemplation,—

that of external causality, in which the train of
thought may be considered as the result of outward
impressions, of accidental combinations, of fancy,
or the associations of the memory,—and on the
other hand, that of internal causality, or of the energy of the will on the mind itself.   Thought,
therefore, might thus be regarded as passive or active; and the same faculties may in a popular sense
be expressed as perception or observation, fancy or
imagination, memory or recollection.

LECTURE XII.

*Dreams — Apparitions — Alchemists — Person-
ality of the Evil Being — Bodily Identity.*

IT is a general, but, as it appears to me, a mistaken opinion, that in our ordinary dreams we
judge the objects to be real.   I say our ordinary
dreams;—because as to the night-mair the opinion
is to a considerable extent just. But the night-mair
is not a mere dream. but takes place when the waking state of the brain is recommencing, and most
often during a rapid alternation, a twinkling, as it
were, of sleeping and waking;—while either from
pressure on, or from some derangement in, the
stomach or other digestive organs acting on the external skin (which is still in sympathy with the
stomach and bowels,) and benumbing it, the sensa-

tions sent up to the brain by double touch (that is, when my own hand touches my side or breast,) are so faint as to be merely equivalent to the sensation given by single touch, as when another person's hand touches me. The mind, therefore, which at all times, with and without our distinct consciousness, seeks for, and assumes, some outward cause for every impression from without, and which in sleep, by aid of the imaginative faculty, converts its judgments respecting the cause into a personal image as being the cause,—the mind, I say, in this case, deceived by past experience, attributes the painful sensation received to a correspondent agent, —an assassin, for instance, stabbing at the side, or a goblin sitting on the breast. Add too that the impressions of the bed, curtains, room, &c. received by the eyes in the half-moments of their opening, blend with, and give vividness and appropriate distance to, the dream image which returns when they close again; and thus we unite the actual perceptions, or their immediate reliques, with the phantoms of the inward sense; and in this manner so confound the half-waking, half-sleeping, reasoning power, that we actually do pass a positive judgment on the reality of what we see and hear, though often accompanied by doubt and self-questioning, which, as I have myself experienced, will at times become strong enough, even before we awake, to convince us that it is what it is—namely, the night-mair.

In ordinary dreams we do not judge the objects

to be real;—we simply do not determine that they are unreal. The sensations which they seem to produce, are in truth the causes and occasions of the images; of which there are two obvious proofs: first, that in dreams the strangest and most sudden metamorphoses do not create any sensation of surprise: and the second, that as to the most dreadful images, which during the dream were accompanied with agonies of terror, we merely awake, or turn round on the other side, and off fly both image and agony, which would be impossible if the sensations were produced by the images. This has always appeared to me an absolute demonstration of the true nature of ghosts and apparitions—such I mean of the tribe as were not pure inventions. Fifty years ago, (and to this day in the ruder parts of Great Britain and Ireland, in almost every kitchen and in too many parlours it is nearly the same,) you might meet persons who would assure you in the most solemn manner, so that you could not doubt their veracity at least, that they had seen an apparition of such and such a person,—in many cases, that the apparition had spoken to them; and they would describe themselves as having been in an agony of terror. They would tell you the story in perfect health. Now take the other class of facts, in which real ghosts have appeared;—I mean, where figures have been dressed up for the purpose of passing for apparitions:—in every instance I have known or heard of (and I have collected very many) the consequence has been either sudden death, or fits, or idiocy, or mania, or a brain fever. Whence comes the difference? evidently from this,—that in the one case the whole of the nervous system has been by slight internal causes gradually and all together brought into a certain state, the sensation of which is extravagantly exaggerated during sleep, and of which the images are the mere effects and exponents, as the motions of the weather-cock are of the wind;—while in the other case, the image rushing through the senses upon a nervous system, wholly unprepared, actually causes the sensation, which is sometimes powerful enough to produce a total check, and almost always a lesion or inflammation. Who has not witnessed the difference in shock when we have leaped down half-a-dozen steps intentionally, and that of having missed a single stair. How comparatively severe the latter is! The fact really is, as to apparitions, that the terror produces the image instead of the contrary; for *in omnem actum perceptionis influit imaginatio*, as says Wolfe.

O, strange is the self-power of the imagination— when painful sensations have made it their interpreter, or returning gladsomeness or convalescence has made its chilled and evanished figures and landscape bud, blossom, and live in scarlet, green, and snowy white (like the fire-screen inscribed with the nitrate and muriate of cobalt,)—strange is the power to represent the events and circumstances,

2   L

even to the anguish or the triumph of the *quasi*-credent soul, while the necessary conditions, the only possible causes of such contingencies, are known to be in fact quite hopeless;—yea, when the pure mind would recoil from the eve-lengthened shadow of an approaching hope, as from a crime:—and yet the effect shall have place, and substance, and living energy, and, on a blue islet of ether, in a whole sky of blackest cloudage, shine like a first-ling of creation!

To return, however to apparitions, and by way of an amusing illustration of the nature and value of even contemporary testimony upon such subjects, I will present you with a passage, literally trans-lated by my friend, Mr. Southey, from the well known work of Bernal Dias, one of the companions of Cortez, in the conquest of Mexico:

Here it is that Gomara says, that Francisco de Morla rode forward on a dappled grey horse, before Cortes and the ca-valry came up, and that the apostle St. Iago, or St. Peter, was there. I must say that all our works and victories are by the hand of our Lord Jesus Christ, and that in this bat-tle there were for each of us so many Indians, that they could have covered us with handfuls of earth, if it had not been that the great mercy of God helped us in every thing. And it may be that he of whom Gomara speaks, was the glorious Santiago or San Pedro, and I, as a sinner, was not worthy to see him; but he whom I saw there and knew, was Francisco de Morla on a chesnut horse, who came up with Cortes. And it seems to me that now while I am writing this, the whole war is represented before these sinful eyes, just in the manner as we then went through it. And though

I, as an unworthy sinner, might not deserve to see either of
these glorious apostles, there were in our company above
four hundred soldiers and Cortes, and many other knights;
and it would have been talked of and testified, and they
would have made a church when they peopled the town,
which would have been called Santiago de la Vittoria, or
San Pedro de la Vittoria, as it is now called, Santa Maria
de la Vittoria. And if it was, as Gomara says, bad Christians must we have been when our Lord God sent us his
holy apostles, not to acknowledge his great mercy, and vene-
rate his church daily. And would to God, it had been, as
the Chronicler says!—but till I read his Chronicle, I never
heard such a thing from any of the conquerors who were
there.

Now, what if the odd accident of such a man as
Bernal Dias' writing a history had not taken place!
Gomara's account, the account of a contemporary,
which yet must have been read by scores who were
present, would have remained uncontradicted. I
remember the story of a man, whom the devil met
and talked with, but left at a particular lane;—the
man followed him with his eyes, and when the devil
got to the turning or bend of the lane, he vanished!
The devil was upon this occasion drest in a blue
coat, plush waistcoat, leather breeches and boots,
and talked and looked just like a common man,
except as to a particular lock of hair which he had.
" And how do you know then that it was the devil?"
" How do I know," replied the fellow,—" why, if
it had not been the devil, being drest as he was, and
looking as he did, why should I have been sore
stricken with fright when I first saw him? and why

should I be in such a tremble all the while he
talked? And, moreover, he had a particular sort
of a kind of a look, and when I groaned and said,
upon every question he asked me, Lord have mercy
upon me! or, Christ have mercy upon me! it was
plain enough that he did not like it, and so he left
me!"—The man was quite sober when he related
this story; but as it happened to him on his return
from market, it is probable that he was then muddled.   As for myself, I was actually seen in Newgate in the winter of 1798;—the person who saw
me there, said he had asked my name of Mr. A. B.
a known acquaintance of mine, who told him that
it was young Coleridge, who had married the eldest
Miss ——.   " Will you go to Newgate, Sir ?" said
my friend; for I assure you that Mr. C. is now in
Germany."   " Very willingly," replied the other,
and away they went to Newgate, and sent for A. B.
" Coleridge," cried he, " in Newgate ! God forbid!"
I said, " young Col—— who married the eldest
Miss ——."   The names were something similar.
And yet this person had himself really seen me at
one of my lectures.

   I remember, upon the occasion of my inhaling
the nitrous oxide at the Royal Institution, about
five minutes afterwards, a gentleman came from the
other side of the theatre and said to me, — " Was
it not ravishingly delightful, Sir ?"—" It was highly
pleasurable, no doubt." — " Was it not very like
sweet music?"—" I cannot say I perceived any

analogy to it."—" Did you not say it was very like Mrs. Billington singing by your ear!"—" No Sir, I said that while I was breathing the gas, there was a singing in my ears."

To return, however, to dreams, I not only believe, for the reasons given, but have more than once actually experienced that the most fearful forms, when produced simply by association, instead of causing fear, operate no other effect than the same would do if they had passed through my mind as thoughts, while I was composing a faery tale; the whole depending on the wise and gracious law in our nature, that the actual bodily sensations, called forth according to the law of association by thoughts and images of the mind, never greatly transcend the limits of pleasurable feeling in a tolerably healthy frame, unless when an act of the judgment supervenes and interprets them as purporting instant danger to ourselves.

* There have been very strange and incredible stories told of and by the alchemists. Perhaps in some of them there may have been a specific form of mania, originating in the constant intension of the mind on an imaginary end, associated with an immense variety of means, all of them substances not familiar to men in general, and in forms strange and unlike to those of ordinary nature. Sometimes, it seems as if the alchemists wrote like the Pytha-

---

* From Mr. Green's note.

goreans on music, imagining a metaphysical and
inaudible music as the basis of the audible. It is
clear that by sulphur they meant the solar rays or
light, and by mercury the principle of ponderability,
so that their theory was the same with that of the
Heraclitic physics, or the modern German *Natur-
philosophie*, which deduces all things from light
and gravitation, each being bipolar; gravitation=
north and south, or attraction and repulsion; light
=east and west, or contraction and dilation; and
gold being the tetrad, or interpenetration of both,
as water was the dyad of light, and iron the dyad
of gravitation.

It is, probably, unjust to accuse the alchemists
generally of dabbling with attempts at magic in the
common sense of the term. The supposed exercise
of magical power always involved some moral guilt,
directly or indirectly, as in stealing a piece of meat
to lay on warts, touching humours with the hand of
an executed person, &c. Rites of this sort and other
practices of sorcery have always been regarded with
trembling abhorrence by all nations, even the most
ignorant, as by the Africans, the Hudson's Bay
people and others. The alchemists were, no doubt,
often considered as dealers in art magic, and many
of them were not unwilling that such a belief should
be prevalent; and the more earnest among them
evidently looked at their association of substances,
fumigations, and other chemical operations as merely ceremonial, and seem, therefore, to have had a

deeper meaning, that of evoking a latent power. It would be profitable to make a collection of all the cases of cures by magical charms and incantations; much useful information might, probably, be derived from it; for it is to be observed that such rites are the form in which medical knowledge would be preserved amongst a barbarous and ignorant people.

Note.* June, 1827.

The apocryphal book of Tobit consists of a very simple, but beautiful and interesting, family-memoir, into which some later Jewish poet or fabulist of Alexandria wove the ridiculous and frigid machinery, borrowed from the popular superstitions of the Greeks (though, probably, of Egyptian origin), and accommodated, clumsily enough, to the purer monotheism of the Mosaic law. The Rape of the Lock is another instance of a simple tale thus enlarged at a later period, though in this case by the same author, and with a very different result. Now unless Mr. Hillhouse is Romanist enough to receive this nursery-tale garnish of a domestic incident as grave history and holy writ, (for which, even from learned Roman Catholics, he would gain more credit as a very obedient child of the Church than as a biblical critic), he will find it no easy matter to support this assertion of his by the passages of

---

* Written in a copy of Mr. Hillhouse's Hadad. *Ed.*

Scripture here referred to, consistently with any sane interpretation of their import and purpose.

: I. The Fallen Spirits.

This is the mythological form, or, if you will, the symbolical representation, of a profound idea necessary as the *præ-suppositum* of the Christian scheme, or a postulate of reason, indispensable, if we would render the existence of a world of finites compatible with the assumption of a super-mundane God, not one with the world. In short, this idea is the condition under which alone the reason of man can retain the doctrine of an infinite and absolute Being, and yet keep clear of pantheism as exhibited by Benedict Spinosa.

II. The Egyptian Magicians.

This whole narrative is probably a relic of the old diplomatic *lingua-arcana*, or state-symbolique —in which the prediction of events is expressed as the immediate causing of them. Thus the prophet is said to destroy the city, the destruction of which he predicts. The word which our version renders by "*enchantments*" signifies "flames or burnings," by which it is probable that the Egyptians were able to deceive the spectators, and substitute serpents for staves. See Parkhurst *in voce.*

And with regard to the possessions in the Gospels, bear in mind first of all, that spirits are not necessarily souls or *I's (ich-heiten* or *self-consciousnesses)*, and that the most ludicrous absurdities would follow from taking them as such in the Gos-

pel instances ; and secondly, that the Evangelist,
who has recorded the most of these incidents, himself speaks of one of these possessed persons as a
lunatic ;— (σεληνιάζεται —ἐξῆλθεν ἀπ᾽ αὐτοῦ τὸ
δαιμόνιον. Matt. xvii. 15. 18) while St. John names
them not at all, but seems to include them under
the description of diseased or deranged persons.
That madness may result from spiritual causes, and
not only or principally from physical ailments, may
readily be admitted.   Is not our will itself a spiritual power? Is it not the spirit of the man? The
mind of a rational and responsible being (that is, of
a free-agent) is a spirit, though it does not follow
that all spirits are minds.   Who shall dare determine what spiritual influences may not arise out of
the collective evil wills of wicked men? Even the
bestial life, sinless in animals and their nature, may
when awakened in the man and by his own act admitted into his will, become a spiritual influence.
He receives a nature into his will, which by this
very act becomes a corrupt will; and *vice versa*,
this will becomes his nature, and thus a corrupt
nature.   This may be conceded; and this is all
that the recorded words of our Saviour absolutely
require in order to receive an appropriate sense;
but this is altogether different from making spirits
to be devils, and devils self-conscious individuals.

Notes.* March, 1824.

A Christian's conflicts and conquests, p. 459. By the devil we are to understand that apostate spirit which fell from God, and is always designing to hale down others from God also. The Old Dragon (mentioned in the Revelation) with his tail drew down the third part of the stars of heaven and cast them to the earth.

How much it is to be regretted, that so enlightened and able a divine as Smith, had not philosophically and scripturally enucleated this so difficult yet important question,—respecting the personal existence of the evil principle ; that is, whether as τὸ θεῖον of paganism is ὁ θεὸς in Christianity, so the τὸ πονηρὸν is to be ὁ πονηρὸς,—and whether this is an express doctrine of Christ, and not merely a Jewish dogma left undisturbed to fade away under the increasing light of the Gospel, instead of assuming the former, and confirming the position by a verse from a poetic tissue of visual symbols,— a verse alien from the subject, and by which the Apocalypt enigmatized the Neronian persecutions and the apostasy through fear occasioned by it in a large number of converts.

Ib. p. 463. When we say, the devil is continually busy with us, I mean not only some apostate spirit as one particular being, but that spirit of apostasy which is lodged in all

---

* Written in a copy of " Select Discourses by John Smith, of Queen's College, Cambridge, 1660," and communicated by the Rev. Edward Coleridge. *Ed.*

men's natures; and this may seem particularly to be aimed
at in this place, if we observe the context:—as the scripture
speaks of Christ not only as a particular person, but as a
divine principle in holy souls.

Indeed the devil is not only the name of one particular
thing, but a nature.

May I not venture to suspect that this was
Smith's own belief and judgment? and that his
conversion of the Satan, that is, *circuitor*, or minister of police (what our Sterne calls the accusing
angel) in the prologue to Job into the devil was a
mere condescension to the prevailing prejudice?
Here, however, he speaks like himself, and like a
true religious philosopher, who felt that the personality of evil spirits is a trifling question, compared
with the personality of the evil principle. This is
indeed most momentous.

NOTE ON A PASSAGE IN THE LIFE OF HENRY EARL OF MORLAND. 20th June, 1827.

The defect of this and all similar theories that I
am acquainted with, or rather, let me say, the desideratum, is the neglect of a previous definition of
the term " body." What do you mean by it? The
immediate grounds of a man's size, visibility, tangibility, &c?—But these are in a continual flux even
as a column of smoke. The material particles of
carbon, nitrogen, oxygen, hydrogen, lime, phospho-
rus, sulphur, soda, iron, that constitute the ponderable organism in May, 1827, at the moment of

Pollio's death in his 70th year, have no better
claim to be called his " body," than the numerical
particles of the same names that constituted the
ponderable mass in May, 1787, in Pollio's prime of
manhood in his 30th year;—the latter no less than
the former go into the grave, that is, suffer dissolu-
tion, the one in a series, the other simultaneously.
The result to the particles is precisely the same in
both, and of both therefore we must say with holy
Paul,—" *Thou fool! that which thou sowest, thou
sowest not that body that shall be,* &c.   Neither
this nor that is the body that abideth.   Abideth, I
say; for that which riseth again must have remained, though perhaps in an inert state.—It is not
dead, but sleepeth;—that is, it is not dissolved any
more than the exterior or phenomenal organism
appears to us dissolved when it lieth in apparent
inactivity during our sleep.

Sound reasoning this, to the best of my judgment, as far as it goes.   But how are we to explain
the reaction of this fluxional body on the animal?
In each moment the particles by the informing
force of the living principle constitute an organ not
only of motion and sense, but of consciousness.
The organ plays on the organist.   How is this
conceivable?   The solution requires a depth, still-
ness, and subtlety of spirit not only for its discovery, but even for the understanding of it when
discovered, and in the most appropriate words
enunciated.   I can merely give a hint.   The par-

ticles themselves must have an interior and gravitate being, and the multeity must be a removable or at least suspensible accident.

LECTURE XIII.*

On Poesy or Art. (*a.*)

MAN communicates by articulation of sounds, and paramountly by the memory in the ear; nature by the impression of bounds and surfaces on the eye, and through the eye it gives significance and appropriation, and thus the conditions of memory, or the capability of being remembered, to sounds, smells, &c. Now Art, used collectively for painting, sculpture, architecture and music, is the mediatress between, and reconciler of, nature and man. (*b.*) It is, therefore, the power of humanizing nature, of infusing the thoughts and passions of man into every thing which is the object of his contemplation; colour, form, motion and sound are the elements which it combines, and it stamps them into unity in the mould of a moral idea.

The primary art is writing;—primary, if we regard the purpose abstracted from the different modes of realizing it, those steps of progression of which the instances are still visible in the lower

---

* For the Notes to this Lecture, containing references to Schelling's oration on the Forming or Imaging Arts, with extracts from the same, see the end of the volume.

degrees of civilization.   First, there is mere gesti-
culation; then rosaries or *wampun ;* then picture-
language; then hieroglyphics, and finally alphabe-
tic letters.   These all consist of a translation of
man into nature, of a substitution of the visible for
the audible.

The so called music of savage tribes as little deserves the name of art for the understanding as the
ear warrants it for music.   Its lowest state is a
mere expression of passion by sounds which the
passion itself necessitates ; — the highest amounts
to no more than a voluntary reproduction of these
sounds in the absence of the occasioning causes, so
as to give the pleasure of contrast, — for example,
by the various outcries of battle in the song of se-
curity and triumph.   Poetry also is purely human;
for all its materials are from the mind, and all its
products are for the mind.   But it is the apotheosis
of the former state, in which by excitement of the
associative power passion itself imitates order, and
the order resulting produces a pleasurable passion,
and thus it elevates the mind by making its feelings
the object of its reflexion.   So likewise, whilst it
recalls the sights and sounds that had accompanied
the occasions of the original passions, poetry im-
pregnates them with an interest not their own by
means of the passions, and yet tempers the passion
by the calming power which all distinct images exert on the human soul.   In this way poetry is the
preparation for art, inasmuch as it avails itself of

the forms of nature to recall, to express, and to modify the thoughts and feelings of the mind. Still, however, poetry can only act through the intervention of articulate speech, which is so peculiarly human, that in all languages it constitutes the ordinary phrase by which man and nature are contradistinguished. It is the original force of the word ' brute ;' and even ' mute,' and ' dumb' do not convey the absence of sound, but the absence of articulated sounds.

As soon as the human mind is intelligibly addressed by an outward image exclusively of articulate speech, so soon does art commence. But please to observe that I have laid particular stress on the words ' human mind,' meaning to exclude thereby all results common to man and all other sentient creatures, and consequently confining myself to the effect produced by the congruity of the animal impression with the reflective powers of the mind; so that not the thing presented, but that which is represented by the thing shall be the source of the pleasure. In this sense nature itself is to a religious observer the art of God; and for the same cause art itself might be defined as of a middle quality between a thought and a thing, or; as I said before, the union and reconciliation of that which is nature with that which is exclusively human. It is the figured language of thought, and is distinguished from nature by the unity of all the parts in one thought or idea. Hence nature itself would give

us the impression of a work of art if we could see
the thought which is present at once in the whole
and in every part; and a work of art will be just in
proportion as it adequately conveys the thought,
and rich in proportion to the variety of parts which
it holds in unity.

If, therefore, the term ' mute' be taken as opposed not to sound but to articulate speech, the
old definition of painting will in fact be the true
and best definition of the Fine Arts in general, that
is, *muta poesis*, mute poesy, and so of course poesy.
(c.) And, as all languages perfect themselves by a
gradual process of desynonymizing words originally
equivalent, I have cherished the wish to use the
word ' poesy' as the generic or common term, and
to distinguish that species of poesy which is not
muta poesis by its usual name ' poetry ;' while of
all the other species which collectively form the
Fine Arts, there would remain this as the common
definition,—that they all, like poetry, are to express
intellectual purposes, thoughts, conceptions, and
sentiments which have their origin in the human
mind, not, however, as poetry does, by means of
articulate speech, but as nature or the divine art
does, by form, colour, magnitude, proportion, or by
sound, that is, silently or musically. (d.)

Well! it may be said—but who has ever thought
otherwise! We all know that art is the imitatress
of nature. And, doubtless, the truths which I
hope to convey, would be barren truisms, if all men

meant the same by the words ‘imitate’ and ‘nature.’ (e) But it would be flattering mankind at large, to presume that such is the fact. First, to imitate. The impression on the wax is not an imitation, but a copy, of the seal; the seal itself is an imitation. But, further, in order to form a philosophic conception, we must seek for the kind, as the heat in ice, invisible light, &c. whilst, for practical purposes, we must have reference to the degree. It is sufficient that philosophically we understand that in all imitation two elements must coexist, and not only coexist, but must be perceived as coexisting. These two constituent elements are likeness and unlikeness, or sameness and difference. and in all genuine creations of art there must be a union of these disparates. The artist may take his point of view where he pleases, provided that the desired effect be perceptibly produced, — that there be likeness in the difference, difference in the likeness, and a reconcilement of both in one. If there be likeness to nature without any check of difference, the result is disgusting, and the more complete the delusion, the more loathsome the effect. (f) Why are such simulations of nature, as wax-work figures of men and women, so disagreeable? Because, not finding the motion and the life which we expected, we are shocked as by a falsehood, every circumstance of detail, which before induced us to be interested, making the distance from truth more palpable. You set out with a supposed reality

2   M

and are disappointed and disgusted with the decep-
tion; whilst, in respect to a work of genuine imitation, you begin with an acknowledged total difference,
and then every touch of nature gives you the pleasure of an approximation to truth.   The fundamental principle of all this is undoubtedly the hor-
ror of falsehood and the love of truth inherent in
the human breast.   The Greek tragic dance rested
on these principles, and I can deeply sympathize in
imagination with the Greeks in this favourite part
of their theatrical exhibitions, when I call to mind
the pleasure I felt in beholding the combat of the
Horatii and Curiatii most exquisitely danced in
Italy to the music of Cimarosa.

Secondly, as to nature. We must imitate nature!
yes, but what in nature,—all and everything? No,
the beautiful in nature. (*g*)   And what then is the
beautiful?   What is beauty?   It is, in the abstract,
the unity of the manifold, the coalescence of the diverse; in the concrete, it is the union of the shapely
(*formosum*) with the vital.   In the dead organic it
depends on regularity of form, the first and lowest
species of which is the triangle with all its modifications, as in crystals, architecture, &c.; in the
living organic it is not mere regularity of form,
which would produce a sense of formality; neither
is it subservient to any thing beside itself. (*h*)   It
may be present in a disagreeable object, in which
the proportion of the parts constitutes a whole; it
does not arise from association, as the agreeable

does, but sometimes lies in the rupture of association; it is not different to different individuals and
nations, as has been said, nor is it connected with
the ideas of the good, or the fit, or the useful. The
sense of beauty is intuitive, and beauty itself is all
that inspires pleasure without, and aloof from, and
even contrarily to, interest.

If the artist copies the mere nature, the *natura
naturata*, what idle rivalry! If he proceeds only
from a given form, which is supposed to answer to
the notion of beauty, what an emptiness, what an
unreality there always is in his productions, as in
Cipriani's pictures! Believe me, you must master
the essence, the *natura naturans*, which presup-
poses a bond between nature in the higher sense
and the soul of man. (*i*)

The wisdom in nature is distinguished from that
in man, by the co-instantaneity of the plan and the
execution; the thought and the product are one, or
are given at once; but there is no reflex act, and
hence there is no moral responsibility. In man
there is reflexion, freedom, and choice; he is, therefore, the head of the visible creation. (*j*) In the
objects of nature are presented, as in a mirror, all
the possible elements, steps, and processes of intellect antecedent to consciousness, and therefore to
the full development of the intelligential act; and
man's mind is the very focus of all the rays of intellect which are scattered throughout the images
of nature. Now so to place these images, totalized,

and fitted to the limits of the human mind, as to elicit from, and to superinduce upon, the forms themselves the moral reflexions to which they approximate, to make the external internal, the internal external, to make nature thought, and thought nature,—this is the mystery of genius in the Fine Arts. Dare I add that the genius must act on the feeling, that body is but a striving to become mind, that it is mind in its essence ! (*k*)

In every work of art there is a reconcilement of the external with the internal; the conscious is so impressed on the unconscious as to appear in it; as compare mere letters inscribed on a tomb with figures themselves constituting the tomb. He who combines the two is the man of genius; and for that reason he must partake of both. Hence there is in genius itself an unconscious activity; nay, that is the genius in the man of genius. (*l*) And this is the true exposition of the rule that the artist must first eloign himself from nature in order to return to her with full effect. Why this? Because if he were to begin by mere painful copying, he would produce masks only, not forms breathing life. He must out of his own mind create forms according to the severe laws of the intellect, in order to generate in himself that co-ordination of freedom and law, that involution of obedience in the prescript, and of the prescript in the impulse to obey, which assimilates him to nature, and enables him to understand her. He merely absents himself for a season from her, that his own spirit, which has the same ground with nature, may learn her unspoken language in its main radicals, before he approaches to her endless compositions of them. (*m*) Yes, not to acquire cold notions—lifeless technical rules—but living and life-producing ideas, which shall contain their own evidence, the certainty that they are essentially one with the germinal causes in nature—his consciousness being the focus and mirror of both,— for this does the artist for a time abandon the external real in order to return to it with a complete sympathy with its internal and actual. For of all we see, hear, feel and touch the substance is and must be in ourselves; and therefore there is no alternative in reason between the dreary (and thank heaven! almost impossible) belief that every thing around us is but a phantom, or that the life which is in us is in them likewise; * and that to know is to resemble, when we speak of objects out of ourselves, even as within ourselves to learn is, according to Plato, only to recollect;—the only effective answer to which, that I have been fortunate enough to meet with, is that which Pope has consecrated for future use in the line—

And coxcombs vanquish Berkeley with a grin!

The artist must imitate that which is within the thing, that which is active through form and figure,

---

* See the *Biographia Literaria* of Mr. Coleridge, chap. xii. vol. i. p. 241, and Schelling's *Transcendental Idealism.*

and discourses to us by symbols—the *Natur-geist*,
or spirit of nature, as we unconsciously imitate those
whom we love; for so only can he hope to produce
any work truly natural in the object and truly human in the effect. (*n*) The idea which puts the
form together cannot itself be the form. It is above
form, and is its essence, the universal in the individual, or the individuality itself,—the glance and
the exponent of the indwelling power. (*o*)

Each thing that lives has its moment of self-
exposition, and so has each period of each thing, if
we remove the disturbing forces of accident. To
do this is the business of ideal art, whether in images of childhood, youth, or age, in man or in woman.
(*p*) Hence a good portrait is the abstract of the
personal; it is not the likeness for actual comparison,
but for recollection. This explains why the likeness of a very good portrait is not always recog-
nized; because some persons never abstract, and
amongst these are especially to be numbered the
near relations and friends of the subject, in consequence of the constant pressure and check exercised on their minds by the actual presence of the
original. And each thing that only appears to live
has also its possible position of relation to life, as
nature herself testifies, who, where she cannot be,
prophesies her being in the crystallized metal, or
the inhaling plant.

The charm, the indispensable requisite, of sculpture is unity of effect. But painting rests in a ma-

terial remoter from nature, and its compass is therefore greater.(*q*) Light and shade give external, as well as internal, being even with all its accidents, whilst sculpture is confined to the latter. And here I may observe that the subjects chosen for works of art, whether in sculpture or painting, should be such as really are capable of being expressed and conveyed within the limits of those arts. Moreover they ought to be such as will affect the spectator by their truth, their beauty, or their sublimity, and therefore they may be addressed to the judgment, the senses, or the reason. The peculiarity of the impression which they may make, may be derived either from colour and form, or from proportion and fitness, or from the excitement of the moral feelings; or all these may be combined. Such works as do combine these sources of effect must have the preference in dignity.

Imitation of the antique may be too exclusive, and may produce an injurious effect on modern sculpture;—1st, generally, because such an imitation cannot fail to have a tendency to keep the attention fixed on externals rather than on the thought within;—2ndly, because, accordingly, it leads the artist to rest satisfied with that which is always imperfect, namely, bodily form, and circumscribes his views of mental expression to the ideas of power and grandeur only;—3rdly, because it induces an effort to combine together two incongruous things, that is to say, modern feelings in antique forms;—

4thly, because it speaks in a language, as it were, learned and dead, the tones of which, being unfamiliar, leave the common spectator cold and unimpressed; (r)—and lastly, because it necessarily causes a neglect of thoughts, emotions and images of profounder interest and more exalted dignity, as motherly, sisterly, and brotherly love, piety, devotion, the divine become human,—the Virgin, the Apostle, the Christ. The artist's principle in the statue of a great man should be the illustration of departed merit; and I cannot but think that a skilful adoption of modern habiliments would, in many instances, give a variety and force of effect which a bigoted adherence to Greek or Roman costume precludes. It is, I believe, from artists finding Greek models unfit for several important modern purposes, that we see so many allegorical figures on monuments and elsewhere. Painting was, as it were, a new art, and being unshackled by old models it chose its own subjects, and took an eagle's flight. And a new field seems opened for modern sculpture in the symbolical expression of the ends of life, as in Guy's monument, Chantrey's children in Worcester Cathedral, &c.

Architecture exhibits the greatest extent of the difference from nature which may exist in works of art. It involves all the powers of design, and is sculpture and painting inclusively. It shews the greatness of man, and should at the same time teach him humility.

Music is the most entirely human of the fine
arts, and has the fewest *analoga* in nature. Its
first delightfulness is simple accordance with the
ear; but it is an associated thing, and recalls the
deep emotions of the past with an intellectual sense
of proportion. Every human feeling is greater and
larger than the exciting cause, —a proof, I think,
that man is designed for a higher state of existence;
and this is deeply implied in music, in which there
is always something more and beyond the immediate
expression.

With regard to works in all the branches of the
fine arts, I may remark that the pleasure arising
from novelty must of course be allowed its due
place and weight. This pleasure consists in the
identity of two opposite elements, that is to say—
sameness and variety. If in the midst of the variety there be not some fixed object for the attention, the unceasing succession of the variety will
prevent the mind from observing the difference of
the individual objects; and the only thing remaining will be the succession, which will then produce
precisely the same effect as sameness. This we
experience when we let the trees or hedges pass
before the fixed eye during a rapid movement in a
carriage, or on the other hand, when we suffer a
file of soldiers or ranks of men in procession to go
on before us without resting the eye on any one in
particular. In order to derive pleasure from the
occupation of the mind, the principle of unity must

always be present, so that in the midst of the multeity the centripetal force be never suspended, nor
the sense be fatigued by the predominance of the
centrifugal force.   This unity in multeity I have
elsewhere stated as the principle of beauty.   It is
equally the source of pleasure in variety, and in
fact a higher term including both.   What is the
seclusive or distinguishing term between them !

Remember that there is a difference between
form as proceeding, and shape as superinduced;—
the latter is either the death or the imprisonment
of the thing;—the former is its self-witnessing and
self-effected sphere of agency.(s) Art would or should
be the abridgment of nature.   Now the fulness of
nature is without character, as water is purest when
without taste, smell, or colour;(t) but this is the highest, the apex only,—it is not the whole.   The object of art is to give the whole *ad hominem;* hence
each step of nature hath its ideal, and hence the
possibility of a climax up to the perfect form of a
harmonized chaos.

To the idea of life victory or strife is necessary;
as virtue consists not simply in the absence of vices,
but in the overcoming of them.   So it is in beauty
The sight of what is subordinated and conquered
heightens the strength and the pleasure; and this
should be exhibited by the artist either inclusively
in his figure, or else out of it and beside it to act
by way of supplement and contrast.   And with a
view to this, remark the seeming identity of body

and mind in infants, and thence the loveliness of
the former ; the commencing separation in boyhood,
and the struggle of equilibrium in youth : thence
onward the body is first simply indifferent ; then
demanding the translucency of the mind not to be
worse than indifferent ; and finally all that presents
the body as body becoming almost of an excremental
nature.

LECTURE XIV.

On Style.

I HAVE, I believe, formerly observed with regard to the character of the governments of
the East, that their tendency was despotic, that is,
towards unity ; whilst that of the Greek governments, on the other hand, leaned to the manifold
and the popular, the unity in them being purely
ideal, namely of all as an identification of the whole.
In the northern or Gothic nations the aim and purpose of the government were the preservation of
the rights and interests of the individual in conjunction with those of the whole. The individual
interest was sacred. In the character and tendency
of the Greek and Gothic languages there is precisely the same relative difference. In Greek the
sentences are long, and the structure architectural,
so that each part or clause is insignificant when
compared with the whole. The result is every

thing, the steps and processes nothing. But in the
Gothic and, generally, in what we call the modern,
languages, the structure is short, simple, and complete in each part, and the connexion of the parts
with the sum total of the discourse is maintained
by the sequency of the logic, or the community of
feelings excited between the writer and his readers.
As an instance equally delightful and complete, of
what may be called the Gothic structure as contradistinguished from that of the Greeks, let me cite
a part of our famous Chaucer's character of a parish priest as he should be. Can it ever be quoted
too often?

> A good man thér was of religioün
> That was a pouré Parsone of a toun,
> But riche he was of holy thought and werk;
> He was alsó a lerned man, a clerk,
> That Cristés gospel trewély wolde preche;
> His párishens[1] devoutly wolde he teche;
> Benigne he was, and wonder[2] diligent,
> And in adversite ful patient,
> And swiche[3] he was ypreved[4] often sithes[5];
> Ful loth were him to cursen for his tithes,
> But rather wolde he yeven[6] out of doute
> Unto his pouré párishens aboute
> Of hís offríng, and eke of his substánce;
> He coude in litel thing have suffisance:
> Wide was his parish, and houses fer asonder,
> But he ne[7] left nought for no rain ne[8] thonder,

---

[1] Parishioners.　[2] Wondrous.　[3] Such.
[4] Proved.　[5] Times.　[6] Give or have given.
[7] Not.　[8] Nor.

In sikenesse and in mischief to visíte
The ferrest[9] in his parish moche and lite[10]
Upon his fete, and in his hand a staf:
This noble ensample to his shepe he yaf,[11]
That first he wrought, and afterward he taught,
Out of the gospel he the wordés caught,
And this figúre he added yet thereto,
That if gold rusté, what should iren do.

   He setté not his benefice to hire,
And lette[12] his shepe accombred[13] in the mire,
And ran untó Londón untó Seint Poules,
To seken him a chantérie for soules,
Or with a brotherhede to be withold,
But dwelt at home, and kepté wel his fold,
So that the wolf ne made it not miscarie :
He was a shepherd and no mercenarie ;
And though he holy were and vertuous,
He was to sinful men not dispitous,[14]
Ne of his speché dangerous ne digne,[15]
But in his teching discrete and benigne,
To drawen folk to heven with fairénesse,
By good ensample was his besinesse ;
But it were any persone obstinat,
What so he were of high or low estat,
Him wolde he snibben[16] sharply for the nones :
A better preest I trowe that no wher non is ;
He waited after no pompe ne reverence,
He maked him no spiced conscience,
But Cristés love and his apostles' twelve
He taught, but first he folwed it himselve.*

Such change as really took place in the style of
our literature after Chaucer's time is with difficulty

---

* Farthest.   [10] Great and small.   [11] Gave.   [12] Left.
[13] Encumbered.   [14] Despiteous.   [15] Proud.
[16] Reprove.   * Prologue to Canterbury Tales.

perceptible, on account of the (death) of writers, during the civil wars of the 15th century.   But the
transition was not very great; and accordingly we
find in Latimer and our other venerable authors
about the time of Edward VI. as in Luther, the
general characteristics of the earliest manner;—
that is, every part popular, and the discourse addressed to all degrees of intellect;—the sentences
short, the tone vehement, and the connexion of the
whole produced by honesty and singleness of purpose, intensity of passion, and pervading importance
of the subject.

Another and a very different species of style is
that which was derived from, and founded on, the
admiration and cultivation of the classical writers,
and which was more exclusively addressed to the
learned class in society.   I have previously mentioned Boccaccio as the original Italian introducer
of this manner, and the great models of it in English are Hooker, Bacon, Milton, and Taylor, although it may be traced in many other authors of
that age.   In all these the language is dignified
but plain, genuine English, although elevated and
brightened by superiority of intellect in the writer.
Individual words themselves are always used by
them in their precise meaning, without either affectation or slipslop.   The letters and state papers of
Sir Francis Walsingham are remarkable for excellence in style of this description.   In Jeremy Taylor the sentences are often extremely long, and yet

are generally so perspicuous in consequence of their logical structure, that they require no perusal to be understood ; and it is for the most part the same in Milton and Hooker.

Take the following sentence as a specimen of the sort of style to which I have been alluding :—

Concerning Faith, the principal object whereof is that eternal verity which hath discovered the treasures of hidden wisdom in Christ; concerning Hope, the highest object whereof is that everlasting goodness which in Christ doth quicken the dead ; concerning Charity, the final object whereof is that incomprehensible beauty which shineth in the countenance of Christ, the Son of the living God : concerning these virtues, the first of which beginning here with a weak apprehension of things not seen, endeth with the intuitive vision of God in the world to come; the second beginning here with a trembling expectation of things far removed, and as yet but only heard of, endeth with real and actual fruition of that which no tongue can express ; the third beginning here with a weak inclination of heart towards him unto whom we are not able to approach, endeth with endless union, the mystery whereof is higher than the reach of the thoughts of men ; concerning that Faith, Hope, and Charity, without which there can be no salvation, was there ever any mention made saving only in that Law which God himself hath from Heaven revealed? There is not in the world a syllable muttered with certain truth concerning any of these three, more than hath been supernaturally received from the mouth of the eternal God.

Eccles. Pol. I. a. 11.

The unity in these writers is produced by the unity of the subject, and the perpetual growth and evolution of the thoughts, one generating, and explaining, and justifying, the place of another, not,

as it is in Seneca, where the thoughts, striking as
they are, are merely strung together like beads,
without any causation or progression. The words
are selected because they are the most appropriate,
regard being had to the dignity of the total impression, and no merely big phrases are used where
plain ones would have sufficed, even in the most
learned of their works.

There is some truth in a remark, which I believe
was made by Sir Joshua Reynolds, that the greatest man is he who forms the taste of a nation, and
that the next greatest is he who corrupts it. The
true classical style of Hooker and his fellows
was easily open to corruption; and Sir Thomas
Brown it was, who, though a writer of great genius, first effectually injured the literary taste of
the nation by his introduction of learned words,
merely because they were learned. It would be
difficult to describe Brown adequately; exuberant
in conception and conceit, dignified, hyperlatinistic,
a quiet and sublime enthusiast; yet a fantast, a humourist, a brain with a twist; egotistic like Mon-
taigne, yet with a feeling heart and an active curiosity, which, however, too often degenerates into a
hunting after oddities. In his *Hydriotaphia* and,
indeed, almost all his works the entireness of his
mental action is very observable; he metamorphoses
every thing, be it what it may, into the subject under consideration. But Sir Thomas Brown with
all his faults had a genuine idiom; and it is the

existence of an individual idiom in each, that makes the principal writers before the Restoration the great patterns or integers of English style. In them the precise intended meaning of a word can never be mistaken; whereas in the latter writers, as especially in Pope, the use of words is for the most part purely arbitrary, so that the context will rarely show the true specific sense, but only that something of the sort is designed. A perusal of the authorities cited by Johnson in his dictionary under any leading word, will give you a lively sense of this declension in etymological truth of expression in the writers after the Restoration, or perhaps, strictly, after the middle of the reign of Charles II.

The general characteristic of the style of our literature down to the period which I have just mentioned, was gravity, and in Milton and some other writers of his day there are perceptible traces of the sternness of republicanism. Soon after the Restoration a material change took place, and the cause of royalism was graced, sometimes disgraced, by every shade of lightness of manner. A free and easy style was considered as a test of loyalty, or at all events, as a badge of the cavalier party; you may detect it occasionally even in Barrow, who is, however, in general remarkable for dignity and logical sequency of expression; but in L'Estrange, Collyer, and the writers of that class, this easy manner was carried out to the utmost extreme of slang and ribaldry. Yet still the works, even of

2 N

these last authors, have considerable merit in one point of view; their language is level to the under-standings of all men; it is an actual transcript of the colloquialism of the day, and is accordingly full of life and reality. Roger North's life of his brother, the Lord Keeper, is the most valuable specimen of this class of our literature; it is delightful, and much beyond any other of the writings of his con-temporaries.

From the common opinion that the English style attained its greatest perfection in and about Queen Ann's reign I altogether dissent; not only because it is in one species alone in which it can be pre-tended that the writers of that age excelled their predecessors; but also because the specimens them-selves are not equal, upon sound principles of judg-ment, to much that had been produced before. The classical structure of Hooker — the impetuous, thought-agglomerating flood of Taylor — to these there is no pretence of a parallel; and for mere ease and grace, is Cowley inferior to Addison, be-ing as he is so much more thoughtful and full of fancy? Cowley, with the omission of a quaintness here and there, is probably the best model of style for modern imitation in general. Taylor's periods have been frequently attempted by his admirers; you may, perhaps, just catch the turn of a simile or single image, but to write in the real manner of Jeremy Taylor would require as mighty a mind as his. Many parts of Algernon Sidney's treatises

afford excellent exemplars of a good modern practical style; and Dryden in his prose works, is a still
better model, if you add a stricter and purer grammar.   It is, indeed, worthy of remark that all our
great poets have been good prose writers, as Chaucer, Spenser, Milton; and this probably arose from
their just sense of metre.   For a true poet will
never confound verse and prose; whereas it is almost characteristic of indifferent prose writers that
they should be constantly slipping into scraps of
metre.   Swift's style is, in its line, perfect; the
manner is a complete expression of the matter, the
terms appropriate, and the artifice concealed.   It is
simplicity in the true sense of the word.

After the Revolution, the spirit of the nation became much more commercial, than it had been before; a learned body, or clerisy, as such, gradually
disappeared, and literature in general began to be
addressed to the common miscellaneous public.
That public had become accustomed to, and required, a strong stimulus; and to meet the requisi-
tions of the public taste, a style was produced which
by combining triteness of thought with singularity
and excess of manner of expression, was calculated
at once to soothe ignorance and to flatter vanity.
The thought was carefully kept down to the immediate apprehension of the commonest understanding, and the dress was as anxiously arranged for
the purpose of making the thought appear something very profound.   The essence of this style

consisted in a mock antithesis, that is, an opposition of mere sounds, in a rage for personification,
the abstract made animate, far-fetched metaphors,
strange phrases, metrical scraps, in every thing, in
short, but genuine prose. (Style is, of course, nothing else but the art of conveying the meaning
appropriately and with perspicuity, whatever that
meaning may be, and one criterion of style is that
it shall not be translateable without injury to the
meaning.) Johnson's style has pleased many from
the very fault of being perpetually translateable; he
creates an impression of cleverness by never saying
any thing in a common way. The best specimen
of this manner is in Junius, because his antithesis
is less merely verbal than Johnson's. Gibbon's
manner is the worst of all; it has every fault of
which this peculiar style is capable. Tacitus is
an example of it in Latin; in coming from Cicero
you feel the *falsetto* immediately.

In order to form a good style, the primary rule
and condition is, not to attempt to express ourselves
in language before we thoroughly know our own
meaning :—when a man perfectly understands himself, appropriate diction will generally be at his
command either in writing or speaking. In such
cases the thoughts and the words are associated.
In the next place preciseness in the use of terms is
required, and the test is whether you can translate
the phrase adequately into simpler terms, regard
being had to the feeling of the whole passage. Try

this upon Shakspeare, or Milton, and see if you can substitute other simpler words in any given passage without a violation of the meaning or tone. The source of bad writing is the desire to be something more than a man of sense, — the straining to be thought a genius; and it is just the same in speech-making. If men would only say what they have to say in plain terms, how much more eloquent they would be! Another rule is to avoid converting mere abstractions into persons. I believe you will very rarely find in any great writer before the Revolution the possessive case of an inanimate noun used in prose instead of the dependent case, as 'the watch's hand,' for 'the hand of the watch.' The possessive or Saxon genitive was confined to persons, or at least to animated subjects. And I cannot conclude this Lecture without insisting on the importance of accuracy of style as being near akin to veracity and truthful habits of mind; he who thinks loosely will write loosely, and, perhaps, there is some moral inconvenience in the common forms of our grammars which give children so many obscure terms for material distinctions. Let me also exhort you to careful examination of what you read, if it be worth any perusal at all; such examination will be a safeguard from fanaticism, the universal origin of which is in the contemplation of phenomena without investigation into their causes.

PROMETHEUS OF ÆSCHYLUS:

An Essay, preparatory to a series of disquisitions respecting
the Egyptian, in connexion with the sacerdotal, theology,
and in contrast with the mysteries of ancient Greece. Read
at the Royal Society of Literature, May 18, 1825.

THE French *savans* who went to Egypt in the
train of Buonaparte, Denon, Fourrier, and
Dupuis, (it has been asserted,) triumphantly vin-
dicated the chronology of Herodotus, on the authority of documents that cannot lie;—namely the inscriptions and sculptures on those enormous masses
of architecture, that might seem to have been built
in the wish of rivalling the mountains, and at some
unknown future to answer the same purpose, that
is, to stand the gigantic tombstones of an elder
world. It is decided, say the critics, whose words
I have before cited, that the present division of the
zodiac had been already arranged by the Egyptians
fifteen thousand years before the Christian era, and
according to an inscription ' which cannot lie' the
temple of Esne is of eight thousand years standing.

Now, in the first place, among a people who had
placed their national pride in their antiquity, I do
not see the impossibility of an inscription lying;
and, secondly, as little can I see the improbability
of a modern interpreter misunderstanding it; and
lastly, the incredibility of a French infidel's partak-

ing of both defects, is still less evident to my understanding. The inscriptions may be, and in some instances, very probably are, of later date than the temples themselves, — the offspring of vanity or priestly rivalry, or of certain astrological theories; or the temples themselves may have been built in the place of former and ruder structures, of an earlier and ruder period, and not impossibly under a different scheme of hieroglyphic or significant characters; and these may have been intentionally, or ignorantly, miscopied or mistranslated.

But more than all the preceding,—I cannot but persuade myself, that for a man of sound judgment and enlightened common sense—a man with whom the demonstrable laws of the human mind, and the rules generalized from the great mass of facts respecting human nature, weigh more than any two or three detached documents or narrations, of whatever authority the narrator may be, and however difficult it may be to bring positive proofs against the antiquity of the documents—I cannot but persuade myself, I say, that for such a man, the relation preserved in the first book of the Pentateuch, —and which, in perfect accordance with all analogous experience, with all the facts of history, and all that the principles of political economy would lead us to anticipate, conveys to us the rapid progress in civilization and splendour from Abraham and Abimelech to Joseph and Pharaoh,—will be worth a whole library of such inferences.

I am aware that it is almost universal to speak
of the gross idolatry of Egypt; nay, that arguments
have been grounded on this assumption in proof of
the divine origin of the Mosaic monotheism.   But
first, if by this we are to understand that the great
doctrine of the one Supreme Being was first revealed to the Hebrew legislator, his own inspired
writings supply abundant and direct confutation of
the position.   Of certain astrological superstitions,
—of certain talismans connected with star-magic,—
plates and images constructed in supposed harmony
with the movements and influences of celestial
bodies, — there doubtless exist hints, if not direct
proofs, both in the Mosaic writings, and those next
to these in antiquity.   But of plain idolatry in
Egypt, or the existence of a polytheistic religion,
represented by various idols, each signifying a several deity, I can find no decisive proof in the
Pentateuch; and when I collate these with the
books of the prophets, and the other inspired writings subsequent to the Mosaic, I cannot but regard
the absence of any such proof in the latter, compared with the numerous and powerful assertions,
or evident implications, of Egyptian idolatry in
the former, both as an argument of incomparably
greater value in support of the age and authenticity
of the Pentateuch; and as a strong presumption in
favour of the hypothesis on which I shall in part
ground the theory which will pervade this series of
disquisitions;—namely, that the sacerdotal religion

of Egypt had, during the interval from Abimelech
to Moses, degenerated from the patriarchal monotheism into a pantheism, cosmotheism, or worship
of the world as God.

The reason or pretext, assigned by the Hebrew
legislator to Pharaoh for leading his countrymen
into the wilderness to join with their brethren, the
tribes who still sojourned in the nomadic state,
namely, that their sacrifices would be an abomina-
tion to the Egyptians, may be urged as inconsistent
with, nay, as confuting this hypothesis.   But to
this I reply, first, that the worship of the ox and
cow was not, in and of itself, and necessarily, a
contravention of the first commandment, though a
very gross breach of the second;—for it is most
certain that the ten tribes worshipped the Jehovah,
the God of Abraham, Isaac, and Jacob, under the
same or similar symbols:—secondly that the cow,
or Isis, and the Io of the Greeks, truly represented,
in the first instance, the earth or productive nature,
and afterwards the mundane religion grounded on
the worship of nature, or the $\tau \grave{o} \ \pi \bar{a} \nu$, as God.   In
after times, the ox or bull was added, representing
the sun, or generative force of nature, according to
the habit of male and female deities, which spread
almost over the whole world,—the positive and
negative forces in the science of superstition;—for
the pantheism of the sage necessarily engenders
polytheism as the popular creed.   But lastly, a very
sufficient reason may, I think, be assigned for the

choice of the ox or cow, as representing the very
life of nature, by the first legislators of Egypt,
and for the similar sacred character in the Brach-
manic tribes of Hindostan.   The progress from
savagery to civilization is evidently first from the
hunting to the pastoral state, a process which even
now is going on, within our own times, among the
South American Indians in the vast tracts between
Buenos Ayres and the Andes: but the second and
the most important step, is from the pastoral, or
wandering, to the agricultural, or fixed, state.
Now, if even for men born and reared under European civilization, the charms of a wandering life
have been found so great a temptation, that few
who have taken to it have been induced to return
(see the confession in the preamble to the statute
respecting the gipsies); *—how much greater must
have been the danger of relapse in the first formation of fixed states with a condensed population?
And what stronger prevention could the ingenuity
of the priestly kings—(for the priestly is ever the
first form of government)—devise, than to have
made the ox or cow the representatives of the divine principle in the world, and, as such, an object
of adoration, the wilful destruction of which was

---

* The Act meant is probably the 5. Eliz. c. 20, enforcing
the two previous Acts of Henry VIII. and Philip and Mary,
and reciting that natural born Englishmen had ' become of
the fellowship of the said vagabonds, by transforming or
disguising themselves in their apparel,' &c.—*Ed.*

sacrilege?—For this rendered a return to the pastoral state impossible; in which the flesh of these animals and the milk formed almost the exclusive food of mankind; while, in the meantime, by once compelling and habituating men to the use of a vegetable diet, it enforced the laborious cultivation of the soil, and both produced and permitted a vast and condensed population. In the process and continued subdivisions of polytheism, this great sacred Word,—for so the consecrated animals were called, ἱεροὶ λόγοι,—became multiplied, till almost every power and supposed attribute of nature had its symbol in some consecrated animal from the beetle to the hawk. Wherever the powers of nature had found a cycle for themselves, in which the powers still produced the same phenomenon during a given period, whether in the motions of the heavenly orbs, or in the smallest living organic body, there the Egyptian sages predicated life and mind. Time, cyclical time, was their abstraction of the deity, and their holidays were their gods.

The diversity between theism and pantheism may be most simply and generally expressed in the following *formula*, in which the material universe is expressed by W, and the deity by G.

$$W - G = O ;$$

or the World without God is an impossible conception. This position is common to theist and pantheist. But the pantheist adds the converse—

$$G - W = O ;$$

for which the theist substitutes—

$$G - W = G ;$$

or that—

$$\overline{G = G}, \text{ anterior and irrelative to the existence of the world, is equal to } G + W.*$$

Before the mountains were, Thou art.—I am not about to lead the society beyond the bounds of my subject into divinity or theology in the professional sense. But without a precise definition of pantheism, without a clear insight into the essential distinction between it and the theism of the Scriptures, it appears to me impossible to understand either the import or the history of the polytheism of the great historical nations. I beg leave, therefore, to repeat, and to carry on my former position, that the religion of Egypt, at the time of the Exodus of the Hebrews, was a pantheism, on the point of passing into that polytheism, of which it afterwards afforded a specimen, gross and distasteful even to polytheists themselves of other nations.

The objects which, on my appointment as Royal Associate of the Royal Society of Literature, I proposed to myself were, 1st. The elucidation of the

---

* Mr. Coleridge was in the constant habit of expressing himself on paper by the algebraic symbols. They have an uncouth look in the text of an ordinary essay, and I have sometimes ventured to render them by the equivalent words. But most of the readers of these volumes will know that — means *less by*, or, *without ;* + *more by*, or, *in addition to ;* = *equal to*, or, *the same as.*— Ed.

purpose of the Greek drama, and the relations in which it stood to the mysteries on the one hand, and to the state or sacerdotal religion on the other :— 2nd. The connection of the Greek tragic poets with philosophy as the peculiar offspring of Greek genius : —3rd. The connection of the Homeric and cyclical poets with the popular religion of the Greeks : and, lastly from all these,—namely, the mysteries, the sacerdotal religion; their philosophy before and after Socrates, the stage, the Homeric poetry and the legendary belief of the people, and from the sources and productive causes in the derivation and confluence of the tribes that finally shaped themselves into a nation of Greeks—to give a juster and more distinct view of this singular people, and of the place which they occupied in the history of the world, and the great scheme of divine providence, than I have hitherto seen,—or rather let me say, than it appears to me possible to give by any other process.

The present Essay, however, I devote to the purpose of removing, or at least invalidating, one objection that I may reasonably anticipate, and which may be conveyed in the following question :—What proof have you of the fact of any connection between the Greek drama, and either the mysteries, or the philosophy, of Greece? What proof that it was the office of the tragic poet, under a disguise of the sacerdotal religion, mixed with the legendary or popular belief, to reveal as much of the mysteries interpreted by philosophy, as would counteract the

demoralizing effects of the state religion, without
compromising the tranquillity of the state itself, or
weakening that paramount reverence, without which
a republic, (such I mean, as the republics of ancient
Greece were) could not exist?

I know no better way in which I can reply to
this objection, than by giving, as my proof and instance, the Prometheus of Æschylus, accompanied
with an exposition of what I believe to be the intention of the poet, and the mythic import of the
work; of which it may be truly said, that it is more
properly tragedy itself in the plenitude of the idea,
than a particular tragic poem; and as a preface to
this exposition, and for the twin purpose of render-
ing it intelligible, and of explaining its connexion
with the whole scheme of my Essays, I entreat permission to insert a quotation from a work of my
own, which has indeed been in print for many years,
but which few of my auditors will probably have
heard of, and still fewer, if any, have read.

" As the representative of the youth and approaching manhood of the human intellect we have
ancient Greece, from Orpheus, Linus, Musæus, and
the other mythological bards, or, perhaps, the bro-
therhoods impersonated under those names, to the
time when the republics lost their independence,
and their learned men sank into copyists of, and
commentators on, the works of their forefathers.
That we include these as educated under a distinct

providential, though not miraculous, dispensation, will surprise no one, who reflects, that in whatever has a permanent operation on the destinies and intellectual condition of mankind at large,—that in all which has been manifestly employed as a co-agent in the mightiest revolution of the moral world, the propagation of the Gospel, and in the intellectual progress of mankind in the restoration of philosophy, science, and the ingenuous arts — it were irreligion not to acknowledge the hand of divine providence.   The periods, too, join on to each other.   The earliest Greeks took up the religious and lyrical poetry of the Hebrews ; and the schools of the prophets were, however partially and imperfectly, represented by the mysteries derived through the corrupt channel of the Phœnicians ! With these secret schools of physiological theology, the mythical poets were doubtless in connexion, and it was these schools which prevented polytheism from producing all its natural barbarizing effects. The mysteries and the mythical hymns and pæans shaped themselves gradually into epic poetry and history on the one hand, and into the ethical tragedy and philosophy on the other.   Under their protection, and that of a youthful liberty, secretly controlled by a species of internal theocracy, the sciences, and the sterner kinds of the fine arts, that is, architecture and statuary, grew up together, followed, indeed, by painting, but a statuesque, and austerely idealized, painting, which did not degenerate into mere copies of the sense, till the process for which Greece existed had been completed."*

The Greeks alone brought forth philosophy in the proper and contra-distinguishable sense of the term, which we may compare to the coronation medal with its symbolic characters, as contrasted with the coins, issued under the same sovereign, current in the market. In the primary sense, philosophy had for its aim and proper subject the τὰ περὶ ἀρχῶν, *de originibus rerum*, as far as man proposes to discover the same in and by the pure reason alone. This, I say, was the offspring of Greece, and elsewhere adopted only. The predisposition appears in their earliest poetry.

The first object, (or subject matter) of Greek philosophizing was in some measure philosophy itself;—not, indeed, as a product, but as the producing power—the productivity. Great minds turned inward on the fact of the diversity between man and beast; a superiority of kind in addition to that of degree; the latter, that is, the difference in degree comprehending the more enlarged sphere and the multifold application of faculties common to man and brute animals;—even this being in great measure a transfusion from the former, namely, from the superiority in kind;—for only by its coexistence with reason, free will, self-consciousness,

---

* Friend, III. Essay 9.

the contra-distinguishing attributes of man, does the instinctive intelligence manifested in the ant, the dog, the elephant, &c. become human understanding. It is a truth with which Heraclitus, the senior, but yet contemporary, of Æschylus, appears, from the few genuine fragments of his writings that are yet extant, to have been deeply impressed,— that the mere understanding in man, considered as the power of adapting means to immediate purposes, differs, indeed, from the intelligence displayed by other animals, and not in degree only; but yet does not differ by any excellence which it derives from itself, or by any inherent diversity, but solely in consequence of a combination with far higher powers of a diverse kind in one and the same subject.

Long before the entire separation of metaphysics from poetry, that is, while yet poesy, in all its several species of verse, music, statuary, &c. continued mythic;—while yet poetry remained the union of the sensuous and the philosophic mind;— the efficient presence of the latter in the *synthesis* of the two, had manifested itself in the sublime *mythus περὶ γενέσεως τοῦ νοῦ ἐν ἀνθρωποῖς*, concerning the *genesis*, or birth of the *νους* or reason in man. This the most venerable, and perhaps the most ancient, of Grecian *mythi*, is a philosopheme, the very same in subject matter with the earliest record of the Hebrews, but most characteristically different in tone and conception;—for the patriarchal religion, as the antithesis of pantheism, was

2   O

necessarily personal; and the doctrines of a faith,
the first ground of which and the primary enuncia-
tion, is the eternal I AM, must be in part historic
and must assume the historic form. Hence the
Hebrew record is a narrative, and the first instance
of the fact is given as the origin of the fact.

That a profound truth — a truth that is, indeed,
the grand and indispensable condition of all moral
responsibility — is involved in this characteristic of
the sacred narrative, I am not alone persuaded, but
distinctly aware. This, however, does not preclude
us from seeing, nay, as an additional mark of the
wisdom that inspired the sacred historian, it rather
supplies a motive to us, impels and authorizes us,
to see, in the form of the vehicle of the truth, an
accommodation to the then childhood of the human
race. Under this impression we may, I trust, safely
consider the narration, — introduced, as it is here
introduced, for the purpose of explaining a mere
work of the unaided mind of man by comparison,—
as an ἔπος ἱερογλυφικὸν,—and as such (apparently,
I mean, not actually) a *synthesis* of poesy and philosophy, characteristic of the childhood of nations.

In the Greek we see already the dawn of approaching manhood. The substance, the stuff, is
philosophy; the form only is poetry. The Prometheus is a *philosophema ταυτηγορικὸν,*—the tree
of knowledge of good and evil, — an allegory, a
προπαίδευμα, though the noblest and the most
pregnant of its kind.

The generation of the νοῦς, or pure reason in
man. 1. It was superadded or infused, *a supra*
to mark that it was no mere evolution of the animal
basis;—that it could not have grown out of the
other faculties of man, his life, sense, understanding, as the flower grows out of the stem, having
pre-existed potentially in the seed: 2. The νοῦς, or
fire, was ' stolen,'—to mark its *hetero*—or rather
its *allo*-geneity, that is, its diversity, its difference
in kind, from the faculties which are common to
man with the nobler animals: 3. And stolen 'from
Heaven,'—to mark its superiority in kind, as well
as its essential diversity: 4. And it was a ' spark,'
—to mark that it is not subject to any modifying
reaction from that on which it immediately acts;
that it suffers no change, and receives no accession,
from the inferior, but multiplies itself by conversion,
without being alloyed by, or amalgamated with, that
which it potentiates, ennobles, and transmutes: 5.
And lastly, (in order to imply the homogeneity of
the donor and of the gift) it was stolen by a 'god,'
and a god of the race before the dynasty of Jove,—
Jove the binder of reluctant powers, the coercer and
entrancer of free spirits under the fetters of shape,
and mass, and passive mobility; but likewise by a
god of the same race and essence with Jove, and
linked of yore in closest and friendliest intimacy
with him. This, to mark the pre-existence, in order
of thought, of the *nous*, as spiritual, both to the objects of sense, and to their products, formed as it

were, by the precipitation, or, if I may dare adopt
the bold language of Leibnitz, by a coagulation of
spirit.* In other words this derivation of the spark
from above, and from a god anterior to the Jovial
dynasty—(that is, to the submersion of spirits in
material forms),—was intended to mark the trans-
cendency of the *nous*, the contra-distinctive faculty
of man, as timeless, ἄχρονόν τι, and, in this negative sense, eternal. It signified, I say, its superiority to, and its diversity from, all things that sub-
sist in space and time, nay, even those which, though
spaceless, yet partake of time, namely, souls or un-
derstandings. For the soul, or understanding, if it
be defined physiologically as the principle of sensibility, irritability, and growth, together with the
functions of the organs, which are at once the representatives and the instruments of these, must be
considered *in genere*, though not in degree or dignity, common to man and the inferior animals. It
was the spirit, the *nous*, which man alone possessed.
And I must be permitted to suggest that this notion deserves some respect, were it only that it can
shew a semblance, at least, of sanction from a far
higher authority.

---

* Schelling ascribes this expression, which I have not been
able to find in the works of Leibnitz, to Hemsterhuis:
" When Leibnitz," says he, " calls matter the sleep-state of
the Monads, or when Hemsterhuis calls it *curdled spirit*,—
den geronnenen Geist. —In fact, matter is no other than spirit contemplated in the equilibrium of its activities." *Transl.
Transfc. Ideal.* p. 190. S. C.

The Greeks agreed with the cosmogonies of the
East in deriving all sensible forms from the indistinguishable.   The latter we find designated as the
τὸ ἄμορφον, the ὕδωρ προκοσμικὸν, the χάος, as the
essentially unintelligible, yet necessarily presumed;
basis or sub-position of all positions.   That it is,
scientifically considered, an indispensable idea for
the human mind, just as the mathematical point,
&c. for the geometrician;—of this the various systems of our geologists and cosmogonists, from Bur-
net to La Place, afford strong presumption.   As an
idea, it must be interpreted as a striving of the mind
to distinguish being from existence,—or potential
being, the ground of being containing the possibility
of existence, from being actualized.   In the language of the mysteries, it was the *esurience*, the
πόθος or *desideratum*, the unfuelled fire, the Ceres,
the ever-seeking maternal goddess, the origin and
interpretation of whose name is found in the Hebrew root signifying hunger, and thence capacity.
It was, in short, an effort to represent the universal
ground of all differences distinct or opposite, but in
relation to which all *antithesis* as well as all *anti-
theta*, existed only potentially.   This was the con-
tainer and withholder, (such is the primitive sense
of the Hebrew word rendered darkness (Gen. 1. 2.))
out of which light, that is, the *lux lucifica*, as distinguished from *lumen seu lux phænomenalis*, was
produced;—say, rather, that which, producing itself
into light as the one pole or antagonist power, remained in the other pole as darkness, that is, gra-

vity, or the principle of mass, or wholeness without distinction of parts.

And here the peculiar, the philosophic, genius of Greece began its fœtal throb. Here it individualized itself in contra-distinction from the Hebrew archology, on the one side, and from the Phœnician, on the other. The Phœnician confounded the indistinguishable with the absolute, the *Alpha* and *Omega*, the ineffable *causa sui*. It confounded, I say, the multeity below intellect, that is, unintelligible from defect of the subject, with the absolute identity above all intellect, that is, transcending comprehension by the plenitude of its excellence. With the Phœnician sages the cosmogony was their theogony and *vice versa*. Hence, too, flowed their theurgic rites, their magic, their worship *(cultus et apotheosis)* of the plastic forces, chemical and vital, and these, or their notions respecting these, formed the hidden meaning, the soul, as it were, of which the popular and civil worship was the body with its drapery.

The Hebrew wisdom imperatively asserts an unbeginning creative One, who neither became the world; nor is the world eternally; nor made the world out of himself by emanation, or evolution;—but who willed it, and it was ! Τὰ ἄθεα ἐγένετο, καὶ ἐγένετο χάος,—and this chaos, the eternal will, by the spirit and the word, or express *fiat*,—again acting as the impregnant, distinctive, and ordonnant power,—enabled to become a world—κοσμεῖσθαι. So must it be when a religion, that shall preclude superstition on the one hand, and brute indifference on the other, is to be true for the meditative sage, yet intelligible, or at least apprehensible, for all but the fools in heart.

The Greek philosopheme, preserved for us in the Æschylean Prometheus, stands midway betwixt both, yet is distinct in kind from either. With the Hebrew or purer Semitic, it assumes an X Y Z, — (I take these letters in their algebraic application) —an indeterminate *Elohim*, antecedent to the matter of the world, ὕλη ἄκοσμος—no less than to the ὕλη κεκοσμημένη. In this point, likewise, the Greek accorded with the Semitic, and differed from the Phœnician — that it held the antecedent X Y Z to be super-sensuous and divine. But on the other hand, it coincides with the Phœnician in considering this antecedent ground of corporeal matter,— τῶν σωμάτων καὶ τοῦ σωματικοῦ,—not so properly the cause of the latter, as the occasion and the still continuing substance. *Materia substat adhuc.* The corporeal was supposed co-essential with the antecedent of its corporeity. Matter, as distinguished from body, was a *non ens*, a simple apparition, *id quod mere videtur ;* but to body the elder physico-theology of the Greeks allowed a participation in entity. It was *spiritus ipse, oppressus, dormiens, et diversis modis somnians.* In short, body was the productive power suspended, and as it were, quenched in the product. This may be rendered plainer by reflecting, that, in the pure Semitic scheme there are four terms introduced in the so-

lution of the problem, 1.. the beginning, self-suffi-
cing, and immutable Creator; 2. the antecedent
night as the identity, or including germ, of the light
and darkness, that is, gravity; 3. the chaos; and
4. the material world resulting from the powers
communicated by the divine *fiat*. In the Phœnician scheme there are in fact but two—a self-or-
ganizing chaos, and the omniform nature as the
result. In the Greek scheme we have three terms,
1. the *hyle* ὕλη, which holds the place of the chaos,
or the waters, in the true system; 2. τὰ σώματα,
answering to the Mosaic heaven and earth; and
3. the Saturnian χρόνοι ὑπερχρόνιοι, — which answer to the antecedent darkness of the Mosaic
scheme, but to which the elder physico-theologists
attributed a self-polarizing power—a *natura ge-
mina quæ fit et facit, agit et patitur*. In other
words, the *Elohim* of the Greeks were still but a
natura deorum, τὸ θεῖον, in which a vague plurality
adhered; or if any unity was imagined, it was not
personal — not a unity of excellence, but simply an
expression of the negative—that which was to pass,
but which had not yet passed, into distinct form.

All this will seem strange and obscure at first
reading,—perhaps fantastic. But it will only seem
so. Dry and prolix, indeed, it is to me in the writing, full as much as it can be to others in the attempt to understand it. But I know that, once
mastered, the idea will be the key to the whole cy-
pher of the Æschylean mythology. The sum stated
in the terms of philosophic logic is this: First, what

Moses appropriated to the chaos itself: what Moses made passive and a *materia subjecta et lucis et tenebrarum*, the containing προθέμενον of the *thesis* and *antithesis ;*—this the Greek placed anterior to the chaos;—the chaos itself being the struggle between the *hyperchronia*, the ἰδέαι πρόνομοι, as the unevolved, unproduced, *prothesis*, of which ἰδέα καὶ νόμος — (idea and law) — are the *thesis* and *antithesis*. (I use the word ' produced' in the mathematical sense, as a point elongating itself to a bipolar line.) Secondly, what Moses establishes, not merely as a transcendant *Monas*, but as an individual Ἑνὰς likewise ; — this the Greek took as a harmony, θεοὶ ἀθάνατοι, τὸ θεῖον, as distinguished from ὁ θεὸς—or, to adopt the more expressive language of the Pythagoreans and cabalists *numen numerantis ;* and these are to be contemplated as the identity.

Now according to the Greek philosopheme or *mythus*, in these, or in this identity, there arose a war, schism, or division, that is, a polarization into *thesis* and *antithesis*. In consequence of this schism in the τὸ θεῖον, the *thesis* becomes *nomos*, or law, and the *antithesis* becomes *idea*, but so that the *nomos* is *nomos*, because, and only because, the *idea* is *idea :* the *nomos* is not idea, only because the idea has not become *nomos*. And this *not* must be heedfully borne in mind through the whole interpretation of this most profound and pregnant philosopheme. The *nomos* is essentially idea, but existentially it is idea *substans*, that is, *id quod stat subtus*, understanding *sensu generalissimo*. The *idea*, which now is no longer idea, has substantiated itself, become real as opposed to idea, and is henceforward, therefore, *substans in substantiato*. The first product of its energy is the thing itself: *ipsa se posuit et jam facta est ens positum*. Still, however, its productive energy is not exhausted in this product, but overflows, or is effluent, as the specific forces, properties, faculties, of the product. It re-appears, in short, in the body, as the function of the body. As a sufficient illustration, though it cannot be offered as a perfect instance, take the following.

' In the world we see every where evidences of a unity, which the component parts are so far from explaining, that they necessarily presuppose it as the cause and condition of their existing as those parts, or even of their existing at all. This antecedent unity, or cause and principle of each union, it has since the time of Bacon and Kepler, been customary to call a law. This crocus, for instance, or any flower the reader may have in sight or choose to bring before his fancy; —that the root, stem, leaves, petals, &c. cohere as one plant, is owing to an antecedent power or principle in the seed, which existed before a single particle of the matters that constitute the size and visibility of the crocus had been attracted from the surrounding soil, air, and moisture. Shall we turn to the seed? Here too

the same necessity meets us, an antecedent unity
(I speak not of the parent plant, but of an agency
antecedent in order of operance, yet remaining present as the conservative and reproductive power,)
must here too be supposed. Analyze the seed with
the finest tools, and let the solar microscope come
in aid of your senses,—what do you find?—means
and instruments, a wondrous fairy-tale of nature,
magazines of food, stores of various sorts, pipes,
spiracles, defences, — a house of many chambers,
and the owner and inhabitant invisible.'* Now,
compare a plant thus contemplated with an animal.
In the former, the productive energy exhausts itself,
and as it were, sleeps in the product or *organismus*
—in its root, stem, foliage, blossoms, seed. Its
balsams, gums, resins, *aromata*, and all other bases
of its sensible qualities, are, it is well known, mere
excretions from the vegetable, eliminated, as lifeless, from the actual plant. The qualities are not
its properties, but the properties, or far rather, the
dispersion and volatilization of these extruded and
rejected bases. But in the animal it is otherwise.
Here the antecedent unity — the productive and
self-realizing idea — strives, with partial success to
re-emancipate itself from its product, and seeks
once again to become *idea :* vainly indeed: for in
order to this, it must be retrogressive, and it hath

---

* Aids to Réflection. Moral and Religious Aphorisms.
Aphorism VI. *Ed.*

subjected itself to the fates, the evolvers of the endless thread — to the stern necessity of progression.
Idea itself it cannot become, but it may in long and
graduated process, become an image, an ANALOGON,
an anti-type of IDEA.   And this εἴδωλον may approximate to a perfect likeness.   *Quod est simile,
nequit esse idem.*   Thus, in the lower animals, we
see this process of emancipation commence with the
intermediate link, or that which forms the transition
from properties to faculties, namely, with sensation.
Then the faculties of sense, locomotion, construction, as, for instance, webs, hives, nests, &c.   Then
the functions; as of instinct, memory, fancy, instinctive intelligence, or understanding, as it exists
in the most intelligent animals.   Thus the idea
(henceforward no more idea, but irrecoverable by
its own fatal act) commences the process of its own
transmutation, as *substans in substantiato*, as the
enteleche, or the *vis formatrix*, and it finishes the
process as *substans e substantiato*, that is, as the
understanding.

If, for the purpose of elucidating this process, I
might be allowed to imitate the symbolic language
of the algebraists, and thus to regard the successive
steps of the process as so many powers and digni-
ties of the *nomos* or law, the scheme would be represented thus :—

Nomos^1 = Product: N^2 = Property: N^3 =
Faculty: N^4 = Function: N^5 = Understanding ;—

which is, indeed, in one sense, itself a *nomos*, inasmuch as it is the index of the *nomos*, as well as its highest function; but, like the hand of a watch, it is likewise a *nomizomenon*.   It is a verb, but still a verb passive.

On the other hand, idea is so far co-essential with *nomos*, that by its co-existence—(not confluence) —with the *nomos ἐν νομιζομένοις* (with the *organismus* and its faculties and functions in the man,) it becomes itself a *nomos*.   But, observe, a *nomos autonomos*, or containing its law in itself likewise; —even as the *nomos* produces for its highest product the understanding, so the idea, in its opposition and, of course, its correspondence to the *nomos*, begets in itself an *analogon* to product; and this is self-consciousness.   But as the product can never become idea, so neither can the idea (if it is to remain idea) become or generate a distinct product. This *analogon* of product is to be itself; but were it indeed and substantially a product, it would cease to be self.   It would be an object for a subject, not (as it is and must be) an object that is its own subject, and *vice versa;* a conception which, if the uncombining and infusile genius of our language allowed it, might be expressed by the term subject-object.   Now, idea, taken in indissoluble connection with this *analogon* of product is mind, that which knows itself, and the existence of which may be inferred, but cannot appear or become a *phenomenon*.

By the benignity of Providence, the truths of

most importance in themselves, and which it most
concerns us to know, are familiar to us, even from
childhood. Well for us if we do not abuse this privilege, and mistake the familiarity of words which
convey these truths, for a clear understanding of
the truths themselves! If the preceding disquisition,
with all its subtlety and all its obscurity, should answer no other purpose, it will still have been neither
purposeless, nor devoid of utility, should it only
lead us to sympathize with the strivings of the human intellect, awakened to the infinite importance
of the inward oracle γνῶθι σεαυτόν—and almost
instinctively shaping its course of search in confor-
mity with the Platonic intimation :—ψυχῆς φύσιν
ἀξίως λόγου κατανοῆσαι οἴει δυνατὸν εἶναι, ἄνευ τῆς
τοῦ ὅλου φύσεως; but be this as it may, the ground
work of the Æschylean *mythus* is laid in the definition of idea and law, as correlatives that mutually
interpret each the other ;—an idea, with the adequate
power of realizing itself being a law, and a law considered abstractedly from, or in the absence of, the
power of manifesting itself in its appropriate product being an idea. Whether this be true philosophy, is not the question. The school of Aristotle
would, of course, deny, the Platonic affirm it; for
in this consists the difference of the two schools.
Both acknowledge ideas as distinct from the mere
generalizations from objects of sense: both would
define an idea as an *ens rationale*, to which there
can be no adequate correspondent in sensible ex-

perience. But, according to Aristotle, ideas are
regulative only, and exist only as functions of the
mind: — according to Plato, they are constitutive
likewise, and one in essence with the power and
life of nature; — ἐν λόγῳ ζωὴ ἦν, καὶ ἡ ζωὴ ἦν τὸ
φῶς τῶν ἀνθρώπων. And this I assert, was the
philosophy of the mythic poets, who, like Æschylus,
adapted the secret doctrines of the mysteries as the
(not always safely disguised) antidote to the deba-
sing influences of the religion of the state.

But to return and conclude this preliminary explanation. We have only to substitute the term
will, and the term constitutive power, for *nomos* or
law, and the process is the same. Permit me to
represent the identity or *prothesis* by the letter Z
and the *thesis* and *antithesis* by X and Y respec-
tively. Then I say X by not being Y, but in consequence of being the correlative opposite of Y, is
will; and Y, by not being X, but the correlative
and opposite of X, is nature, — *natura naturans,*
νόμος φυσικός. Hence we may see the necessity
of contemplating the idea now as identical with the
reason, and now as one with the will, and now as
both in one, in which last case I shall, for conve-
nience sake, employ the term *Nous*, the rational
will, the practical reason.

We are now out of the holy jungle of transcendental metaphysics; if indeed, the reader's patience
shall have had strength and persistency enough to
allow me to exclaim—

Ivimus ambo
Per densas umbras : at tenet umbra Deum.

Not that I regard the foregoing as articles of faith,
or as all true ;—I have implied the contrary by con-
trasting it with, at least, by shewing its disparate-
ness from, the Mosaic, which, *bona fide*, I do regard as the truth.   But I believe there is much,
and profound, truth in it, *supra captum* ψιλοσόφων,
*qui non agnoscunt divinum, ideoque nec naturam,
nisi nomine, agnoscunt ; sed res cunctas ex sensu-
ali corporeo cogitant, quibus hac ex causa inte-
riora clausa manent, et simul cum illis exteriora
quæ proxima interioribus sunt !*   And with no less
confidence do I believe that the positions above
given, true or false, are contained in the Prome-
thean *mythus.*

In this *mythus,* Jove is the impersonated representation or symbol of the *nomos — Jupiter est
quodcunque vides.*   He is the *mens agitans molem,* but at the same time, the *molem corpoream
ponens et constituens.*   And so far the Greek philosopheme does not differ essentially from the cosmotheism, or identification of God with the universe, in which consisted the first apostacy of mankind after the flood, when they combined to raise a
temple to the heavens, and which is still the favored religion of the Chinese.   Prometheus, in
like manner, is the impersonated representative of
Idea, or of the same power as Jove, but contemplated as independent and not immersed in the

product,—as law *minus* the productive energy. As such it is next to be seen what the several signifi-cances of each must or may be according to the philosophic conception; and of which significances, therefore, should we find in the philosopheme a correspondent to each, we shall be entitled to assert that such are the meanings of the fable. And first of Jove:—

Jove represents 1. *Nomos* generally, as opposed to Idea or *Nous:* 2. *Nomos archinomos*, now as the father, now as the sovereign, and now as the in-cluder and representative of the νόμοι οὐράνιοι κοσ-μικοί, or *dii majores*, who, had joined or come over to Jove in the first schism: 3. *Nomos* δαμνητής—the subjugator of the spirits, of the ἰδέαι πρόνομοι, who, thus subjugated, became νόμοι ὑπονόμιοι ὑπο-σπόνδοι, *Titanes pacati*, *dii minores*, that is, the elements considered as powers reduced to obedience under yet higher powers than themselves: 4. *No-mos* πολιτικός, law in the Pauline sense, νόμος αλ-λοτριόνομος in antithesis to νόμος αὐτόνομος.

COROLLARY.

It is in this sense that Jove's jealous, ever-quar-relsome, spouse represents the political sacerdotal *cultus*, the church, in short, of republican pagan-ism;—a church by law established for the mere purposes of the particular state, unennobled by the consciousness of instrumentality to higher purposes;

2   P

—at once unenlightened and unchecked by revelation. Most gratefully ought we to acknowledge
that since the completion of our constitution in
1688, we may, with unflattering truth, elucidate
the spirit and character of such a church by the
contrast of the institution, to which England owes
the larger portion of its superiority in that, in which
alone superiority is an unmixed blessing,—the dif-
fused cultivation of its inhabitants. But previously
to this period, I shall offend no enlightened man if
I say without distinction of parties — *intra muros
peccatur et extra;* —that the history of Christendom presents us with too many illustrations of this
Junonian jealousy, this factious harassing of the
sovereign power as soon as the latter betrayed any
symptoms of a disposition to its true policy, namely,
to privilege and perpetuate that which is best, — to
tolerate the tolerable,—and to restrain none but
those who would restrain all, and subjugate even
the state itself. But while truth extorts this confession, it, at the same time, requires that it should
be accompanied by an avowal of the fact, that the
spirit is a relic of Paganism; and with a bitter smile
would an Æschylus or a Plato in the shades, listen
to a Gibbon or a Hume vaunting the mild and to-
lerant spirit of the state religions of ancient Greece
or Rome. Here we have the sense of Jove's intrigues with Europa, Io, &c. whom the god, in his
own nature a general lover, had successively taken
under his protection. And here, too, see the full

appropriateness of this part of the *mythus*, in which symbol fades away into allegory, but yet in reference to the working cause, as grounded in humanity, and always existing either actually or potentially, and thus never ceases wholly to be a symbol or taute-gory.

Prometheus represents, 1. *sensu generali*, Idea πρόνομος, and in this sense he is a θεὸς ὁμόφυλος, a fellow-tribesman both of the *dii majores*, with Jove at their head, and of the Titans or *dii pacati:* 2. He represents Idea φιλόνομος, νομοδείκτης; and in this sense the former friend and counsellor of Jove or *Nous uranius:* 3. Λόγος φιλάνθρωπος, the divine humanity, the humane God, who retained unseen, kept back, or (in the *catachresis* character-istic of the Phœnicio-Grecian mythology) stole, a portion or *ignicula* from the living spirit of law, which remained with the celestial gods unexpended ἐν τῷ νομίζεσθαι.   He gave that which, according to the whole analogy of things, should have existed either as pure divinity, the sole property and birth-right of the *Dii Joviales*, the *Uranions*, or was conceded to inferior beings as a *substans in sub-stantiato.*   This spark divine Prometheus gave to an elect, a favored animal, not as a *substans* or un-derstanding, commensurate with, and confined by, the constitution and conditions of this particular organism, but as *aliquid superstans, liberum, non subactum, invictum, impacatum,* μὴ νομιζόμενον. This gift, by which we are to understand reason

theoretical and practical, was therefore a *νόμος αὐ-*
τόνομος—unapproachable and unmodifiable by the
animal basis — that is, by the pre-existing *substans*
with its products, the animal *organismus* with its
faculties and functions; but yet endowed with the
power of potentiating, ennobling, and prescribing
to, the substance ; and hence, therefore, a *νόμος*
νομοπείθης, lex legisuada : 4. By a transition, ordinary even in allegory, and appropriate to mythic
symbol, but especially significant in the present
case—the transition, I mean, from the giver to the
gift—the giver, in very truth, being the gift,
' whence the soul receives reason : and reason is
her being,' says our Milton.   Reason is from God,
and God is reason, *mens ipsissima.*

5. Prometheus represents, *Νοῦς ἐν ἀνθρώπῳ—*
νοῦς ἀγωνιστὴς.   Thus contemplated, the *Nous* is
of necessity, powerless ; for all power, that is, productivity, or productive energy, is in Law, that is,
νόμος ἀλλοτριόνομος : * still, however, the Idea in
the Law, the *numerus numerans* become *νόμος*, is
the principle of the Law ; and if with Law dwells
power, so with the knowledge or the Idea *scientia-*
lis of the Law, dwells prophecy and foresight.   A
perfect astronomical time-piece in relation to the
motions of the heavenly bodies, or the magnet in

---

* I scarcely need say, that I use the word *ἀλλοτριόνομος*
as a participle active, as exercising law on another, not as
receiving law from another, though the latter is the classical
force, (1 suppose) of the word.

the mariner's compass in relation to the magnetism
of the earth, is a sufficient illustration.

6. Both νόμος and Idea (or *Nous*) are the *verbum;* but, as in the former, it is *verbum fiat* 'the
Word of the Lord,'—in the latter it must be the
verbum fiet or, 'the Word of the Lord in the mouth
of the prophet.'   *Pari argumento,* as the knowledge is therefore not power, the power is not knowledge.   The νόμος, the Ζεῦς ταντοκράτωρ, seeks to
learn, and, as it were, to wrest the secret, the hate-
ful secret, of his own fate, namely, the transitori-
ness adherent to all antithesis; for the identity or
the absolute is alone eternal.   This secret Jove
would extort from the *Nous,* or Prometheus, which
is the sixth representment of Prometheus.

7. Introduce but the least of real as opposed to
ideal, the least speck of positive existence, even
though it were but the mote in a sun beam, into the
sciential *contemplamen* or theorem, and it ceases
to be science.   *Ratio desinit esse pura ratio et fit
discursus, stat subter et fit ὑποθετικὸν:—non su-
perstat.*   The *Nous* is bound to a rock, the im-
movable firmness of which is indissolubly connected
with its barrenness, its non-productivity.   Were it
productive it would be *Nomos;* but it is *Nous,* because it is not *Nomos.*

8. Solitary ἀβάτῳ ἐν ἐρημίᾳ.   Now I say that
the *Nous,* notwithstanding its diversity from the
Nomizomeni, is yet, relatively to their supposed
original essence, πᾶσι τοῖς νομιζομένοις ταυτογενὴς,

of the same race or *radix :* though in another sense,
namely, in relation to the πᾶν θεῖον—the pantheis-.
tic *Elohim*, it is conceived·anterior to the schism,
and to the conquest and enthronization of Jove who
succeeded.   Hence the Prometheus of the great.
tragedian is θεὸς συγγενής.   The kindred deities
come to him, some to soothe, to condole ; others to
give weak, yet friendly, counsels of submission ;
others to tempt, or insult.   The most prominent of
the latter, and the most odious to the imprisoned
and insulated *Nous,* is Hermes, the impersonation
of interest with the entrancing and serpentine *Ca-
duceus,* and, as interest or motives intervening between the reason and its immediate self-determina-
tions, with the antipathies to the νόμος αὐτονόμος.
The Hermes impersonates the eloquence of cupi-
dity, the cajolement of power regnant; and in a
larger sense, custom, the irrational in language,
ῥήματα τὰ ῥητόρικα, the fluent, from ῥέω—the
rhetorical in opposition to λόγοι, τὰ νοητά.   But,
primarily, the Hermes is the symbol of interest.
He is the messenger, the inter-nuncio, in the low
but expressive phrase, the go-between, to beguile
or insult.   And for the other visitors of Prometheus, the elementary powers, or spirits of the elements, *Titanes pacati,* θεοὶ ὑπονόμιοι, vassal potentates, and their solicitations, the noblest interpretation will be given, if I repeat the lines of our great
contemporary poet : —

Earth fills her lap with pleasures of her own :
Yearnings she hath in her own natural kind,
And e'en with something of a mother's mind,
   And no unworthy aim,
The homely nurse doth all she can
To make her foster-child, her inmate, Man
   Forget the glories he hath known
   And that imperial palace whence he came : —
                        WORDSWORTH.

which exquisite language is prefigured in coarser clay, indeed, and with a less lofty spirit, but yet excellently in their kind, and even more fortunately for the illustration and ornament of the present commentary, in the fifth, sixth, and seventh stanzas of Dr. Henry More's poem on the Pre-existence of the Soul : —

Thus groping after our own center's near
And proper substance, we grew dark, contract,
Swallow'd up of earthly life ! Ne what we were
Of old, thro' ignorance can we detect.
Like noble babe, by fate or friends' neglect
Left to the care of sorry salvage wight,
Grown up to manly years cannot conject
His own true parentage, nor read aright
What father him begot, what womb him brought to light.

So we, as stranger infants elsewhere born,
Cannot divine from what spring we did flow ;
Ne dare these base alliances to scorn,
Nor lift ourselves a whit from hence below ;
Ne strive our parentage again to know,
Ne dream we once of any other stock,

Since foster'd upon Rhea's* knees we grow,
In Satyrs' arms with many a mow and mock
Oft danced; and hairy Pan our cradle oft hath rock'd!

But Pan nor Rhea be our parentage!
We been the offspring of the all seeing Nous, &c.

To express the supersensual character of the reason, its abstraction from sensation, we find the Prometheus ἀτερπῆ,—while in the yearnings accompanied with the remorse incident to, and only possible in consequence of the Nous being, the rational, self-conscious, and therefore responsible will, he is γυπὶ διακναιόμενος.

If to these contemplations we add the control and despotism exercised on the free reason by Jupiter in his symbolical character, as νόμος πολιτικὸς; —by custom (Hermes); by necessity, βία καὶ κρατὸς;—by the mechanic arts and powers, συγγενεῖς τῷ Νῷ though they are, and which are symbolized in Hephaistos,—we shall see at once the propriety of the title, Prometheus, δεσμώτης.

9. Nature, or *Zeus* as the νόμος ἐν νομιζομένοις, knows herself only, can only come to a knowledge

---

* Rhea (from ῥέω, *fluo*), that is, the earth as the transitory, the ever-flowing nature, the flux and sum of *phenomena*, or objects of the outward sense, in contradistinction from the earth as Vesta, as the firmamental law that sustains and disposes the apparent world! The Satyrs represent the sports and appetences of the sensuous nature (φρόνημα σαρκὸς)— Pan, or the total life of the earth, the presence of all in each, the universal *organismus* of bodies and bodily energy.

of herself, in man! And even in man, only as man
is supernatural, above nature, noetic. But this
knowledge man refuses to communicate; that is,
the human understanding alone is at once self-conscious and conscious of nature. And this high prerogative it owes exclusively to its being an assessor
of the reason. Yet even the human understanding
in its height of place seeks vainly to appropriate
the ideas of the pure reason, which it can only represent by *idola*. Here, then, the *Nous* stands as
Prometheus ἀντίπαλος, *renuens*—in hostile opposition to Jupiter *Inquisitor*.

10. Yet finally, against the obstacles and even
under the fostering influences of the *Nomos*, τοῦ
νομίμου, a son of Jove himself, but a descendant
from Io, the mundane religion, as contra-distin-
guished from the sacerdotal *cultus*, or religion of
the state, an Alcides *Liberator* will arise, and the
Nous or divine principle in man, will be Prometheus
ἐλευθερώμενος.

Did my limits or time permit me to trace the
persecutions, wanderings, and migrations of the Io,
the mundane religion, through the whole map
marked out by the tragic poet, the coincidences
would bring the truth, the unarbitrariness, of the
preceding exposition as near to demonstration as
can rationally be required on a question of history,
that must, for the greater part, be answered by
combination of scattered facts. But this part of
my subject, together with a particular exemplifica-

tion of the light which my theory throws both on the sense and the beauty of numerous passages of this stupendous poem, I must reserve for a future communication.

NOTES. *

v. 15. φάραγγι :—' in a coomb, or combe.'
v. 17.

$$\text{ἐξωριάζειν γὰρ πατρὸς λόγους βαρύ.}$$

εὐωριάζειν, as the editor confesses, is a word in-troduced into the text against the authority of all editions and manuscripts. I should prefer ἐξωριάζειν, notwithstanding its being a ἅπαξ λεγόμενον. The εὐ—seems to my tact too free and easy a word ;— and yet our ' to trifle with' appears the exact mean-ing.

SUMMARY OF AN ESSAY

ON THE FUNDAMENTAL POSITION OF THE MYS-TERIES IN RELATION TO GREEK TRAGEDY.

THE Position, to the establishment of which Mr. Coleridge regards his essay as the Pro-legomena, is : that the Greek Tragedy stood in the same relation to the Mysteries, as the Epic Song,

---

* Written in Bp. Blomfield's edition, and communicated by Mr. Cary. *Ed.*

and the Fine Arts to the Temple Worship, or the
Religion of the State; that the proper function of
the Tragic Poet was under the disguise of popular
superstitions, and using the popular Mythology as
his stuff and drapery to communicate so much and
no more of the doctrines preserved in the Mysteries
as should counteract the demoralizing influence of
the state religion, without disturbing the public
tranquillity, or weakening the reverence for the
laws, or bringing into contempt the ancestral and
local usages and traditions on which the patriotism
of the citizens mainly rested, or that nationality
in its intensest form which was little less than essential in the constitution of a Greek republic.   To
establish this position it was necessary to explain
the nature of these secret doctrines, or at least the
fundamental principles of the faith and philosophy
of Elensis and Samothrace.   The Samothracian
Mysteries Mr. Coleridge supposes to have been of
Phœnician origin, and both these and the Elensi-
nian to have retained the religious belief of the
more ancient inhabitants of the Peloponnesus, prior
to their union with the Hellenes and the Egyptian
colonies: that it comprised sundry relics and fragments of the Patriarchal Faith, the traditions historical and prophetic of the Noetic Family, though
corrupted and depraved by their combination with
the system of Pantheism, or the Worship of the
Universe as God *(Jupiter est quodcunque vides)*
which Mr. Coleridge contends to have been the

first great Apostacy of the Ancient World. But a
religion founded on Pantheism, is of necessity a
religion founded on philosophy, i. e. an attempt to
determine the origin of nature by the unaided
strength of the human intellect, however unsound
and false that philosophy may have been. And of
this the sacred books of the Indian Priests afford
at once proof and instance. Again: the earlier the
date of any philosophic scheme, the more *subjective*
will it be found—in other words the earliest rea-
soners sought in their own minds the form, measure
and substance of all other power. Abstracting from
whatever was individual and accidental, from whatever distinguished one human mind from another,
they fixed their attention exclusively on the characters which belong to all rational beings, and
which therefore they contemplated as mind itself,
mind in its essence. And however averse a scholar
of the present day may be to these first fruits of
speculative thought, as metaphysics, a knowledge
of their contents and distinctive tenets is indispensable as history. At all events without this
knowledge he will in vain attempt to understand
the spirit and genius of the arts, institutions and
governing minds of ancient Greece. The difficulty
of comprehending any scheme of opinion is proportionate to its greater or lesser unlikeness to the
principles and modes of reasoning in which our
own minds have been formed. Where the difference is so great as almost to amount to contrariety,

no clearness in the exhibition of the scheme will remove the sense, or rather, perhaps the *sensation*, of strangeness from the hearer's mind. Even beyond its utmost demerits it will appear obscure, unreal, visionary. This difficulty the author anticipates as an obstacle to the ready comprehension of the first principles of the eldest philosophy, and the esoteric doctrines of the Mysteries; but to the necessity of overcoming this the only obstacle, the thoughtful inquirer must resign himself, as the condition under which alone he may expect to solve a series of problems the most interesting of all that the records of ancient history propose or suggest.

The fundamental position of the Mysteries, Mr. Coleridge contends, consists in affirming that the productive powers or laws of nature are essentially the same with the active powers of the mind —in other words that mind, or Nous, under which term they combine the universal attributes of reason and will, is a principle of forms or patterns, endued with a tendency to manifest itself as such; and that this mind or eternal essence exists in two modes of being. Namely, either the form and the productive power, which gives it outward and phœnomenal reality, are united in equal and adequate proportions, in which case it is what the eldest philosophers, and the moderns in imitation of them, call a *law* of nature: or the *form* remaining the same, but with the productive power in unequal or inadequate proportions, whether the diminution be

effected by the mind's own act or original determination not to put forth this inherent power, or whether the power have been repressed, and as it were
driven inward by the violence of a superior force
from without,—and in this case it was called by the
most Ancient School " Intelligible Number," by a
later School " Idea," or *Mind*—κατ' ἐξοχην.　To
this position a second was added, namely, that the
form could not put forth its productive or self-realizing power without ceasing at the same moment
to exist *for* itself,—i. e. to exist, and know itself as
existing.　The formative power was as it were alie-
nated from itself and absorbed in the product.　It
existed as an instinctive, essentially intelligential,
but not self-knowing, power.　It was law, Jupiter,
or (when contemplated plurally) the Dii Majores.
On the other hand, to possess its own being consciously, the form must remain single and only inwardly
productive.　To exist *for* itself, it must continue to
exist *by* itself.　It must be an *idea ;* but an idea
in the primary sense of the term, the sense attached
to it by the oldest Italian School and by Plato,—
not as a synonyme of, but in contra-distinction from,
image, conception or notion : as a true entity of all
entities the most actual, of all essences the most
essential.

Now on this Antithesis of idea and law, that is
of mind as an unproductive but self-knowing power,
and of mind as a productive but unconscious power,
the whole religion of pantheism as disclosed in the
Mysteries turns, as on its axis, bi-polar.

FRAGMENT OF AN ESSAY ON
TASTE. 1810.

THE same arguments that decide the question, whether taste has any fixed principles, may probably lead to a determination of what those principles are. First then, what is taste in its metaphorical sense, or, which will be the easiest mode of arriving at the same solution, what is there in the primary sense of the word, which may give to its metaphorical meaning an import different from that of sight or hearing, on the one hand, and of touch or smell on the other? And this question seems the more natural, because in correct language we confine beauty, the main subject of taste, to objects of sight and combinations of sounds, and never, except sportively or by abuse of words, speak of a beautiful flavour, or a beautiful scent.

Now the analysis of our senses in the commonest books of anthropology has drawn our attention to the distinction between the perfectly organic, and the mixed senses; — the first presenting objects, as distinct from the perception ;—the last as blending the perception with the sense of the object. Our eyes and ears—(I am not now considering what is or is not the case really, but only that of which we are regularly conscious as appearances,) our eyes most often appear to us perfect organs of the sentient principle, and wholly in action, and our hearing so much more so than the three other senses, and in all the ordinary exertions of that sense, perhaps, equally so with the sight, that all languages place them in one class, and express their different modifications by nearly the same metaphors. The three remaining senses appear in part passive, and combine with the perception of the outward object a distinct sense of our own life. Taste, therefore, as opposed to vision and sound, will teach us to expect in its metaphorical use a certain reference of any given object to our own being, and not merely a distinct notion of the object as in itself, or in its independent properties. From the sense of touch, on the other hand, it is distinguishable by adding to this reference to our vital being some degree of enjoyment, or the contrary,— some perceptible impulse from pleasure or pain to complacency or dislike. The sense of smell, indeed, might perhaps have furnished a metaphor of the same import with that of taste; but the latter was naturally chosen by the majority of civilized nations on account of the greater frequency, importance, and dignity of its employment or exertion in human nature.

By taste, therefore, as applied to the fine arts, we must be supposed to mean an intellectual perception of any object blended with a distinct reference to our own sensibility of pain or pleasure, or, *vice versa*, a sense of enjoyment or dislike co-instantaneously combined with, and appearing to proceed from, some

intellectual perception of the object;—intellectual
perception, I say; for otherwise it would be a definition of taste in its primary rather than in its metaphorical sense. Briefly, taste is a metaphor taken
from one of our mixed senses, and applied to objects
of the more purely organic senses, and of our moral
sense, when we would imply the co-existence of immediate personal dislike or complacency. In this
definition of taste, therefore, is involved the definition of fine arts, namely, as being such the chief
and discriminative purpose of which it is to gratify
the taste,—that is, not merely to connect, but to
combine and unite, a sense of immediate pleasure
in ourselves, with the perception of external arrangement.

The great question, therefore, whether taste in
any one of the fine arts has any fixed principle or
ideal, will find its solution in the ascertainment of
two facts:—first, whether in every determination
of the taste concerning any work of the fine arts,
the individual does not, with or even against the
approbation of his general judgment, involuntarily
claim that all other minds ought to think and feel
the same; whether the common expressions, ' I
dare say I may be wrong, but that is my particular
taste;'—are uttered as an offering of courtesy, as
a sacrifice to the undoubted fact of our individual
fallibility, or are spoken with perfect sincerity, not
only of the reason but of the whole feeling, with
the same entireness of mind and heart, with which

we concede a right to every person to differ from
another in his preference of bodily tastes and fla-
vours. If we should find ourselves compelled to
deny this, and to admit that, notwithstanding the
consciousness of our liability to error, and in spite
of all those many individual experiences which may
have strengthened the consciousness, each man does
at the moment so far legislate for all men, as to
believe of necessity that he is either right or wrong,
and that if it be right for him, it is universally right,
— we must then proceed to ascertain :— secondly,
whether the source of these phenomena is at all to
be found in those parts of our nature, in which each
intellect is representative of all,—and whether
wholly, or partially.   No person of common reflection demands even in feeling, that what tastes pleasant to him ought to produce the same effect on all
living beings; but every man does and must expect and demand the universal acquiescence of all
intelligent beings in every conviction of his understanding.

*   *   *   *   *

FRAGMENT OF AN ESSAY ON
BEAUTY. 1818.

THE only necessary, but this the absolutely necessary, pre-requisite to a full insight into the
grounds of the beauty in the objects of sight, is—
the directing of the attention to the action of those

thoughts in our own mind which are not consciously distinguished.   Every man may understand this, if he will but recall the state of his feelings in endeavouring to recollect a name, which he is quite sure that he remembers, though he cannot force it back into consciousness.   This region of unconscious thoughts, oftentimes the more working the more indistinct they are, may, in reference to this subject, be conceived as forming an ascending scale from the most universal associations of motion with the functions and passions of life,—as when, on passing out of a crowded city into the fields on a day in June, we describe the grass and king-cups as nodding their heads and dancing in the breeze,—up to the half perceived, yet not fixable, resemblance of a form to some particular object of a diverse class, which resemblance we need only increase but a little, to destroy, or at least injure, its beauty-enhancing effect, and to make it a fantastic intrusion of the accidental and the arbitrary, and consequently a disturbance of the beautiful.   This might be abundantly exemplified and illustrated from the paintings of Salvator Rosa.

I am now using the term beauty in its most comprehensive sense, as including expression and artistic interest,—that is, I consider not only the living balance, but likewise all the accompaniments that even by disturbing are necessary to the renewal and continuance of the balance.   And in this sense I proceed to show, that the beautiful in the object

may be referred to two elements,—lines and colours;
the first belonging to the shapely *(forma, formalis,
formosus)*, and in this, to the law, and the reason;
and the second, to the lively, the free, the spontaneous, and the self-justifying. As to lines, the rec-
tilineal are in themselves the lifeless, the determined
ab extra, but still in immediate union with the cy-
cloidal, which are expressive of function. The curve
line is a modification of the force from without by
the force from within, or the spontaneous. These
are not arbitrary symbols, but the language of nature, universal and intuitive, by virtue of the law
by which man is impelled to explain visible motions
by imaginary causative powers analogous to his own
acts, as the Dryads, Hamadryads, Naiads, &c.

The better way of applying these principles will
be by a brief and rapid sketch of the history of the
fine arts,—in which it will be found, that the beautiful in nature has been appropriated to the works
of man, just in proportion as the state of the mind
in the artists themselves approached to the subjective beauty. Determine what predominance in the
minds of the men is preventive of the living balance
of excited faculties, and you will discover the exact
counterpart in the outward products. Egypt is an
illustration of this. Shapeliness is intellect without
freedom; but colours are significant. The introduction of the arch is not less an epoch in the fine
than in the useful arts.

Order is beautiful arrangement without any purpose *ad extra;*—therefore there is a beauty of order, or order may be contemplated exclusively as beauty.

The form given in every empirical intuition,—the stuff, that is, the quality of the stuff, determines the agreeable: but when a thing excites us to receive it in such and such a mould, so that its exact correspondence to that mould is what occupies the mind,—this is taste or the sense of beauty. Whether dishes full of painted wood or exquisite viands were laid out on a table in the same arrangement, would be indifferent to the taste, as in ladies' patterns; but surely the one is far more agreeable than the other. Hence observe the disinterestedness of all taste; and hence also a sensual perfection with intellect is occasionally possible without moral feeling. So it may be in music and painting, but not in poetry. How far it is a real preference of the refined to the gross pleasures, is another question, upon the supposition that pleasure, in some form or other, is that alone which determines men to the objects of the former;—whether experience does not show that if the latter were equally in our power, occasioned no more trouble to enjoy, and caused no more exhaustion of the power of enjoying them by the enjoyment itself, we should in real practice prefer the grosser pleasure. It is not, therefore, any excellence in the quality of the refined pleasures themselves, but the advantages and facilities in the means of enjoying them, that give them the pre-eminence.

This is, of course, on the supposition of the absence of all moral feeling. Suppose its presence, and then there will accrue an excellence even to the quality of the pleasures themselves; not only, however, of the refined, but also of the grosser kinds, —inasmuch as a larger sweep of thoughts will be associated with each enjoyment, and with each thought will be associated a number of sensations; and so, consequently, each pleasure will become more the pleasure of the whole being. This is one of the earthly rewards of our being what we ought to be, but which would be annihilated, if we attempted to be it for the sake of this increased enjoyment. Indeed it is a contradiction to suppose it. Yet this is the common *argumentum in circulo*, in which the eudæmonists flee and pursue.

*　　*　　*　　*

NOTES ON CHAPMAN'S HOMER.

Extract of a Letter sent with the Volume.* 1807.

CHAPMAN I have sent in order that you might read the Odyssey; the Iliad is fine, but less equal in the translation, as well as less interesting in itself. What is stupidly said of Shak-

---

* Communicated through Mr. Wordsworth. *Ed.*

speare, is really true and appropriate of Chapman;
mighty faults counterpoised by mighty beauties.
Excepting his quaint epithets which he affects to
render literally from the Greek, a language above
all others blest in the "happy marriage of sweet
words," and which in our language are mere
printer's compound epithets—such as quaffed divine *joy-in-the-heart-of-man-infusing* wine, (the
undermarked is to be one word, because one sweet
mellifluous word expresses it in Homer);—excepting this, it has no look, no air, of a translation. It
is as truly an original poem as the Faery Queene;
—it will give you small idea of Homer, though a
far truer one than Pope's epigrams, or Cowper's
cumbersome most anti-Homeric Miltonism.   For
Chapman writes and feels as a poet,—as Homer
might have written had he lived in England in the
reign of Queen Elizabeth.   In short, it is an exquisite poem, in spite of its frequent and perverse
quaintnesses and harshnesses, which are, however,
amply repaid by almost unexampled sweetness and
beauty of language, all over spirit and feeling.   In
the main it is an English heroic poem, the tale of
which is borrowed from the Greek.   The dedication to the Iliad is a noble copy of verses, especially
those sublime lines beginning,—

O! 'tis wondrous much
(Through nothing prisde) that the right vertuous touch
Of a well written·soule, to vertue moves.
Nor haue we soules to purpose, if their loves

Of fitting objects be not so inflam'd.
How much then, were this kingdome's maine soul maim'd,
To want this great inflamer of all powers
That move in humane soules! All realmes but yours,
Are honor'd with him; and hold blest that state
That have his workes to reade and contemplate.
In which, humanitie to her height is raisde;
Which all the world (yet, none enough) hath praisde.
Seas, earth, and heaven, he did in verse comprize;
Out sung the Muses, and did equalise
Their king Apollo; being so farre from cause
Of princes light thoughts, that their gravest lawes
May finde stuffe to be fashiond by his lines.
Through all the pompe of kingdomes still he shines
And graceth all his gracers.   Then let lie
Your lutes, and viols, and more loftily
Make the heroiques of your Homer sung,
To drums and trumpets set his Angels tongue:
And with the princely sports of haukes you use,
Behold the kingly flight of his high Muse:
And see how like the Phœnix she renues
Her age, and starrie feathers in your sunne;
Thousands of yeares attending; everie one
Blowing the holy fire, and throwing in
Their seasons, kingdomes, nations that have bin
Subverted in them; lawes, religions, all
Offerd to change, and greedie funerall;
Yet still your Homer lasting, living, raigning.—

and likewise the 1st, the 11th, and last but one, of the prefatory sonnets to the Odyssey. Could I have foreseen any other speedy opportunity, I should have begged your acceptance of the volume in a somewhat handsomer coat; but as it is, it will better represent the sender,—to quote from my- self—

A man disherited, in form and face,
By nature and mishap, of outward grace.

Chapman in his moral heroic verse, as in this *Dedication to Prince Henry.*
dedication and the prefatory sonnets to his Odyssey,
stands above Ben Jonson; there is more dignity,
more lustre, and equal strength; but not midway
quite between him and the sonnets of Milton.   I
do not know whether I give him the higher praise,
in that he reminds me of Ben Jonson with a sense
of his superior excellence, or that he brings Milton
to memory notwithstanding his inferiority.   His
moral poems are not quite out of books like Jonson's, nor yet do the sentiments so wholly grow up
out of his own natural habit and grandeur of thought,
as in Milton.   The sentiments have been attracted
to him by a natural affinity of his intellect, and so
combined;—but Jonson has taken them by individual and successive acts of choice.

All this and the preceding is well felt and vigo- *Epistle Dedi- catorie to the Odyssey.*
rously, though harshly, expressed, respecting sub-
lime poetry *in genere;* but in reading Homer I
look about me, and ask how does all this apply here.
For surely never was there plainer writing; there
are a thousand charms of sun and moonbeam, rip-
ple, and wave, and stormy billow, but all on the
surface.   Had Chapman read Proclus and Porphy-
ry?—and did he really believe them,—or even that
they believed themselves?   They felt the immense
power of a Bible, a Shaster, a Koran.   There was
none in Greece or Rome, and they tried therefore

by subtle allegorical accommodations to conjure the poem of Homer into the βίβλιον θεοπαράδοτον of Greek faith.

Epistle Dedi-catorie to the Batrachomy-omachia.

Chapman's identification of his fate with Homer's, and his complete forgetfulness of the distinction between Christianity and idolatry, under the general feeling of some religion, is very interesting. It is amusing to observe, how familiar Chapman's fancy has become with Homer, his life and its circumstances, though the very existence of any such individual, at least with regard to the Iliad and the Hymns, is more than problematic. N. B. The rude engraving in the page was designed by no vulgar hand. It is full of spirit and passion.

End of the Batrachomy-omachia.

I am so dull, that neither in the original nor in any translation could I ever find any wit or wise purpose in this poem. The whole humour seems to lie in the names. The frogs and mice are not frogs or mice, but men, and yet they do nothing that conveys any satire. In the Greek there is much beauty of language, but the joke is very flat. This is always the case in rude ages ;—their serious vein is inimitable,—their comic low and low indeed. The psychological cause is easily stated, and copiously exemplifiable.

NOTE IN CASAUBON'S PERSIUS.
1807.

THERE are six hundred and sixteen pages in this volume, of which twenty-two are text; and five hundred and ninety-four commentary and introductory matter. Yet when I recollect, that I have the whole works of Cicero, Livy, and Quinctilian, with many others,—the whole works of each in a single volume, either thick quarto with thin paper and small yet distinct print, or thick octavo or duodecimo of the same character, and that they cost me in the proportion of a shilling to a guinea for the same quantity of worse matter in modern books, or editions,—I a poor man, yet one whom βιβλίων κτήσεως ἐκ παιδαρίου δεινὸς ἐκράτησε πόθος, feel the liveliest gratitude for the age, which produced such editions, and for the education, which by enabling me to understand and taste the Greek and Latin writers, has thus put it in my power to collect on my own shelves, for my actual use, almost all the best books in spite of my small income. Somewhat too I am indebted to the ostentation of expense among the rich, which has occasioned these cheap editions to become so disproportionately cheap.

NOTES ON BARCLAY'S ARGENIS.

1803.*

HEAVEN forbid that this work should not exist in its present form and language! Yet I cannot avoid the wish that it had, during the reign of James I., been moulded into an heroic poem in English octave stanza, or epic blank verse; —which, however, at that time had not been invented, and which, alas! still remains the sole property of the inventor, as if the Muses had given him an unevadible patent for it. Of dramatic blank verse we have many and various specimens ;—for example, Shakspeare's as compared with Massinger's, both excellent in their kind:—of lyric, and of what may be called Orphic, or philosophic, blank verse, perfect models may be found in Wordsworth: of colloquial blank verse there are excellent, though not perfect, examples in Cowper;—but of epic blank verse, since Milton, there is not one.

It absolutely distresses me when I reflect that this work, admired as it has been by great men of all ages, and lately, I hear, by the poet Cowper, should be only not unknown to general readers. It has been translated into English two or three times—how, I know not, wretchedly, I doubt not. It affords matter for thought that the last transla-

---

* Communicated by the Rev. Derwent Coleridge.

tion (or rather, in all probability, miserable and
faithless abridgment of some former one) was given
under another name.   What a mournful proof of
the incelebrity of this great and amazing work
among both the public and the people! For as
Wordsworth, the greater of the two great men of
this age,—(at least, except Davy and him, I have
known, read of, heard of, no others)—for as Wordsworth did me the honour of once observing to me,
the people and the public are two distinct classes,
and, as things go, the former is likely to retain a
better taste, the less it is acted on by the latter.
Yet Telemachus is in every mouth, in every school-
boy's and schoolgirl's hand! It is awful to say of a
work, like the Argenis, the style and Latinity of
which, judged (not according to classical pedantry,
which pronounces every sentence right which can
be found in any book prior to Boetius, however
vicious the age, or affected the author, and every
sentence wrong, however natural and beautiful,
which has been of the author's own combination,—
but) according to the universal logic of thought as
modified by feeling, is equal to that of Tacitus in
energy and genuine conciseness, and is as perspicuous as that of Livy, whilst it is free from the affecta-
tions, obscurities, and lust to surprise of the former,
and seems a sort of antithesis to the slowness and
prolixity of the latter;—(this remark does not,
however, impeach even the classicality of the language, which, when the freedom and originality, the

easy motion and perfect command of the thoughts,
are considered, is truly wonderful):—of such a
work it is awful to say, that it would have been well
if it had been written in English or Italian verse!
Yet the event seems to justify the notion. Alas!
it is now too late. What modern work, even of the
size of the Paradise Lost—much less of the Faery
Queene—would be read in the present day, or even
bought or be likely to be bought, unless it were an
instructive work, as the phrase is, like Roscoe's
quartos of Leo X., or entertaining like Boswell's
three of Dr. Johnson's conversations. It may be
fairly objected—what work of surpassing merit has
given the proof?—Certainly, none. Yet still there
are ominous facts, sufficient, I fear, to afford a certain prophecy of its reception, if such were produced.

NOTES ON CHALMERS'S LIFE OF
SAMUEL DANIEL.

The justice of these remarks cannot be disputed, though some
of them are too figurative for sober criticism.

MOST genuine! a figurative remark! If this
strange writer had any meaning, it must be:
—Headly's criticism is just throughout, but conveyed
in a style too figurative for prose composition.
Chalmers's own remarks are wholly mistaken ; too
silly for any criticism, drunk or sober, and in lan-

guage too flat for any thing. In Daniel's Sonnets there is scarcely one good line; while his Hymen's Triumph, of which Chalmers says not one word, exhibits a continued series of first-rate beauties in thought, passion, and imagery, and in language and metre is so faultless, that the style of that poem may without extravagance be declared to be imperishable English. 1820.

BISHOP CORBET.

I ALMOST wonder that the inimitable humour, and the rich sound and propulsive movement of the verse, have not rendered Corbet a popular poet. I am convinced that a reprint of his poems, with illustrative and chit-chat biographical notes, and cuts by Cruikshank, would take with the public uncommonly well. September, 1823.

NOTES ON SELDEN'S TABLE TALK.*

THERE is more weighty bullion sense in this book, than I ever found in the same number of pages of any uninspired writer.

OPINION.

Opinion and affection extremely differ. I may affect a woman best, but it does not follow I must think her the

---

* These remarks on Selden were communicated by Mr. Cary. *Ed.*

handsomest woman in the world. * * * Opinion is something wherein I go about to give reason why all the world should think as I think. Affection is a thing wherein I look after the pleasing of myself.

Good! This is the true difference betwixt the beautiful and the agreeable, which Knight and the rest of that πλῆθος ἄθεον have so beneficially confounded, *meretricibus scilicet et Plutoni.*

O what an insight the whole of this article gives into a wise man's heart, who has been compelled to act with the many, as one of the many! It explains Sir Thomas More's zealous Romanism, &c.

PARLIAMENT.

Excellent! O! to have been with Selden over his glass of wine, making every accident an outlet and a vehicle of wisdom!

POETRY.

The old poets had no other reason but this, their verse was sung to music; otherwise it had been a senseless thing to have fettered up themselves.

No man can know all things: even Selden here talks ignorantly. Verse is in itself a music, and the natural symbol of that union of passion with thought and pleasure, which constitutes the essence of all poetry, as contradistinguished from science, and distinguished from history civil or natural. To Pope's Essay on Man, — in short, to whatever is mere metrical good sense and wit, the remark applies.

Ib.

Verse proves nothing but the quantity of syllables; they are not meant for logic.

True; they, that is, verses, are not logic; but they are, or ought to be, the envoys and representatives of that vital passion, which is the practical cement of logic; and without which logic must remain inert.

NOTES ON TOM JONES.*

MANNERS change from generation to generation, and with manners morals appear to change,—actually change with some, but appear to change with all but the abandoned. A young man of the present day who should act as Tom Jones is supposed to act at Upton, with Lady Bellaston, &c. would not be a Tom Jones; and a Tom Jones of the present day, without perhaps being in the ground a better man, would have perished rather than submit to be kept by a harridan of fortune. Therefore this novel is, and, indeed, pretends to be, no exemplar of conduct. But, notwithstanding all this, I do loathe the cant which can recommend Pamela and Clarissa Harlowe as strictly moral, though they poison the imagination of the young with continued

---

* Communicated by Mr. Gillman. *Ed.*

doses of *tinct. lyttæ*, while Tom Jones is prohibited
as loose. I do not speak of young women; — but
a young man whose heart or feelings can be injured, or even his passions excited, by aught in this
novel, is already thoroughly corrupt. There is a
cheerful, sun-shiny, breezy spirit that prevails every-
where, strongly contrasted with the close, hot, day-
dreamy continuity of Richardson. Every indiscretion, every immoral act, of Tom Jones, (and it
must be remembered that he is in every one taken
by surprise — his inward principles remaining firm
—) is so instantly punished by embarrassment
and unanticipated evil consequences of his folly,
that the reader's mind is not left for a moment to
dwell or run riot on the criminal indulgence itself.
In short, let the requisite allowance be made for
the increased refinement of our manners, — and
then I dare believe that no young man who con-
sulted his heart and conscience only, without adverting to what the world would say — could rise
from the perusal of Fielding's Tom Jones, Joseph
Andrews, or Amelia, without feeling himself a better
man : — at least, without an intense conviction that
he could not be guilty of a base act.

If I want a servant or mechanic, I wish to know
what he does : — but of a friend, I must know what
he is. And in no writer is this momentous distinction so finely brought forward as by Fielding.
We do not care what Blifil does; —the deed, as separate from the agent, may be good or ill; but

Blifil is a villain; — and we feel him to be so from the very moment he, the boy Blifil, restores Sophia's poor captive bird to its native and rightful liberty.

Book xiv. ch. 8.

Notwithstanding the sentiment of the Roman satirist, which denies the divinity of fortune; and the opinion of Seneca to the same purpose; Cicero, who was, I believe, a wiser man than either of them, expressly holds the contrary; and certain it is there are some incidents in life so very strange and unaccountable, that it seems to require more than human skill and foresight in producing them.

Surely Juvenal, Seneca, and Cicero, all meant the same thing, namely, that there was no chance, but instead of it providence, either human or divine.

Book xv. ch. 9.

The rupture with Lady Bellaston.

Even in the most questionable part of Tom Jones, I cannot but think, after frequent reflection, that an additional paragraph, more fully and forcibly unfolding Tom Jones's sense of self-degradation on the discovery of the true character of the relation in which he had stood to Lady Bellaston, and his awakened feeling of the dignity of manly chastity, would have removed in great measure any just objections, — at all events relatively to Fielding himself, and with regard to the state of manners in his time.

Book xvi. ch. 5.

That refined degree of Platonic affection which is absolutely detached from the flesh, and is indeed entirely and purely spiritual, is a gift confined to the female part of the creation; many of whom I have heard declare (and doubtless with great truth) that they would, with the utmost readiness, resign a lover to a rival, when such resignation was proved to be necessary for the temporal interest of such lover.

I firmly believe that there are men capable of such a sacrifice, and this, without pretending to, or even admiring or seeing any virtue in, this absolute detachment from the flesh.

ANOTHER SET OF NOTES ON TOM JONES.

Book 1. ch. 4.

" Beyond this the country gradually rose into a ridge of wild mountains, the tops of which were above the clouds."

As this is laid in Somersetshire, the clouds must have been unusually low.   One would be more apt to think of Skiddaw or Ben Nevis, than of Quantock or Mendip Hills.

Book xi. ch. 1.

" Nor can the Devil receive a guest more worthy of him, nor possibly more welcome to him than a slanderer."

The very word Devil, *Diabolus*, means a slanderer.

Book xii. ch. 12.

" And here we will make a concession, which would not perhaps have been expected from us; That no limited form of government is capable of rising to the same degree of perfection, or of producing the same benefits to society with this. Mankind has never been so happy, as when the greatest part of the then known world was under the dominion of a single master; and this state of their felicity continued under the reign of five successive Princes."

Strange that such a lover of political liberty as Fielding should have forgotten that the glaring infamy of the Roman morals and manners immediately on the ascent of Commodus prove, that even five excellent despots in succession were but a mere temporary palliative of the evils inherent in despotism and its causes. Think you that all the sub-despots were Trojans and Antonines? No! Rome was left as it was found by them, incapable of freedom.

Book xviii. ch. 4.

Plato himself concludes his Phædon with declaring, that his best argument amounts only to raise a probability; and Cicero himself seems rather to profess an inclination to believe, than any actual belief, in the doctrines of immortality.

No! Plato does not say so, but speaks as a philosophic Christian would do of the best arguments of the scientific intellect. The assurance is derived from a higher principle. If this be Methodism Plato and Socrates were arrant Methodists and New Light men; but I would ask Fielding what ratiocinations do more than raise a high degree of probability. But assuredly an historic belief is far different from Christian *faith*.

No greater proof can be conceived of the strength

of the instinctive anticipation of a future state than that it was believed at all by the Greek Philoso‐ phers, with their vague and (Plato excepted) Pan‐ theistic conception of the First Cause.   S. T. C.

JONATHAN WILD.*

JONATHAN WILD is assuredly the best of all the fictions in which a villain is throughout the prominent character.   But how impossible it is by any force of genius to create a sustained attractive interest for such a ground-work, and how the mind wearies of, and shrinks from, the more than painful interest, the μισητὸν, of utter depravity,—Fielding himself felt and endeavoured to mitigate and remedy by the (on all other principles) far too large a pro‐ portion, and too quick recurrence, of the interposed chapters of moral reflection, like the chorus in the Greek tragedy, — admirable specimens as these chapters are of profound irony and philosophic satire. Chap. VI. Book 2, on Hats,*—brief as it is, ex‐ ceeds any thing even in Swift's Lilliput, or Tale of the Tub.   How forcibly it applies to the Whigs, Tories, and Radicals of our own times.

Whether the transposition of Fielding's scorching

---

* Communicated by Mr. Gillman. *Ed.*

† ' In which our hero makes a speech well worthy to be celebrated; and the behaviour of one of the gang, perhaps more unnatural than any other part of this history.'

wit (as B. III. c. xiv.) to the mouth of his hero be objectionable on the ground of *incredulus odi,* or is to be admired as answering the author's purpose by unrealizing the story, in order to give a deeper reality to the truths intended,—I must leave doubtful, yet myself inclining to the latter judgment. 27th Feb. 1832.

NOTES ON JUNIUS.   1807.

Stat nominis umbra.

AS he never dropped the mask, so he too often used the poisoned dagger of an assassin.

Dedication to the English nation.

The whole of this dedication reads like a string of aphorisms arranged in chapters, and classified by a resemblance of subject, or a cento of points.

Ib. If an honest, and I may truly affirm a laborious, zeal for the public service has given me any weight in your esteem, let me exhort and conjure you never to suffer an invasion of your political constitution, however minute the instance may appear, to pass by, without a determined persevering resistance.

A longer sentence and proportionately inelegant.

Ib. If you reflect that in the changes of administration which have marked and disgraced the present reign, although your warmest patriots have, in their turn, been invested with the lawful and unlawful authority of the crown, and though other reliefs or improvements have been held forth to the people, yet that no one man in office has ever promoted or encouraged a bill for shortening the duration of parliaments, but that (whoever was minister) the opposition to this measure, ever since the septennial act passed, has been constant and uniform on the part of government.

Long, and as usual, inelegant. Junius cannot manage a long sentence; it has all the *ins* and *outs* of a snappish figure-dance.

Preface.

. An excellent preface, and the sentences not so snipt as in the dedication. The paragraph near the conclusion beginning with " some opinion may now be expected," &c. and ending with " relation between guilt and punishment," deserves to be quoted as a master-piece of rhetorical ratiocination in a series of questions that permit no answer; or (as Junius says) carry their own answer along with them. The great art of Junius is never to say too much, and to avoid with equal anxiety a commonplace manner, and matter that is not common-place. If ever he deviates into any originality of thought, he takes care that it shall be such as excites surprise for its acuteness, rather than admiration for its profundity. He takes care? say rather that nature took care for him. It is impossible to detract from the merit of these Letters: they are suited to their purpose, and perfect in their kind. They impel to action, not thought. Had they been profound or subtle in thought, or majestic and sweeping in composition, they would have been adapted for the closet of a Sydney, or for a House

of Lords such as it was in the time of Lord Bacon;
but they are plain and sensible whenever the author
is in the right, and whether right or wrong, always
shrewd and epigrammatic, and fitted for the coffee-
house, the exchange, the lobby of the House of
Commons, and to be read aloud at a public meeting.
When connected, dropping the forms of connexion,
desultory without abruptness or appearance of dis-
connexion, epigrammatic and antithetical to excess,
sententious and personal, regardless of right or
wrong, yet well-skilled to act the part of an honest
warm-hearted man, and even when he is in the
right, saying the truth but never proving it, much
less attempting to bottom it,—this is the character
of Junius;—and on this character, and in the
mould of these writings must every man cast himself, who would wish in factious times to be the important and long remembered agent of a faction.
I believe that I could do all that Junius has done,
and surpass him by doing many things which he
has not done: for example,—by an occasional in-
duction of startling facts, in the manner of Tom
Paine, and lively illustrations and witty applications
of good stories and appropriate anecdotes in the
manner of Horne Tooke. I believe I could do it
if it were in my nature to aim at this sort of excellence, or to be enamoured of the fame, and immediate influence, which would be its consequence and
reward. But it is not in my nature. I not only
love truth, but I have a passion for the legitimate

investigation of truth.   The love of truth conjoined
with a keen delight in a strict and skilful yet impassioned argumentation, is my master-passion, and
to it are subordinated even the love of liberty and
all my public feelings—and to it whatever I labour
under of vanity, ambition, and all my inward im-
pulses.

Letter I.   From this Letter all the faults and
excellencies of Junius may be exemplified.   The
moral and political aphorisms are just and sensible,
the irony in which his personal satire is conveyed
is fine, yet always intelligible; but it approaches too
nearly to the nature of a sneer; the sentences are
cautiously constructed without the forms of connection ; the *he* and *it* every where substituted for the
who and *which;* the sentences are short, laboriously
balanced, and the antitheses stand the test of analysis much better than Johnson's.   These are all
excellencies in their kind;—where is the defect?
In this :—there is too much of each, and there is a
defect of many things, the presence of which would
have been not only valuable for their own sakes,
but for the relief and variety which they would have
given.   It is observable too that every Letter adds
to the faults of these Letters, while it weakens the
effect of their beauties.

L. III.   A capital letter, addressed to a private
person, and intended as a sharp reproof for intrusion.   Its short sentences, its witty perversions and
deductions, its questions and omissions of connec-

tives, all in their proper places are dramatically good.

L. V. For my own part, I willingly leave it to the public to determine whether your vindication of your friend has been as able and judicious as it was certainly well intended; and you, I think, may be satisfied with the warm acknowledgments he already owes you for making him the principal figure in a piece in which, but for your amicable assistance, he might have passed without particular notice or distinction.

A long sentence and, as usual, inelegant and cumbrous. This Letter is a faultless composition with exception of the one long sentence.

L. VII. These are the gloomy companions of a disturbed *imagination*; the melancholy madness of poetry, without the *inspiration*.

The rhyme is a fault. 'Fancy' had been better; though but for the rhyme, imagination is the fitter word.

Ib. Such a question might perhaps discompose the gravity of his muscles, but I believe it would little affect the tranquillity of his conscience.

A false antithesis, a mere verbal balance; there are far, far too many of these. However, with these few exceptions, this Letter is a blameless composition. Junius may be safely studied as a model for letters where he truly writes letters. Those to the Duke of Grafton and others, are small pamphlets in the form of letters.

L. VIII. To do justice to your Grace's humanity, you felt for Mac Quick as you ought to do; and, if you had been contented to assist him indirectly, without a notorious

denial of justice, or openly insulting the sense of the nation,
you might have satisfied every duty of political friendship,
without committing the honour of your sovereign, or hazarding the reputation of his government.

An inelegant cluster of *withouts*.   Junius asks
questions incomparably well ;—but *ne quid nimis*.

L. IX.   Perhaps the fair way of considering
these Letters would be as a kind of satirical poems; the short, and for ever balanced, sentences
constitute a true metre ; and the connexion is that
of satiric poetry, a witty logic, an association of
thoughts by amusing semblances of cause and effect,
the sophistry of which the reader has an interest in
not stopping to detect, for it flatters his love of
mischief, and makes the sport.

L. XII.   One of Junius's arts, and which gives
me a high notion of his genius, as a poet and satirist, is this :—he takes for granted the existence of
a character that never did and never can exist, and
then employs his wit, and surprises and amuses his
readers with analyzing its incompatibilities.

L. XIV.   Continual sneer, continual irony, all
excellent, if it were not for the ' all;'—but a countenance, with a malignant smile in statuary fixure
on it, becomes at length an object of aversion,
however beautiful the face, and however beautiful
the smile.   We are relieved, in some measure,
from this by frequent just and well expressed moral aphorisms ; but then the preceding and following irony gives them the appearance of proceeding

from the head, not from the heart. This objection
would be less felt, when the Letters were first published at considerable intervals; but Junius wrote
for posterity.

L. XXIII. Sneer and irony continued with such
gross violation of good sense, as to be perfectly
nonsense. The man who can address another on
his most detestable vices in a strain of cold continual irony, is himself a wretch.

L. XXXV. To honour them with a determined predilection and confidence in exclusion of your English subjects,
who placed your family, and, in spite of treachery and rebellion, have supported it upon the throne, is a mistake too
gross even for the unsuspecting generosity of youth.

The words ' upon the throne,' stand unfortu-
nately for the harmonious effect of the balance of
' placed' and ' supported.'

This address to the king is almost faultless in
composition, and has been evidently tormented with
the file. But it has fewer beauties than any other
long letter of Junius ; and it is utterly undramatic.
There is nothing in the style, the transitions, or the
sentiments, which represents the passions of a man
emboldening himself to address his sovereign per-
sonally. Like a Presbyterian's prayer, you may
substitute almost every where the third for the
second person without injury. The newspaper,
his closet, and his own person were alone present
to the author's intention and imagination. This
makes the composition vapid. It possesses an Iso-

cratic correctness, when it should have had the
force and drama of an oration of Demosthenes.
From this, however, the paragraph beginning with
the words ' As to the Scotch,' and also the last
two paragraphs must be honourably excepted.
They are, perhaps, the finest passages in the whole
collection.

WONDERFULNESS OF PROSE.

IT has just struck my feelings that the Pherecy-
dean origin of prose being granted, prose must
have struck men with greater admiration than
poetry.   In the latter it was the language of passion
and emotion : it is what they themselves spoke and
heard in moments of exultation, indignation, &c.
But to hear an evolving roll, or a succession of
leaves, talk continually the language of deliberate
reason in a form of continued preconception, of a Z
already possessed when A was being uttered,—this
must have appeared godlike.   I feel myself in the
same state, when in the perusal of a sober, yet elevated and harmonious succession of sentences and
periods, I abstract my mind from the particular passage and sympathize with the wonder of the common
people, who say of an eloquent man :—' He talks
like a book !'

NOTES ON HERBERT'S TEMPLE AND HARVEY'S SYNAGOGUE.

G. HERBERT is a true poet, but a poet *sui generis*, the merits of whose poems will never be felt without a sympathy with the mind and character of the man. To appreciate this volume, it is not enough that the reader possesses a cultivated judgment, classical taste, or even poetic sensibility, unless he be likewise a *Christian*, and both a zealous and an orthodox, both a devout and a *devotional* Christian. But even this will not quite suffice. He must be an affectionate and dutiful child of the Church, and from habit, conviction, and a constitutional predisposition to ceremoniousness, in piety as in manners, find her forms and ordinances aids of religion, not sources of formality; for religion is the element in which he lives, and the region in which he moves.

The Church, say rather the Churchmen of England, under the two first Stuarts, has been charged with a yearning after the Romish fopperies, and even the papistic usurpations; but we shall decide more correctly, as well as more charitably, if for the Romish and papistic we substitute the patristic leaven. There even was (natural enough from their distinguished learning, and knowledge of ecclesiastical antiquities) an overrating of the Church

and of the Fathers, for the first five or even six
centuries; these lines on the Egyptian monks,
" Holy Macarius and great Anthony" (p. 205.)
supply a striking instance and illustration of this.

P. 10.

> If thou be single, all thy goods and ground
> Submit to love; but yet not more than all.
> Give one estate as one life.   None is bound
> To work for two, who brought himself to thrall.
>   God made me one man; love makes me no more,
>   Till labour come, and make my weakness score.

I do not understand this stanza.

P. 41.

> My flesh *began unto my soul* in pain,
> Sicknesses clave my bones, &c.

Either a misprint, or a noticeable idiom of the
word " began?" Yes! and a very beautiful idiom
it is : the first colloquy or address of the flesh.

P. 46.

> What though my body run to dust ?
> Faith cleaves unto it, counting every grain,
> *With an exact and most particular trust,*
> Reserving all for flesh again.

I find few historical facts so difficult of solution
as the continuance, in Protestantism, of this anti-
scriptural superstition.

P. 54.   Second poem on *The Holy Scriptures.*

> This verse marks that, and both do make a motion
> Unto a third that ten leaves off doth lie.

The spiritual unity of the Bible = the order and
connection of organic forms in which the unity of

life is shewn, though as widely dispersed in the world of sight as the text.

Ib.

> Then as dispersed herbs do *watch* a potion,
> These three make up some Christian's destiny.

Some misprint.

P. 87.

> Sweet Spring, full of sweet days and roses,
> A *box* where sweets compacted lie.

Nest.

P. 92. *Man.*

> Each thing is full of duty :
> Waters united are our navigation :
> *Distinguished, our habitation ;*
> Below, our drink ; above, our meat :
> Both are our cleanliness. Hath one such beauty ?
> Then how are all things neat !

' Distinguished.' I understand this but imperfectly. Did they form an island? and the next lines refer perhaps to the then belief that all fruits grow and are nourished by water. But then how is the ascending sap " our cleanliness ?" Perhaps, therefore, the rains.

P. 140.

> But he doth bid us take his blood for wine.

Nay, the contrary; take wine to be blood, and *the* blood of a man who died 1800 years ago. This

2   s

is the faith which even the Church of England demands ; * for consubstantiation only *adds* a mystery
to that of Transubstantiation, which it implies.

P. 175.   The Flower.

A delicious poem.

Ib.

> How fresh, O Lord, how sweet and clear
> Are thy returns ! e'en as the flowers in spring ;
>   To which, besides their own demean,
> The late past frosts tributes of pleasure bring.
>   Grief melts away

---

* This is one of my father's *marginalia*, which I can
hardly persuade myself he would have re-written just as it
stands.   Where does the Church of England affirm that the
wine *per se* literally *is* the blood shed 1800 years ago ?   The
language of our Church is that " we receiving these creatures
of bread and wine, &c. may be partakers of His most blessed
body and blood :" that " to such as rightly receive the same
the cup of blessing is a partaking of the blood of Christ."
Does not this language intimate, that the blood of Christ is
spiritually produced in the soul through a faithful reception
of the appointed symbols, rather than that the wine itself,
apart from the soul, has become the blood ?   In one sense,
indeed, it *is* the blood of Christ to the soul: it may be metaphorically called so, if, by means of it, the blood is *really*,
though spiritually, partaken.   More than this is surely not
affirmed in our formularies, nor taught by our great divines
in general.   I do not write these words by way of *argument*,
but because I cannot re-print such a note of my father's,
which has excited surprise in some of his studious readers,
without a protest.   S. C.

Like snow in May,
As if there were no such cold thing.

"The late-past frosts tributes of pleasure bring."

$$\cup - - - \qquad - \cup\cup \qquad - \cup \qquad -$$

Epitritus primus + Dactyl + Trochee + a long word—syllable, which, together with the pause intervening between it and the word—trochee, equals $\cup\cup\cup$ - form a pleasing variety in the Pentameter Iambic with rhymes. Ex. gr.

Thĕ lāte pāst frōsts | trībutĕs ŏf | plĕāsŭre | brīng.

N. B. First, the difference between - $\cup$ | —and an amphimacer - $\cup$ - | and this not always or necessarily arising out of the latter being one word. It may even consist of three words, yet the effect be the same. It is the pause that makes the difference. Secondly, the expediency, if not necessity, that the first syllable both of the Dactyl and the Trochee should be short by quantity, and only $=$ - by force of accent or position — the Epitrite being true *lengths.*—Whether the last syllable be — or $=$ — the force of the rhymes renders indifferent. Thus,
....

" As if there *were no such cold thing.*" Had been no such thing.

P. 181.

Thou who condemnest Jewish hate, &c.
Call home thine eye, (that busy wanderer,)
That choice may be thy story.

Their choice.

P. 184.

> Nay, thou dost make me sit and dine
> E'en in my enemies' sight.

Foemen's.

P. 201. *Judgment.*

> Almighty Judge, how shall poor wretches brook
>   Thy dreadful look, &c.

> What others mean to do, I know not well ;
>   Yet I here tell,
> That some will turn thee to some leaves therein
>   So void of sin,
>   That they in merit shall excel.

I should not have expected from Herbert so open an avowal of Romanism in the article of *merit.* In the same spirit is " Holy Macarius, and great Anthony," p. 205.*

---

* Herbert however adds :

> But I resolve, when thou shalt call for mine,
>   That to decline,
> And thrust a Testament into thy hand :
>   Let that be scann'd ;
> There thou shalt find my faults are thine."

Martin Luther himself might have penned this concluding stanza.

Since I wrote the above, a note in Mr. Pickering's edition of Herbert has been pointed out to me.

" The Rev. Dr. *Bliss* has kindly furnished the following judicious remark, and which is proved to be correct, as the

P. 237.   The *Communion Table*.

And for the matter whereof it is made,
  The matter is not much,
  Although it be of *tuch*,
Or wood, or metal, what will last, or fade;
    So vanity
And superstition avoided be.

Tuch rhyming to *much*, from the German *tuch*, cloth, I never met with before, as an English word. So I find *platt* for *foliage* in Stanley's Hist. of Philosophy, p. 22.

P. 252.   *The Synagogue*, by Christopher Harvey.

The Bishop.

But who can show of old that ever any
Presbyteries without their bishops were:
Though bishops without presbyteries many, &c.

---

word is printed 'heare' in the first edition (1633). He says, "Let me take this opportunity of mentioning what a very learned and able friend pointed out on this note. The fact is, *Coleridge* has been misled by an error of the press.

  What others mean to do, I know not well,
    Yet I here tell, &c. &c.

should be *hear tell*. The sense is then obvious, and *Herbert* is not made to do that which he was the last man in the world to have done, namely, to avow 'Romanism in the article of merit.'"

This suggestion once occurred to myself, and appears to be right, as it is verified by the first edition: but at the time it seemed to me so obvious, that surely the correction would have been made before if there had not been some reason against it. S. C.

An instance of *proving too much.* If Bishop
without Presb. B.=Presb. i. e. no Bishop.

P. 253.   The *Bishop.*

> To rule and to be ruled are distinct,
> And several duties, severally belong
> To several *persons.*

Functions of times, but not persons, of necessity?
Ex. Bishop to Archbishop.

P. 255.   *Church Festivals.*

> Who loves not you, doth but in vain profess
> That he loves God, or heaven, or happiness.

Equally unthinking and uncharitable;—I approve
of them;—but yet remember Roman Catholic
idolatry, and that it originated in such high-flown
metaphors as these.

P. 255.   *The Sabbath, or Lord's Day.*

Hail	Vail
Holy	Wholly
King of days, &c.	To thy praise, &c.

Make it sense and lose the rhyme; or make it
rhyme and lose the sense.

P. 258.   *The Nativity,* or *Christmas Day.*

> Unfold thy face, unmask thy ray,
> Shine forth, bright sun, double the day,
> Let no malignant misty fume, &c.

The only poem in *The Synagogue* which possesses
poetic merit; with a few changes and additions this
would be a striking poem.

Substitute the following for the fifth to the eighth line.

> To sheath or blunt one happy ray,
> That wins new splendour from the day.
> This day that gives thee power to rise,
> And shine on hearts as well as eyes:
> This birth-day of all souls, when first
> On eyes of flesh and blood did burst
> That primal great lucific light,
> That rays to thee, to us gave sight.

P. 267.   *Whit-Sunday.*

> Nay, startle not to hear that rushing wind,
>   Wherewith this place is shaken, &c.

> To hear at once so great variety
>   Of language from them come, &c.

The spiritual miracle was the descent of the Holy Ghost: the outward the wind and the tongues: and so St. Peter himself explains it. That each individual obtained the power of speaking all languages, is neither contained in, nor fairly deducible from, St. Luke's account.

P. 269.   *Trinity Sunday.*

> The Trinity
> In Unity,
> And Unity
> In Trinity,
> All reason doth *transcend.*

Most true, but not *contradict.* Reason is to faith, as the eye to the telescope.

EXTRACT FROM A LETTER

OF S. T. COLERIDGE TO W. COLLINS, R. A.
PRINTED IN THE LIFE OF COLLINS
BY HIS SON.   VOL. I.

December, 1818.

TO feel the full force o' the Christian religion it is perhaps necessary, for many tempers, that they should first be made to feel, experimentally, the hollowness of human friendship, the presumptuous emptiness of human hopes. I find more substantial comfort now in pious George Herbert's Temple, which I used to read to amuse myself with his quaintness, in short, only to laugh at, than in all the poetry since the poems of Milton. If you have not read Herbert I can recommend the book to you confidently. The poem entitled "The Flower" is especially affecting, and to me such a phrase as " *and relish versing*" expresses a sincerity and reality, which I would unwillingly exchange for the more dignified " and once more love the Muse," &c. and so with many other of Herbert's homely phrases.

NOTES ON MATHIAS' EDITION OF GRAY.

On a distant prospect of Eton College.

Vol. 1. p. 9.

> Wanders the hoary Thames along
> His silver-winding way.   GRAY.

W E want, methinks, a little treatise from some
man of flexible good sense, and well versed
in the Greek poets, especially Homer, the choral,
and other lyrics, containing first a history of compound epithets, and then the laws and licenses.   I
am not so much disposed as I used to be to quarrel
with such an epithet as " silver-winding ;" ungram-
matical as the hyphen is, it is not wholly *illogical*,
for the phrase conveys more than silvery and winding.   It gives, namely, the unity of the impression,
the co-inherence of the brightness, the motion, and
the line of motion.

P. 10.

> Say, Father Thames, for thou hast seen
>   Full many a sprightly race
> Disporting on thy margent green,
>   The paths of pleasure trace ;
> Who foremost now delight to cleave,
> With pliant arm, thy glassy wave ?
>   The captive linnet which enthral ?
> What idle progeny succeed

> To chase the rolling circle's speed,
> Or urge the flying ball?   GRAY.

This is the only stanza that appears to me very objectionable in point of diction.   This, I must confess, is not only *falsetto* throughout, but is at once harsh and feeble, and very far the worst ten lines in all the works of Mr. Gray, English or Latin, prose or verse.

P. 12.

> And envy wan, and faded care,[1]
> Grim-visaged comfortless despair,[2]
> And sorrow's piercing dart.[3]

[1] Bad in the first, [2] in the second, [3] in the last degree.

P. 15.

> The proud are taught to *taste of pain*.   GRAY.

There is a want of dignity—a sort of irony in this phrase to my feeling that would be more proper in dramatic than in lyric composition.

On Gray's *Platonica*, vol. 1. p. 299.—547.

Whatever might be expected from a scholar, a gentleman, a man of exquisite taste, as the quintessence of sane and sound good sense, Mr. Gray appears to me to have performed.   The poet Plato, the orator Plato, Plato the exquisite dramatist of conversation, the seer and the painter of character, Plato the high-bred, highly-educated, aristocratic republican, the man and the gentleman of quality

stands full before us from behind the curtain as
Gray has drawn it back. Even so does Socrates,
the social wise old man, the *practical* moralist.
But Plato the philosopher, but the divine Plato, was
not to be comprehended within the field of vision,
or be commanded by the fixed immoveable telescope
of Mr. Locke's human understanding. The whole
sweep of the best philosophic reflections of French
or English fabric in the age of our scholarly bard,
was not commensurate with the mighty orb. The
little, according to *my* convictions at least, the very
little of proper Platonism contained in the *written*
books of Plato, who himself, in an epistle, the authenticity of which there is no tenable ground for
doubting, as I was rejoiced to find Mr. Gray acknowledge, has declared all he had written to be
substantially Socratic, and not a fair exponent of
his own tenets,* even this little, Mr. Gray has
either misconceived or honestly confessed that, as
he was not one of the initiated, it was utterly beyond
his comprehension. Finally, to repeat the explanation with which I closed the last page of these
notes and extracts,

> Volsimi ———— e vidi Plato
>   (ma non quel Plato)
> Che'n quella schiera andò più presso al segno,

---

* See Plato's second epistle φραστέον δή σοι δι' αἰνιγμῶν
κ. τ. λ. and towards the end τὰ δὲ νῦν λεγόμενα Σωκράτους
ἐστί, κ. τ. λ. See also the 7th Epistle, p. 341.

Al qual' aggiunge, a chì dal Cielo è dato.*

S. T. Coleridge, 1819.

P. 385.   Hippias Major.

We learn from this dialogue in how poor a condition the art of reasoning on moral and abstracted subjects was before the time of Socrates: for it is impossible that Plato should introduce a sophist of the first reputation for eloquence and knowledge in several kinds, talking in a manner below the absurdity and weakness of a child; unless he had really drawn after the life. No less than twenty-four pages are here spent in vain, only to force it into the head of Hippias that there is such a thing as a general idea; and that, before we can dispute on any subject, we should give a definition of it.

Is not this, its improbability out of the question, contradicted by the Protagoras of Plato's own drawing? Are there no authors, no physicians in London at the present moment, of " the first reputation," i. e. whom a certain class cry up: for in no other sense is the phrase *historically* applicable to Hippias, whom a Sydenham redivivus or a new Stahl might not exhibit as pompous ignoramuses ? no *one* Hippias amongst them? But we need not flee to conjectures. The ratiocination assigned by Aristotle and Plato himself to Gorgias and then to the Eleatic school, are positive proofs that Mr. Gray has mistaken the satire of an individual for a characteristic of an age or class.

May I dare whisper to the reeds without proclaiming that I am in the state of Midas, — may I

---

* Petrarch's *Trionfo della Fama*, cap. terz. v. 4-6.

dare to hint that Mr. Gray himself had not, and
through the spectacles of Mr. Locke and his followers, could not have seen the difficulties which
Hippias found in a *general* idea, *secundum Pla-
tonem?* S. T. C.

P. 386. Notes 289. Passages of Heraclitus.

Πιθηκῶν ὁ κάλλιστος αἰσχρὸς ἄλλῳ γένει συμβαλεῖν.—
Ἀνθρώπων ὁ σοφώτατος πρὸς Θεὸν πιθηκὸς φανεῖται.

This latter passage is undoubtedly the original
of that famous thought in Pope's Essay on Man,
B. 2:

" And shewed a Newton as we shew an ape."

I remember to have met nearly the same words
in one of our elder Poets.

P. 390—91.

That a sophist was a kind of merchant, or rather a retailer
of food for the soul, and, like other shopkeepers, would exert
his eloquence to recommend his own goods. The misfortune
was, we could not carry them off, like corporeal viands, set
them by a while, and consider them at leisure, whether they
were wholesome or not, before we tasted them : that in this
case we have no vessel but the soul to receive them in,
which will necessarily retain a tincture, and perhaps, much
to its prejudice, of all which is instilled into it.

Query, if Socrates, himself a scholar of the sophists, is accurate, did not the change of ὁ σοφός into
ὁ Σοφιστής, in the single case of Solon, refer to the
wisdom-causing influences of his legislation? Mem:
—to examine whether Φροντιστής was, or was not,

more generally used at first *in malum sensum*, or rather the proper force originally of the termination ἰστής, ἀστής—whether (as it is evidently verbal) it imply a reflex or a transitive act.

P. 399. Ὅτι Ἀμαθία.

This is the true key and great moral of the dialogue, that knowledge alone is the source of virtue, and ignorance the source of vice; it was Plato's own principle, see Plat. Epist. 7. p. 336. Ἀμαθία, ἐξ ἧς πάντα κακὰ πᾶσιν ἐῤῥίζωται καὶ βλαστάνει καὶ εἰς ὕστερον ἀποτελεῖ καρπὸν τοῖς γεννήσασι πικρότατον. See also *Sophist.* p. 228 and 249, and *Euthyde- mus* from p. 278 to 281, and *De Legib.* L. 3. p. 688.) and proba- bly it was also the principle of Socrates: the consequence of it is, that virtue may be taught, and may be acquired: and that philosophy alone can point us out the way to it.

More than our word, Ignorance, is contained in the Ἀμαθία of Plato. I, however, freely acknow- ledge, that this was the point of view, from which Socrates did *for the most part* contemplate moral good and evil. Now and then he seems to have taken a higher station, but soon quitted it for the lower, more generally intelligible. Hence the va- cillation of Socrates himself: hence, too, the imme- diate opposition of his disciples, Antisthenes and Aristippus. But that this was Plato's own principle I exceedingly doubt. That it was not the principle of Platonism, as taught by the first Academy under Speusippus, I do *not* doubt at all. See the xivth Essay, p. 129-39 of *The Friend*, vol. i. In the sense in which ἀμαθίας πάντα κακὰ ἐῤῥίζωται, κ. τ. λ.

is maintained in that Essay, so and no otherwise can it be truly asserted, and so and no otherwise did ὡς ἐμοί γε δοκεῖ, Plato teach it.

BARRY CORNWALL.*

BARRY CORNWALL is a poet, *me saltem judice:* and in that sense of the term, in which I apply it to C. Lamb and W. Wordsworth. There are poems of great merit, the authors of which I should yet not feel impelled so to designate.

The faults of these poems are no less things of hope, than the beauties; both are just what they ought to be,—that is, now.

If B. C. be faithful to his genius, it in due time will warn him, that as poetry is the identity of all other knowledges, so a poet cannot be a great poet, but as being likewise inclusively an historian and naturalist, in the light, as well as the life, of philosophy: all other men's worlds are his chaos.

Hints *obiter* are:—not to permit delicacy and exquisiteness to seduce into effeminacy. Not to permit beauties by repetition to become manner-isms. To be jealous of fragmentary composition,—as epicurism of genius, and apple-pie made all of quinces. *Item*, that dramatic poetry must be poetry

---

* Written in Mr. Lamb's copy of the ' Dramatic Scenes.' Ed.

hid in thought and passion,—not thought or passion disguised in the dress of poetry. Lastly, to be economic and withholding in similes, figures, &c. They will all find their place, sooner or later, each as the luminary of a sphere of its own. There can be no galaxy in poetry, because it is language,— *ergo* processive,—*ergo* every the smallest star must be seen singly.

There are not five metrists in the kingdom, whose works are known by me, to whom I could have held myself allowed to have spoken so plainly. But B. C. is a man of genius, and it depends on him-self—(competence protecting him from gnawing or distracting cares)—to become a rightful poet,—that is, a great man.

Oh! for such a man worldly prudence is trans-figured into the highest spiritual duty! How gene-rous is self-interest in him, whose true self is all that is good and hopeful in all ages, as far as the language of Spenser, Shakspeare, and Milton shall become the mother-tongue!

A map of the road to Paradise, drawn in Pur-gatory, on the confines of Hell, by S. T. C. July 30, 1819.

ON THE MODE OF STUDYING KÁNT.

EXTRACT FROM A LETTER OF MR. COLERIDGE TO

J. GOODEN, ESQ.*

ACCEPT my thanks for the rules of the harmony. I perceive that the members are chiefly merchants; but yet it were to be wished, that such an enlargement of the society could be brought about as, retaining all its present purposes, might add to them the groundwork of a library of northern literature, and by bringing together the many gentlemen who are attached to it be the means of eventually making both countries better acquainted with the valuable part of each other; especially, the English with the German, for our most sensible men look at the German Muses through a film of prejudice and utter misconception.

With regard to philosophy, there are half a dozen things, good and bad, that in this country are so nick-named, but in the only accurate sense of the term, there neither are, have been, or ever will be but two essentially different schools of phi-

---

* This letter and the following notes on Jean Paul were communicated by Mr. H. C. Robinson. S. C.

2   T

losophy, the Platonic, and the Aristotelian. To
the latter but with a somewhat nearer approach to
the Platonic, Emanuel Kant belonged; to the former Bacon and Leibnitz, and, in his riper and better
years, Berkeley. And to this I profess myself an
adherent—*nihil novum, vel inauditum audemus;*
though, as every man has a face of his own, without being more or less than a man, so is every true
philosopher an original, without ceasing to be an
inmate of Academus or of the Lyceum. But as to
caution, I will just tell you how I proceeded myself
twenty years and more ago, when I first felt a curiosity about Kant, and was fully aware that to master his meaning, as a system, would be a work of
great labour and long time. First, I asked myself,
have I the labour and the time in my power? Secondly, if so, and if it would be of adequate importance to me if true, by what means can I arrive at
a rational presumption for or against? I inquired
after all the more popular writings of Kant—read
them with delight. I then read the Prefaces of
several of his systematic works, as the *Prolego-
mena*, &c. Here too every part, I understood, and
that was nearly the whole, was replete with sound
and plain, though bold and to me novel truths; and
I followed Socrates' adage respecting Heraclitus:
all I understand is excellent, and I am bound to
presume that the rest is at least worth the trouble
of trying whether it be not equally so. In other
words, until I understand a writer's ignorance, I
presume myself ignorant of his understanding. Per-

mit me to refer you to a chapter on this subject in my Literary Life.*

Yet I by no means recommend to you an extension of your philosophic researches beyond Kant. In him is contained all that can be *learned*, and as to the results, you have a firm faith in God, the responsible Will of Man and Immortality; and Kant will demonstrate to you, that this faith is acquiesced in, indeed, nay, confirmed by the Reason and Understanding, but grounded on Postulates authorized and substantiated solely by the *Moral* Being. There are likewise *mine:* and whether the Ideas are regulative only, as Aristotle and Kant teach, or constitutive and actual, as Pythagoras and Plato, is of living interest to the philosopher by profession alone. Both systems are equally true, if only the former abstain from denying *universally* what is denied individually. He, for whom Ideas are constitutive, will in effect be a Platonist; and in those for whom they are regulative only, Platonism is but a hollow affectation. Dryden *could* not have been a Platonist: Shakspeare, Milton, Dante, Michael Angelo and Rafael could not have been other than Platonists. Lord Bacon, who never read Plato's works, taught pure Platonism in his *great* work, the *Novum Organum*, and abuses his divine predecessor for fantastic nonsense, which he had been the first to explode. Accept my best respects, &c.

S. T. COLERIDGE.

14 Jan. 1814.   Highgate.

* *Biographia Literaria*, vol. i. chap. xii. p. 242.   S. C.

NOTES ON THE PALINGENESIEN OF
JEAN PAUL.

Written in the blank leaf at the beginning.

——S ist zu merken, dass die Sprache in diesem Buch nicht sey wie in gewöhnlich Bette, darin der Gedankenstrom ordentlich and chrbar hinströmt, sondern wie cin Verwüstung in Damm and Dei-chen.*

Preface p. xxxi.

Two Revolutions, the Gallican, which sacrifices the indi-viduals to the Idea or to the State, and in time of need, even the latter themselves ;— and the Kantian-Moralist, (Kantisch-Moralische), which abandons the affection of human Love altogether, because it can so little be described as merit ; these draw and station us forlorn human creatures ever further and more lonesomely one from another, each on a frosty uninhabited island : nay the Gallican, which ex-cites and arms feelings against feelings, does it less than the Critical, which teaches us to disarm and to dispense with them altogether; and which neither allows Love to pass for the spring of virtue, nor virtue for the source of Love.† *Transl.*

---

* It is observable that the language in this book is not as in an ordinary channel, wherein the stream of thought flows on in a seemly and regular manner, but like a violent flood rushing against dyke and mole.

† Zwei Revoluzionen, diè gallische, welche der Idee oder dem Staate diè Individuen, and im Nothsal dièsen selber opfert, und die kantisch-moralische, welche den Af-fekt der Menschenliebe liegen lässet, weil er so wenig wie Verdienste geboten werden kan, diese ziehen und stellen

But surely Kant's aim was not to give a full *Sittenlehre,* or system of practical material morality, but the *a priori* form—*Ethice formalis:* which was then a most necessary work, and the only mode of quelling at once both Necessitarians and Meritmongers, and the idol common to both, Eudæmonism. If his followers have stood still in lazy adoration, instead of following up the road thus opened out to them, it is their fault not Kant's.

S. T. C.

FROM BLACKWOOD'S EDINBURGH MAGAZINE, Oct. 1821.

LETTER FROM MR. COLERIDGE.

DEAR Sir,—In the third letter (in the little parcel,) which I have headed with your name, you will find my reasons for wishing these five letters, and a sixth, which will follow in my next, on the plan and code of a Magazine, which should unite the *utile* and *dulce*, to appear in the first instance. My next will consist of very different articles, apparently ; namely, the First Book of

---

uns verlassene Menschen immer weiter und einsamer aus einander, jeden nur auf ein frostiges unbewohntes Eiland ; ja die gallische, die nur Gefühle gegen Gefühle bewafnet und aufhezt, thut es weniger als die kritische, die sie entwafnen und entbehren lehrt, und die weder die Liebe als Quelle der Tugend noch diese als Quelle von jener gelten lassen kan.

my True History from Fairy Land, or the World Without, and the World Within. 2. The commencement of the Annals and Philosophy of Superstition; for the completion of which I am waiting only for a very curious folio, in Mr **********'s possession. 3. The life of Holty, a German poet, of true genius, who died in early manhood; with specimens of his poems, translated, or freely imitated in English verse. It would have been more in the mode to have addressed myself to the Editor, but I could not give up this one opportunity of assuring you that I am, my dear Sir,

With every friendly wish, your obliged,

Mr. Blackwood.   S. T. COLERIDGE.

Selection from Mr. Coleridge's Literary Correspondence with Friends, and Men of Letters.

No. I.

LETTER I.   *From a Professional Friend.*

MY DEAR AND HONOURED SIR,—I was much struck with your Excerpta from Porta, Eckartshausen, and others, as to the effect of the ceremonial drinks and unguents, on the (female) practitioners of the black arts, whose witchcraft you believe to have consisted in the unhappy craft of bewitching themselves. I at least know of no reason, why to these *toxications*, (especially when

taken through the skin, and to the cataleptic state
induced by them,) we should not attribute the poor
wretches' own belief of their guilt. I can conceive,
indeed, of no other mode of accounting—I do not
say for their suspicious last dying avowals at the
stake; but—for their private and voluntary con-
fessions on their death-beds, which made a convert
of your old favourite, Sir T. Brown.   Perhaps my
professional pursuits, and medical studies, may have
predisposed me to be interested ; but my mind has
been in an eddy ever since I left you. The con-
nections of the subject with classical and with
druidical superstitions, pointed out by you —the
Circeia pocula—the herbal spells of the Haxæ, or
Druidesses—the somniloquism of the prophetesses,
under the coercion of the Scandinavian enchanters
—the dependence of the Greek oracles on mineral
waters, and stupifying vapours from the earth, as
stated by Plutarch, and more than once alluded to
by Euripides—the vast spread of the same, or similar usages, from Greenland even to the south-
ernmost point of America ;— you sent me home
with enough to think of!—But, more than all, I
was struck and interested with your concluding remark, that these, and most other superstitions, were,
in your belief, but the CADAVER ET PUTRIMENTA
OF A DEFUNCT NATURAL PHILOSOPHY.—Why
not rather the imperfect rudiments ? I asked. You
promised me your reasons, and a fuller explanation.
But let me speak out my whole wish ; and call on

you to redeem the pledges you gave, so long back as October 1809, that you would devote a series of papers to the subject of Dreams, Visions, Presentations, Ghosts, Witchcraft, Cures by sympathy, in which you would select and explain the most interesting and best attested facts that have come to your knowledge from books or personal testimony.

You can scarcely conceive how deep an interest I attach to this request; nor how many, beside myself, in the circle of my own acquaintance have the same feeling. Indeed, my dear Sir! when I reflect, that there is scarcely a chapter of history in which superstition of some kind or other does not form or supply a portion of its contents, I look forward, with unquiet anticipation, to the power of explaining the more frequent and best attested narrations, at least without the necessity of having recourse to the supposition of downright tricks and lying, on one side, or to the Devil and his imps on the other. * * * *

Your obliged Pupil,
and affectionate Friend,
J. L——.

P.S.—Dr. L. of the Museum, is quite of your opinion, that little or nothing of importance to the philosophic naturalist can result from Comparative Anatomy on Cuvier's plan; and that its best trophies will be but lifeless skeletons, till it is studied in combination with a Comparative Physiology.

But you ought yourself to vindicate the priority of your claim. But I fear, dear C., that *Sic Vos, non Vobis* was made for your motto throughout life.

LETTER II. *In Answer to the above.*

WELL, my dear pupil and fellow-student! I am willing to make the attempt. If the majority of my readers had but the same personal knowledge of me as you have, I should sit down to the work with good cheer. But this is out of the question. Let me, however, suppose you for the moment, as an *average* reader—address you as such, and attribute to you feelings and language in character.—Do not mistake me, my dear L——. Not even for a moment, nor under the pretext of *mons a non movendo*, would I contemplate in connection with your name " id genus lectorum, qui meliores obtrectare malint quam imitari : et quorum *similitudinem* desperent, eorundem affectent *simultatem*—scilicet uti qui suo nomine obscuri sunt, meo innotescant."* The readers I have in view, are of that class who with a sincere, though not

---

* The passage, which cannot fail to remind you of H—— and his set, is from Apuleius's Lib. Floridorum—the two books of which, by the bye, seem to have been transcribed from his common-place-book of *Good Things*, happy phrases, &c. that he had not had an opportunity of bringing *in* in his set writings.

very strong desire, of acquiring knowledge, have
taken it for granted, that all knowledge of any value
respecting the mind is either to be found in three
or four books, the eldest not a hundred years old,
or may be conveniently taught without any other
terms or previous explanations than these works
have already rendered familiar among men of education.

Well, friendly reader! as the problem of things
little less (it seems to you,) than impossible, yet
strongly and numerously attested by evidence which
it seems impossible to discredit, has interested you,
I am willing to attempt the solution. But then it
must be under certain *conditions*. I must be able
to *hope*, I must have sufficient grounds for hoping,
that I shall be understood, or rather that I shall be
allowed to make myself understood. And as I am
gifted with no magnetic power of throwing my
reader into the state of *clear-seeing* (clairvoyance)
or luminous vision; as I have not the secret of
enabling him to read with the pit of his stomach,
or with his finger-ends, nor of calling into act "the
cuticular faculty," dormant at the tip of his nose;
but must rely on WORDS—I cannot form the hope
rationally, unless the reader will have patience
enough to master the sense in which I use them.

But why employ words that need explanation?
And might I not ask in *my* turn, would you, gentle
reader! put the same question to Sir Edward Smith,
or any other member of the Linnæan Society, to

whom you had applied for instruction in Botany?
And yet he would require of you that you should
attend to a score of technical terms, and make yourself master of the sense of each, in order to your
understanding the distinctive characters of a grass,
a mushroom, and a lichen! Now the psychologist,
or speculative philosopher, will be content with you,
if you will impose on yourself the trouble of understanding and remembering one of the number, in
order to understand your own nature. But I will
meet your question direct. You ask me, why I
use words that need explanation? Because (I reply) on this subject there are no others! Because
the darkness and the main difficulties that attend
it, are owing to the vagueness and ambiguity of the
words in common use; and which preclude all explanation for him who has resolved that none is required. Because there is already a falsity in the
very phrases, " words in *common* use;" "the language of *common* sense." Words of most *frequent* use they may be, *common* they are not; but
the language of the market, and as such, expressing *degrees* only, and therefore incompetent to the
purpose wherever it becomes necessary to designate
the *kind* independent of all degree. The philosopher may, and often does, employ the same words
as in the market; but does this supersede the necessity of a previous explanation? As I referred
you before to the botanist, so now to the chemist.
Light, heat, charcoal, are every man's words. But

fixed or *invisible* light? The *frozen* heat? Charcoal in its simplest form as *diamond*, or as blacklead? Will a stranger to chemistry be worse off, would the chemist's language be less likely to be understood by his using different words for distinct meanings, as carbon, caloric, and the like?

But the case is stronger. The chemist is compelled to make words, in order to prevent or remove some error connected with the common word; and this too an error, the continuance of which was incompatible with the first principles and elementary truths of the science he is to teach. You must submit to regard yourself ignorant even of the words, air and water; and will find, that they are not chemically intelligible without the terms, oxygen, nitrogen, hydrogen, or others equivalent. Now it is even so with the knowledge, which you would have *me* to communicate. There are certain prejudices of the common, *i. e.* of the *average* sense of men, the exposure of which is the first step, the indispensable preliminary, of all rational psychology: and these cannot be exposed but by selecting and adhering to some one word, in which we may be able to trace the growth and modifications of the opinion or belief conveyed in this, or similar words, not by any revolution or positive *change* of the original sense, but by the transfer of this sense and the difference in the application.

Where there is but one word for two or more diverse or disparate meanings in a language, (or

though there should be several, yet if perfect syno-
nimes, they count but for one word,) the language
is so far defective.   And this is a defect of frequent occurrence in all languages, prior to the cultivation of science, logic and philology, especially
of the two latter: and among a free, lively, and ingenious people, such as the Greeks were, sophistry
and the influence of sophists are the inevitable result.   To check this evil by striking at its root in
the ambiguity of words, Plato wrote the greater part
of his published works, which do not so much contain his own system of philosophy, as the negative
conditions of reasoning aright on *any* system.   And
yet more obviously is it the case with the Metaphysics, Analytics, &c. of Aristotle, which have
been well described by Lambert as a dictionary of
general terms, the process throughout being, first,
to discover and establish definite meanings, and
then to appropriate to each a several word.   The
sciences will take care, each of it's own nomenclature ; but the interests of the language at large fall
under the special guardianship of logic and rational
psychology.   Where these have fallen into neglect
or disrepute, from exclusive pursuit of wealth, excess of the commercial spirit, or whatever other
cause disposes men in general to attach an exclusive value to immediate and palpable utility, the
dictionary may swell, but the language will decline.
Few are the books published within the last fifty
years, that would not supply their quota of proofs,

that so it is with our own mother English. The bricks and stones are in abundance, but the cement none or naught. That which is indeed the *common* language exists every where as the menstruum, and no where as the whole—See *Biographia Literaria**—while the language complimented with this name, is, as I have already said, in fact the language of the market. Every science, every trade, has its technical nomenclature; every folly has its *fancy-words;* every vice its own slang— and is the science of humanity to be the one exception? Is philosophy to work without tools? to have no straw wherewith to make the bricks for her mansion-house but what she may pick up on the high road, or steal, with all its impurities and sophistications, from the litter of the cattle market?

For the present, however, my demands on your patience are very limited.—If as the price of much *entertainment* to follow, and I trust of something besides of less *transitory* interest, you will fairly attend to the history of *two* scholastic terms, OB-JECT and SUBJECT, with their derivatives; you shall have my promise that I will not on any future occasion ask you to be attentive, without trying not to be myself dull. That it may cost you no more trouble than necessary, I have brought it under the eye in numbered paragraphs, with *scholia* or commentary to such as seemed to require it.

Your's most affectionately,
S. T. COLERIDGE.

* Vol. ii. p. 61. 2nd. *edit.* S. C.

On the Philosophic import of the Words, OBJECT and SUBJECT.

§ 1.

Existence is a simple intuition, underived and indecomponible. It is no *idea*, no particular form, much less any determination or modification of the possible: it is nothing that can be educed from the logical conception of a thing, as its predicate: it is no *property* of a thing, but its reality itself; or, as the Latin would more conveniently express it— Nulla *rei* proprietas est, sed ipsa ejus *realitas*.

SCHOLIUM.

Herein lies the sophism in Des Cartes' celebrated demonstration of the existence of the Supreme Being from the idea. In the idea of God are contained *all* attributes that belong to the perfection of a being: but existence is such: therefore, God's existence is contained in the idea of God. To this it is a sufficient answer, that existence is not an attribute. It might be shewn too, from the barrenness of the demonstration, by identifying the deduction with the premise, *i. e.* for reducing the minor or term *included* to a mere repetition of the major or term *including*. For in fact the syllogism ought to stand thus: the *idea* of God comprises the *idea* of all attributes that belong to perfection; but the *idea* of existence is such : therefore the idea of his existence is included in the idea of God. — Now, existence is no idea, but a *fact :* or, though we had an *idea* of existence, still the proof of a correspondence to a *reality* would be wanting, *i. e.* the very point would be wanting which it was the purpose of the demonstration to supply. Still the *idea* of the fact is not the fact itself. Besides, the term, idea, is here improperly substituted for the mere *supposition* of a *logical* subject, necessarily presumed in order to the conceivableness *(cogitabilitas)* of *any* qualities, properties, or attributes. But this is a mere *ens logicum*, (vel etiam *grammaticum*,) the result of the thinker's own unity of consciousness, and no less contained in the conception of a plant or of a chimera, than in the idea of the Supreme Being. If Des Cartes could have proved, that his idea of a Supreme Being is universal and necessary, and that the conviction of a reality perfectly coincident with the idea is equally universal and inevitable ; and that these were in truth but one and the same act or intuition, unique, and without analogy, though, from the inadequateness of our minds, from the mechanism of thought, and the structure of language, we are compelled to express it dividually, as consisting of two correlative terms—this would have been something. But then it must be entitled a *statement*, not a demonstration — the necessity of which it would supersede. And something like this may perhaps be found true, where the reasoning

powers are developed and duly exerted; but would
I fear, do little towards settling the dispute between
the religious Theist, and the speculative Atheist or
Pantheist, whether this be *all*, or whether it is even
what we mean, and are bound to mean, by the word
God. The old controversy would be started, what
are the possible perfections of an Infinite Being—
in other words, what the legitimate sense is of the
term, infinite, as applied to Deity, and what is, or is
not compatible with that sense.

§ 2.

I think, and while thinking, I am conscious of
certain workings or movements, as acts or activities
of my being, and feel myself as the power in which
they originate. I feel myself *working;* and the
sense or feeling of this *activity* constitutes the sense
and feeling of EXISTENCE, *i. e.* of my actual being.

SCHOLIUM.

Movements, motions, taken metaphorically, without relation to space or place. Κινήσεις μὴ κατὰ
τόπον; αἱ ὥσπερ κινήσεις, of Aristotle.

§ 3.

In these workings, however, I distinguish a difference. In some I feel myself as the cause and
proper agent, and the movements themselves as the
work of my own power. In others, I feel these

2   U

movements as my own activity; but not as my own
acts. The first we call the active or positive state
of our existence; the second, the passive or negative state. The active power, nevertheless, is felt
in both equally. But in the first I feel it as the
cause acting, in the second, as the *condition*, with
out which I could not be acted on.

Scholium.

It is a truth of highest importance, that *agere et
pati* are not different kinds, but the same kind in
different relations. And this not only in consequence of an immediate re-action, but the act of *receiving* is no less truly an *act*, than the act of in-
fluencing. Thus, the lungs act in being stimulated
by the air, as truly as in the act of breathing, to
which they were stimulated. The Greek verbal
termination, ω, happily illustrates this. Ποιῶ, πράτ-
τω, πάσχω, in philosophical grammar, are all three
verbs active; but the first is the active-*transitive*,
in which the agency passes forth out of the agent
into another. Τί ποιεῖς; what are you doing? The
second is the active-*intransitive*. Τί πράττεις;
how do you do? or how *are* you? The third is the
active-*passive*, or more appropriately the active-*patient*, the verb *recipient* or *receptive*, τί πάσχεις;
what ails you? Or, to take another idiom of our
language, that most livelily expresses the co-pre-
sence of an agent, an agency distinct and alien from
our own, What is the *matter with* you? It would

carry us too far to explain the nature of verbs *passive*, as so called in technical grammar. Suffice, that this class *originated* in the same causes, as led men to make the division of substances into living and dead—a division *psychologically* necessary, but of doubtful philosophical validity.

§ 4.

With the workings and movements, which I refer to myself and my own agency, there alternate— say rather, I find myself alternately conscious of forms (=Impressions, images, or better or less figurative and hypothetical, *presences*, presentations,) and of states or modes, which not feeling as the work or effect of my own power I refer to a power *other* than me, *i. e.* (iu the language derived from my sense of sight) without me. And this is the feeling, I have, of the existence of outward things.

Scholium.

In this superinduction of the sense of *outness* on the feeling of the *actual* arises our notion of the *real* and reality. But as I cannot but reflect, that as the other is to me, so I must be to the other, the terms real and actual, soon become confounded and interchangeable, or only discriminated in the gold scales of metaphysics.

§ 5.

Since both then, the feeling of my own existence and the feeling of the existence of things without, are but this sense of an acting and working—it is clear that to exist is the same as to act or work; *(Quantum operor, tantum sum,)* that whatever exists, works, (= is *in action; actually* is; is *in deed*) that not to work, as agent or patient, is not to exist; and lastly, that patience (= *vis patiendi,*) and the reaction that is its co-instantaneous consequent, is the same activity in opposite and alternating relations.

§ 6.

That which is *inferred* in those acts and workings, the feeling of which is one with the feeling of our own existence, or inferred *from* those which we refer to an agency distinct from our own, but in *both* instances is *inferred*, is the SUBJECT, *i. e.* that which does not appear, but *lies under* (quod *jacet subter*) the appearance.

§ 7.

But in the first instance, that namely which is inferred *in* its effects, and of course therefore *self*-inferred, the subject is a MIND, *i. e.* that which *knows* itself, and may be *inferred* by others; but which cannot appear.

§ 8.

That, in or from which the subject is inferred, is the OBJECT, id quod *jacet ob* oculos, that which lies before us, that which lies straight opposite.

SCHOLIUM.

The terms used in psychology, logic, &c. even those of most frequent occurrence in common life, are, for the most part, of Latin derivation; and not only so, but the original words, such as quantity, quality, subject, object, &c. &c. were formed in the schools of philosophy for scholastic use, and in correspondence to Greek technical terms of the same meaning. Etymology, therefore, is little else than indispensable to an insight into the true force, and, as it were, freshness of the words in question, especially of those that have passed from the schools into the market-place, from the medals and tokens (σύμβολα) of the philosophers' guild or company into the current coin of the land. But the difference between a man, who understands them according to their first use, and seeks to restore the original impress and superscription, and the man who gives and takes them *in small change*, unweighed, and tried only by the *sound*, may be illustrated by imagining the different points of view in which the same *cowry* would appear to a scientific conchologist, and to a chaffering negro. This use of etymology may be exemplified in the present case. The immediate *object* of the mind is always and exclusively the *workings* or *makings* above stated and distinguished into two kinds, § 2, 3, and 4. Where the object consists of the first kind, in which the subject infers its own existence, and which

it refers to its own agency, and identifies with itself,
(feels and contemplates as one with itself, and as
itself,) and yet without confounding the inherent
distinction between subject and object, the subject
witnesses to itself that it is a *mind, i. e.* a subject-
object, or subject that becomes an object to itself.

But where the workings or makings of the second
sort are the object, from objects of this sort we always infer the existence of a subject, as in the former case.   But we infer it *from* them, rather than
in them; or to express the point yet more clearly,
we infer two subjects.   *In* the object, we infer our
own existence and *subjectivity; from* them the existence of a subject, not our own, and to this we
refer the object, as to its proper cause and agent.
Again, we always infer a correspondent *subject;*
but not always a *mind.*   Whether we consider this
other subject as another mind, is determined by the
more or less analogy of the objects or makings of
the second class to those of the first, and not seldom depends on the varying degrees of our attention and previous knowledge.

Add to these differences the modifying influence
of the senses, the sense of sight more particularly,
in consequence of which this subject *other than* we,
is presented as a subject *out of* us.   With the sensuous vividness connected with, and which in part
constitutes, this outness or outwardness, contrast
the exceeding obscurity and dimness in the conception of a subject, not a mind; and reflect, too, that,

to objects of the *first* kind, we cannot attribute actual or separative outwardness; while, in cases of the *second* kind, we are, after a shorter or longer time, compelled by the law of association to transfer this outness from the *inferred* subject to the *present* object. Lastly, reflect that, in the former instance, the object is identified with the subject, both positively by the act of the subject, and negatively by insusceptibility of outness in the object; and that in the latter the very contrary takes place; namely, instead of the object being identified with the subject, the subject is taken up and confounded in the object. In the ordinary and unreflecting states, therefore, of men's minds, it could not be otherwise, but that, in the one instance, the object must be lost, and indistinguishable in the subject; and that, in the other, the subject is lost and forgotten in the object, to which a necessary illusion had already transferred that outness, which, in its origin, and in right of reason, belongs exclusively to the subject, *i. e.* the agent *ab extra* inferred from the object. For *outness* is but the feeling of otherness (alterity), rendered intuitive, or alterity visually represented. Hence, and also because we find this outness and the objects, to which, though they are, in fact, workings in our own being, we transfer it, independent of our will, and apparently common to other minds, we learn to connect therewith the feeling and sense of *reality;* and the objective becomes synonimous first with *external*, then with *real*, and at length it

was employed to express universal and permanent
validity, free from the accidents and particular constitution of *individual* intellects; nay, when taken
in its highest and absolute sense, as free from the
inherent limits, partial perspective, and refracting
media of the human mind *in specie,* (*idola tribûs*
of Lord Bacon,) as distinguished from mind *in toto
genere.* In direct antithesis to these several senses
of the term, objective, the subjective has been used
as synonimous with, first, inward; second, unreal;
and third, that the cause and seat of which are to be
referred to the special or individual peculiarity of
the percipients, mind, organs, or relative position.
Of course, the meaning of the word in any one sentence cannot be *definitely* ascertained but by aid of
the context, and will vary with the immediate purposes, and previous views and persuasions of the
writer. Thus, the egoist, or ultra-idealist, affirms
all objects to be subjective; the disciple of Mal-
branche, or of Berkeley, that the objective subsists
wholly and solely in the universal subject—God.
A lady, otherwise of sound mind, was so affected
by the reported death of her absent husband, that
every night at the same hour she saw a figure at
the foot of her bed, which she identified with him,
and minutely described to the bystanders, during
the continuance of the vision. The husband re-
turned, and previous to the meeting, was advised to
appear for the first time at the foot of the bed, at
the precise instant that the spirit used to appear,

and in the dress described, in the hope that the
original might scare away the counterfeit; or, to
speak more seriously, in the expectation that the
impression on her senses from without would meet
half-way, as it were, and repel, or take the place of,
the image from the brain. He followed the advice;
but the moment he took his position, the lady
shrieked out, " My God! there are *two!* and"—
The story is an old one, and you may end it, happily or tragically, Tate's King Lear or Shakespeare's, according to your taste.   I have brought
it as a good instance of the force of the two words.
You and I would hold the one for a *subjective* phenomenon, the other only for *objective*, and perhaps
illustrate the fact, as I have already done elsewhere, by the case of two appearances seen in
juxta-position, the one by transmitted, and the other
by reflected, light.   A believer, according to the
old style, whose almanack of faith has the one
trifling fault of being for the year of our Lord one
thousand *four*, instead of one thousand *eight* hundred and twenty, would stickle for the *objectivity*
of both.*

---

* Nay, and relate the circumstance for the very purpose
of proving the reality or objective truth of ghosts.   For the
lady saw *both!* But if this were any proof at all, it would at
best be a superfluous proof, and superseded by the bed-posts,
&c. For if she saw the real posts at the same time with the
ghost, that stood betwixt them, or rather if she continued
to see the ghost, spite of the sight of these, how should she

Andrew Baxter, again, would take a different road from either.   He would agree with us in calling the apparition *subjective*, and the figure of the husband *objective*, so far as the *ubi* of the latter, and its position *extra cerebrum*, or in outward spaces, was in question.   But he would differ from us in *not* identifying the agent or proper cause of

---

not see the *real* husband ? What was to make the difference, between the two solids, or intercept the rays from the husband's dressing-gown, while it allowed free passage to those from the bed-curtain ? And yet I first heard this story from one, who, though professedly an unbeliever in this branch of *ancient Pneumatics*, (which stood, however, a niche higher, I suspect, in his good opinion, than Monboddo's *Ancient Metaphysics*,) adduced it as a *something on the other side!*— A puzzling fact ! and challenged me to answer it. And this too, was a man no less respectable for talents, education, and active sound sense, than for birth, fortune, and official rank.   So strangely are the healthiest judgments suspended by any out-of the way combinations, connected with obscure feelings and inferences, when they happen to have occurred within the narrator's own knowledge !—The pith of this argument in support of *ghost*-objects, stands thus : $B = D$: $C = D$: *ergo*, $B = C$.   The D, in this instance, being the equal *visibility* of the figure, and of its *real* duplicate, a logic that would entitle the logician to dine off a neck of mutton in a looking-glass, and to set his little ones in downright earnest to hunt *the rabbits* on the wall by candle-light. Things, that fall under the same definition, belong to the same class ; and visible, yet not tangible, is the generic character of reflections, shadows, and ghosts ; and apparitions, their common, and most certainly their proper, *Christian* name.

the former—*i. e.* the apparition—with the subject
beholding. The shape beheld he would grant to be
a making in the beholder's own brain; but the
facient, he would contend, was a several and *other*
subject, an intrusive supernumerary or *squatter* in
the same tenement and work-shop, and working
with the same tools (ὄργανα,) as the *subject,* their
rightful owner and original occupant. And verily,
I could say something in favour of this theory, if
only I might put my own interpretation on it—
having been hugely pleased with the notion of that
father of oddities, and oddest of the fathers, old
TERTULLIAN, who considers these *soggetti cattivi,*
(that take possession of other folk's kitchens, pan-
tries, sculleries, and water-closets, causing a sad
to-do at *head* quarters,) as creatures of the same
order with the Tæniæ, Lumbrici, and Ascarides—
i. e. the Round, Tape, and Thread-worms.   Dæ-
mones hæc sua corpora dilatant et contrahunt ut
volunt, sicut *Lumbrici et alia quædam insecta.* Be
this as it may, the difference between this last class
of speculators and the common run of ghost-fanci-
ers, will scarcely enable us to exhibit any essential
change in the meaning of the terms.   Both must
be described as asserting the *objective* nature of the
appearance, and in both the term contains the sense
of real as opposed to imaginary, and of *out*ness no
less than of *other*ness, the difference in the former
being only, that, in the vulgar belief, the object is
outward in relation to the whole circle, in Baxter's

to the centre only. The one places the ghost without, the other within, the line of circumference.

I have only to add, that these different shades of meaning form no valid objection to the revival and readoption of these correlative terms in physiology* and mental analytics, as expressing the two poles of all consciousness, in their most general form and highest abstraction. For by the law of association, the same metaphorical changes, or shiftings and ingraftings of the primary sense, must inevitably take place in all terms of greatest comprehensiveness and simplicity. Instead of subject and object, put thought and thing. You will find these liable to the same inconveniences, with the additional one of having no adjectives or adverbs, as substitutes for objective, subjective, objectively, subjectively. It is sufficient that no heterogeneous senses are confounded under the same term, as was the case prior to Bishop Bramhall's controversy with Hobbes, who had availed himself of the (at that time, and in the common usage,) equivalent words, *compel* and oblige, to confound the *thought* of moral obligation with that of compulsion and physical

---

* " Physiology," according to present usage, treats of the laws, organs, functions, &c. of life; " Physics" not so. Now, *quære*: The etymological import of the two words being the same, is the difference in their application accidental and arbitrary, or a hidden irony at the assumption on which the division is grounded? φύσις ἄνευ ζωῆς ἄνευ λόγυ, or Λόγος περὶ φύσεως μὴ ζώσης ἐστὶ λόγος ἄλογος.

necessity. For the rest, the remedy must be provided by a dictionary, constructed on the one only
philosophical principle, which, regarding words as
living growths, offsets, and organs of the human
soul, seeks to trace each historically, through all the
periods of its natural growth, and accidental modifications—a work worthy of a Royal and Imperial
confederacy, and which would indeed *hallow* the
Alliance! A work which, executed for any one
language, would yet be a benefaction to the world,
and to the nation itself a source of immediate honour and of ultimate *weal*, beyond the power of
victories to bestow, or the mines of Mexico to purchase. The realization of this scheme lies in the
far distance; but in the mean time, it cannot but
beseem every individual competent to its further-
ance, to contribute a small portion of the materials
for the future temple—from a polished column to
a hewn stone, or a plank for the scaffolding; and
as they come in, to erect with them sheds for the
workmen, and temporary structures for present use.
The preceding analysis I would have you regard
as my *first* contribution; and the first, because I
have been long convinced that the want of it is a
serious impediment—I will not say, to that self-
knowledge which it concerns all men to attain, but
—to that self-*understanding*, or *insight*, which it
is all men's interest that *some* men should acquire;
that " the heaven-descended, Γνῶθι Σεαυτόν," (Juv.
Sat.) should exist not only as *a wisdom*, but as *a*

science. But every science will have its rules of
art, and with these its technical terms; and in this
best of sciences, its elder nomenclature has fallen
into disuse, and no other been put in its place.
To bring these back into light, as so many delving-
tools dug up from the rubbish of long-deserted
mines, and at the same time to exemplify their use
and handling, I have drawn your attention to the
three questions :—What is the primary and proper
sense of the words Subject and Object, in the technical language of philosophy? In what does *Objectivity* actually exist?—From what is all apparent
or assumed Objectivity derived or transferred?

It is not the age, you have told me, to bring hard
words into fashion.   Are we to account for this
tender-mouthedness on the ground assigned by
your favourite, Persius : (Sat. iii. 113.)

> " Tentemus fauces : tenero latet ulcus in ore
> Putre, quod haud deceat crustosis radere verbis ?"

But is the age so averse to hard words ? Eidoura-
nion; Phantasmagoria; Kaleidoscope ; Marmoro-
kainomenon *(for cleaning mantle-pieces)*; Protox-
ides; Deutoxides; Tritoxides ; and Dr. Thomson's
Latin-greek-english Peroxides ; not to mention the
splashing shoals, that

> "——confound the language of the nation
> With long-tail'd words in *osity* and *ation,*"

(as our great living master of sweet and perfect
English, Hookham Frere, has it,) would seem to

argue the very contrary. In the train of these, methinks, object and subject, with the derivatives, look tame, and claim a place in the last, or, at most, in the humbler seats of the second species, in the *far-noised* classification—the long-tailed pigs, and the short-tailed pigs, and the pigs without a tail. *Aye, but not on such dry topics!*—I submit. You have touched the vulnerable heel—" *Iis, quibus siccum lumen abest,*" they must needs be *dry*. We have Lord Bacon's word for it. A topic that requires stedfast intuitions, clear conceptions, and ideas, as the source and substance of both, and that will admit of no substitute for these, in images, fictions, or factitious facts, must be *dry* as the broad-awake of sight and day-light, and desperately barren of all *that* interest which a busy yet sensual age requires and finds in the " *uda somnia,*" and moist moonshine of an epicurean philosophy. For you, however, and for those who, like you, are not so satisfied with the present doctrines, but that you would fain try " another and an elder lore," (and such there are, I know, and that the number is on the increase,) I hazard this assurance, —That let what will come of the terms, yet without the *truths* conveyed in these terms, there can be no self-knowledge ; and without THIS, no knowledge, of any kind. For the fragmentary recollections and recognitions of empiricism,* usurping the

---

* Let *y* express the *conditions* under which E, (that is, a

name of experience, can amount to opinion only, and that alone is knowledge which is at once real and systematic—or, in one word, *organic.* Let monk and pietist pervert the precept into sickly, brooding, and morbid introversions of consciousness —you have learnt, that, even under the wisest regulations, THINKING can go but *half* way toward this knowledge. To know the *whole* truth, we must likewise ACT: and he alone acts, who *makes* —and this can no man do, estranged from Nature. Learn to know thyself in Nature, that thou mayest understand Nature in thyself.

But I forget myself. My pledge and purpose was to help you over the threshold into the outer court; and here I stand, spelling the dim characters inwoven in the veil of Isis, in the recesses of the temple.

I must conclude, therefore, if only to begin again without too abrupt a *drop*, lest I should remind you of Mr—— in his Survey of Middlesex, who having digressed, for some half a score of pages, into the heights of cosmogony, the old planet between Jupiter and Mars, that *went off*, and split into the four new ones, besides the smaller rubbish for stone showers, the formation of the galaxy, and the other

series of forms, facts, circumstances, &c. presented to the senses of an individual,) will become Experience—and we might, not unaptly, define the two words thus: $E + y = $ Experience; $E - y = $ Empiricism.

world-worlds, on the same *principles*, and by similar accidents, superseding the *hypothesis* of a Creator, and demonstrating the superfluity of *church* tithes and country parsons, takes up the stitch again with—*But to return to the subject of dung*. God bless you and your

Affectionate Friend,

S. T. COLERIDGE.

LETTER III. *To Mr. Blackwood.*

DEAR SIR,—Here have I been sitting, this whole long-lagging, *muzzy*, mizly morning, struggling without success against the insuperable disgust I feel to the task of explaining the abrupt chasm at the outset of our correspondence, and disposed to let your verdict take its course, rather than suffer over again by detailing the causes of the stoppage; though sure by so doing to acquit *my will* of all share in the result. Instead of myself, and of *you*, my dear sir, in relation to myself, I have been thinking, first, of the Edinburgh Magazine; then of the magazines generally and comparatively;— then of a magazine in the abstract; and lastly, of the immense importance and yet strange neglect of that prime dictate of prudence and common sense —DISTINCT MEANS TO DISTINCT ENDS.—But here I must put in one proviso, not in any relation

though to the aphorism itself, which is of universal
validity, but relatively to my intended application
of it. I must assume—I mean, that the individuals
disposed to grant me free access and fair audience
for my remarks, have *a conscience*—such a portion
at least, as being eked out with superstition and
sense of character, will suffice to prevent them from
seeking to realize the *ultimate* end, (i. e. the maxim
of profit) by base or disreputable means. This,
therefore, may be left out of the present argument,
an extensive sale being the common object of all pub-
lishers, of whatever kind the publications may be,
morally considered. Nor do the means appropriate
to this end differ. Be the work good or evil in its
tendency, in both cases alike there is one question
to be predetermined, viz. what class or classes of the
reading world the work is intended for? I made the
proviso, however, because I would not mislead any
man even for an honest cause, and my experience
will not allow me to promise an equal immediate
circulation from a work addressed to the higher interests and blameless predilections of men, as from
one constructed on the plan of flattering the envy
and vanity of sciolism, and gratifying the cravings
of vulgar curiosity. Such may be, and in some instances, I doubt not, has been, the result. But I
dare not answer for it beforehand, even though both
works should be equally well suited to their several
purposes, which will not be thought a probable case,
when it is considered, how much less talent, and of

how much commoner kind, is required in the latter.

On the other hand, however, I am persuaded that a sufficient success, and less liable to draw-backs from competition, would not fail to attend a work on the former plan, if the scheme and execution of the contents were as appropriate to the object, which the purchasers must be supposed to have in view, as the means adopted for its outward attraction and its general circulation were to the interest of its proprietors.

During a long literary life, I have been no inattentive observer of periodical publications; and I can remember no failure, in any work deserving success, that might not have been anticipated from some error or deficiency in the means, either in regard to the mode of circulating the work, (as for instance by the vain attempt to unite the characters of author, editor, and publisher,) or to the typographical appearance; or else from its want of suitableness to the class of readers, on whom, it should have been foreseen, the remunerating sale must principally depend. It would be misanthropy to suppose that the seekers after truth, information, and innocent amusement, are not sufficiently numerous to support a work, in which these attractions are prominent, without the dishonest aid of personality, literary faction, or treacherous invasions of the sacred recesses of private life, without slanders, which both reason and duty command us to *disbelieve* as well as abhor; for what but falsehood, or that half truth, which is falsehood in its most malignant form, can or ought to be expected from a self-convicted traitor and ingrate?

If these remarks are well founded, we may narrow the problem to the few following terms,—it being understood, that the work now in question, is a monthly publication, not devoted to any *one* branch of knowledge or literature, but a magazine of whatever may be supposed to interest readers in general, not excluding the discoveries, or even the speculations of science, that are generally intelligible and interesting, so that the portion devoted to any one subject or department, shall be kept proportionate to the number of readers for whom it may be supposed to have a *particular* interest. Here, however, we must not forget, that however few the actual *dilettanti*, or men of the fancy may be, yet, as long as the articles remain generally intelligible, (in *pugilism*, for instance,) Variety and Novelty communicate attraction that interests all. *Homo sum, nihil humani a me alienum.* If to this we add the exclusion of theological controversy, which is endless, I shall have pretty accurately described the EDINBURGH MAGAZINE, as to its characteristic plan and purposes; which may, I think, be comprised in three terms, as a Philosophical, Philological, and *Æsthetic Miscellany. The word miscella-

---

* I wish I could find a more familiar word than æsthetic, for works of taste and criticism. It is, however, in all respects better, and of more reputable origin, than belletristic.

ny however, must be taken as involving a predicate in itself, in addition to the three preceding epithets, comprehending, namely, all the ephemeral births of intellectual life, which add to the gaiety and variety of the work, without interfering with its express and regular objects.

<hr />

To be sure, there is *tasty;* but that has been long ago emasculated for all unworthy uses by milliners, tailors, and the androgynous correlatives of both, formerly called *its,* and now yclept dandies. As our language, therefore, contains no other *useable* adjective, to express that coincidence of form, feeling, and intellect, that something, which, confirming the inner and outward senses, becomes a new sense in itself, to be tried by laws of its own, and acknowledging the laws of the understanding so far only as not to contradict them ; that faculty which, when possessed in a high degree, the Greeks termed φιλοκαλία but when spoken of generally, or in kind only, τὸ αἰσθητικόν ; and for which even our substantive, Taste, is a—not inappropriate—but very inadequate metaphor ; there is reason to hope, that the term *æsthetic,* will be brought into common use as soon as distinct thoughts and definite expressions shall once more become the requisite accomplishment of a gentleman. So it was in the energetic days, and in the starry court of our *English*-hearted Eliza ; when trade, the nurse of freedom, was the enlivening counterpoise of agriculture, not its alien and usurping spirit ; when commerce had all the enterprize, and more than the romance of war ; when the precise yet pregnant terminology of the schools gave bone and muscle to the diction of poetry and eloquence, and received from them in return passion and harmony ; but, above all, when from the self-evident truth, that what *in kind* constitutes the superiority of man to animal, the same *in degree* must constitute the superiority of men to each other, the practical inference was drawn,

Having thus a sufficiently definite notion of what your Magazine is, and is intended to be, I proposed to myself, as a problem, to find out, *in detail*, what the *means* would be to the most perfect attainment of this end. In other words, what the *scheme*, and of what nature, and in what order and proportion, the *contents* should be of a monthly publication ; in order for it to verify the title of a Philosophical, Philological, and Æsthetic Miscellany and Magazine. The result of my lucubrations I hope to forward in my next, under the title of " The Ideal of a Magazine ;" and to mark those departments, in the filling up of which, I flatter myself with the prospect of being a fellow labourer. But since I began this scrawl, a friend reminded me of a letter

---

that every proof of these distinctive faculties being in a *tense* and *active* state, that even the sparks and crackling of mental electricity, in the sportive approaches and collisions of ordinary intercourse, (such as we have in the wit-combats of Benedict and Beatrice, of Mercutio, and in the dialogues assigned to courtiers and gentlemen, by all the dramatic writers of that reign,) are stronger indications of natural superiority, and, therefore, more becoming signs and accompaniments of *artificial* rank, than apathy, studied mediocrity, and the ostentation of wealth. When I think of the vigour and felicity of style characteristic of the age, from Edward VI. to the restoration of Charles, and observable in the letters and family memoirs of noble families—take, for instance, the life of Colonel Hutchinson, written by his widow—I cannot suppress the wish—O that the *habits* of those days could return, even though they should bring pedantry and Euphuism in their train !

I wrote him many years ago, on the improvement
of the mind, by the habit of commencing our in-
quiries with the attempt to construct the most absolute or perfect form of the object desiderated,
leaving its practicability, in the first instance, unde-
termined. An essay, in short, *de emendatione intel-
lectûs per ideas*—the beneficial influence of which,
on his mind, he spoke of with warmth. The main
contents of the letter, the effect of which, my friend
appreciated so highly, were derived from conversation with a great man, now no more. And as I
have reason to regard that conversation as an epoch
in the history of my own mind, I feel myself encouraged to hope that its publication may not prove
useless to some of your numerous readers, to whom
Nature has given the stream, and nothing is wanting but to be led in the right channel. There is
one other motive to which I must plead conscious,
not only in the following, but in all of these, my
preliminary contributions; viz. That by the reader's agreement with the principles, and sympathy
with the general feelings, which they are meant to
impress, the interest of my future contributions, and
still more, their permanent effect, will be heightened;
and most so in those, in which, as narrative and
imaginative compositions, there is the least shew of
reflection, on my part, and the least necessity for it,
—though I flatter myself not the least opportunity
on the part of my readers.

It will be better too, if I mistake not, both for

your purposes and mine, to have it said hereafter, that he dragged slow and stiff-knee'd up the first hill, but sprang forward as soon as the road was full before him, and *got in* fresh; than that he set off in grand style—broke up midway, and came in broken-winded. *Finis coronat opus.*

Your's, &c.

S. T. COLERIDGE.

LETTER IV.

To a Junior Soph, at Cambridge.

OFTEN, my dear young friend! often, and bitterly, do I regret the stupid prejudice that made me neglect my mathematical studies at Jesus. There is something to me enigmatically attractive and imaginative in the generation of curves, and in the whole geometry of motion. I seldom look at a fine prospect or mountain landscape, or even at a grand picture, without abstracting the lines with a feeling similar to that with which I should contemplate the graven or painted walls of some temple or palace in Mid Africa,—doubtful whether it were mere Arabesque, or undeciphered characters of an unknown tongue, framed when the language of men was nearer to that of nature—a language of symbols and correspondences. I am, therefore, far more disposed to envy, than join in the laugh against your fellow-collegiate, for amusing himself in the geometrical construction of leaves and flowers.

Since the receipt of your last, I never take a turn round the garden without thinking of his billow-lines and shell-lines, under the well-sounding names of Cumäids and Conchoids; they have as much life and poetry for me, as their elder sisters, the Naiads, Nereids, and Hama-dryads. I pray you, present my best respects to him, and tell him, that he brought to my recollection the glorious passage in Plotinus, " Should any one interrogate Nature *how* she works? if graciously she vouchsafe to answer, she will say, It behoves thee to understand me (*or better, and more literally*, to go along with me) in silence, even as I am silent, and work without words;"—but you have a Plotinus, and may construe it for yourself.—(Ennead 3. 1. 8. c. 3.) attending particularly to the comparison of the process pursued by Nature, with that of the geometrician. And now for your questions respecting the moral influence of W.'s minor poems. Of course, this will be greatly modified by the character of the recipient. But that in the majority of instances it has been most salutary, I cannot for a moment doubt. But it is another question, whether verse is the best way of disciplining the mind to that spiritual alchemy, which communicates a sterling value to real or apparent trifles, by using them as moral diagrams, as your friend uses the oak and fig-leaves

as geometrical ones. To have formed the habit of
looking at every thing, not for what it is relative to
the purposes and associations of men in general, but
for the truths which it is suited to represent—to contemplate objects as *words* and pregnant symbols—
the advantages of this, my dear D., are so many,
and so important, so eminently calculated to excite and evolve the power of sound and connected
reasoning, of distinct and clear conception, and of
genial feeling, that there were few of W.'s finest
passages—and who, of living poets, can lay claim to
half the number?—that I repeat so often, as that
homely quatrain,

> O reader! had you in your mind
> Such stores as silent thought can bring;
> O gentle reader! you would find
> A tale in every thing.

You did not know my revered friend and patron;
or rather, you do know the man, and mourn his
loss, from the character I have* lately given of him.
— The following supposed dialogue actually took
place, in a conversation with him; and as in part,
an illustration of what I have already said, and in
part as text and introduction to much I would wish
to say, I entreat you to read it with patience, spite

---

* In the 8th Number of the Friend, as first circulated by
the post. 1 dare assert, that it is worthy of preservation,
and will send a transcript in my next.

of the triviality of the subject, and mock-heroic of
the title.

SUBSTANCE OF A DIALOGUE, WITH A COMMENTARY ON THE SAME.

A. I never found yet, an ink-stand that I was
satisfied with.

B. What would you have an ink-stand to be?
What qualities and properties would you wish to
have combined in an ink-stand? Reflect! Consult
your past experience; taking care, however, not to
desire things demonstrably, or self-evidently incompatible with each other; and the union of these *de-
siderata* will be *your ideal* of an ink-stand. A
friend, perhaps, suggests some additional excellence
that might rationally be desired, till at length the
catalogue may be considered as complete, when
neither yourself, nor others, can think of any *desideratum* not anticipated or precluded by some one
or more of the points already enumerated; and the
conception of all these, as realized in one and the
same artefact, may be fairly entitled, the

IDEAL *of an Ink-stand.*

That the pen should be allowed, without re-
quiring any effort or interruptive act of attention
from the writer, to dip sufficiently low, and yet be
prevented, without injuring its nib, from dipping

too low, or taking up too much ink: that the ink-stand should be of such materials as not to decompose the ink, or occasion a deposition or discolouration of its specific ingredients, as, from what cause I know not, is the fault of the black Wedgewood-ware ink-stands; that it should be so constructed, that on being overturned, the ink cannot escape; and so protected, or made of such stuff, that in case of a blow or a fall from any common height, the ink-stand itself will not be broken;—that from both these qualities, and from its shape, it may be safely and commodiously travelled with, and packed up with books, linen, or whatever else is likely to form the contents of the portmanteau, or travelling trunk; —that it should stand steadily and commodiously, and be of as pleasing a shape and appearance as is compatible with its more important uses; — and, lastly, though of minor regard, and non-essential, that it be capable of including other implements or requisites, always, or occasionally connected with the art of writing, as pen-knife, wafers, &c. without any addition to the size and weight, otherwise desirable, and without detriment to its more important and *proper* advantages.

Now, (continued B.) that we have an adequate notion of what is to be wished, let us try what is to be done! And my friend actually succeeded in constructing an ink-stand, in which, during the twelve years that have elapsed since this conversation, alas! I might almost say since his death, I have never been able, though I have put my wits on the stretch, to detect any thing wanting that an ink-stand could be rationally desired to possess; or even to imagine any addition, detraction, or change, for use or appearance, that I could desire, without involving a contradiction.

HERE! (methinks I hear the reader exclaim) Here's a meditation on a broom-stick with a vengeance! Now, in the first place, I am, and I do not care who knows it, no enemy to meditations on broom-sticks; and though Boyle had been the real author of the article so waggishly passed off for his on poor Lady Berkley; and though that good man had written it in grave good earnest, I am not certain that he would not have been employing his time as creditably to himself, and as profitably for a large class of readers, as the witty dean was while composing the Draper's Letters, though the muses forbid that I should say the same of Mary Cooke's Petition, Hamilton's Bawn, or even the rhyming correspondence with Dr. Sheridan. In hazarding this confession, however, I beg leave to put in a *provided always*, that the said Meditation on Broom-stick, or *aliud quidlibet ejusdem farinæ*, shall be as truly a meditation as the broom-stick is verily a broom-stick—and that the name be not a misnomer of vanity, or fraudulently labelled on a mere compound of brain-dribble and printer's ink. For meditation, I presume, is that act of the mind, by which it seeks *within* either the *law* of the phenomena, which it had *contemplated* without, *(me-ditatio scientifica,)* or semblances, symbols, -and analogies, corresponsive to the same, *(meditatio ethica.)*   At all events, therefore, it implies *think-ing*, and tends to make the reader *think ;* and what-ever does this, does what in the present over-ex-cited state of society is most wanted, though perhaps least desired.   Between the *thinking* of a Harvey or Quarles, and the thinking of a Bacon or a Fene-lon, many are the degrees of difference, and many the differences in degree of depth and originality : but not such as to fill up the chasm *in genere* be-tween thinking and no-thinking, or to render the discrimination difficult for a man of ordinary un-derstanding, not under the same * contagion of vanity as the writer.   Besides, there are shallows for the full-grown, that are the maximum of safe depth for the younglings.   There are truths, quite *common-place* to you and me, that for the unin-structed many would be new and full of wonder, as the common day-light to the Lapland child at the re-ascension of its second summer.   Thanks and honour in the highest to those stars of the first magnitude that shoot their beams downward, and

---

* " Verily, to ask, what meaneth this ? is no Herculean labour.   And the reader languishes under the same vain-glory as his author, and hath laid his head on the other knee of Omphale, if he can mistake the thin vocables of incogi-tance for the consubstantial words which thought begetteth and goeth forth in."—*Sir T. Brown, MSS.*

while in their proper form they stir and invirtuate
the sphere next below them, and natures pre-assi-
milated to their influence, yet call forth likewise,
each after its own *form* or model, whatever is best
in whatever is susceptible to each, even in the lowest.   But, excepting these, I confess that I seldom
look at Harvey's Meditations, or Quarles' Emblems,* without feeling that I would rather be the
author of those books — of the innocent pleasure,
the purifying emotions, and genial awakenings of
the *humanity* through the whole man, which those
books have given to thousands and tens of thousands—than shine the brightest in the constellation
of fame among the heroes and *Dii minores* of literature.   But I have a better excuse, and if not a
better, yet a less general motive, for this solemn
trifling, as it will seem, and one that will, I trust
rescue my ideal of an ink-stand from being doomed

---

* A full collection, a *Bibliotheca Specialis*, of the books
of emblems and symbols, of all sects and parties, moral, theological, or political, including those in the Centenaries and
Jubilee volumes published by the Jesuit and other religious
orders, is a *desideratum* in our library literature that would
well employ the talents of our ingenious masters in wood-en-
graving, etching, and lithography, under the superintendence
of a Dibdin, and not unworthy of royal and noble patronage,
or the attention of a Longman and his compeers. Singly or
jointly undertaken, it would do honour to these princely
merchants in the service of the muses. What stores might
not a Southey contribute as notes or interspersed prefaces ?
I could dream away an hour on the subject.

to the same slut's corner with the *de tribus Capel-
lis*, or *de umbra asini*, by virtue of the process
which it exemplifies; though I should not quarrel
with the allotment, if its risible merits allowed it to
keep company with the ideal immortalized by Rabelais in his disquisition inquisitory *De Rebus op-
time abstergentibus.*

Dared I mention the name of *my Idealizer,* a
name dear to science, and consecrated by discoveries of far-extending utility, it would at least give a
biographical interest to this trifling anecdote, and
perhaps entitle me to claim for it a yet higher, as
a trait *in minimis,* characteristic of a class of powerful and most beneficent intellects.   For to the
same process of thought we owe whatever instruments of power have been bestowed on mankind by
science and genius; and only such deserve the
name of inventions or discoveries.   But even in
those, which chance may seem to claim, " *quæ ho-
mini obvenisse* videantur potius quam homo *venire
in* ea"—which come to us rather than we to them
—this process will *most* often be found as the indispensable *antecedent* of the discovery—as the
condition, without which the suggesting accident
would have whispered to deaf ears, unnoticed; or,
like the faces in the fire, or the landscapes made
by damp on a white-washed wall, noticed for their
oddity alone.   To the birth of the tree a prepared
soil is as necessary as the falling seed.   A Daniel
was present; or the fatal characters in the ban-

quet-hall of Belshazzar might have struck more
terror, but would have been of no more import than
the trail of a luminous worm. · In the far greater
number, indeed, of these asserted boons of chance,
it is the accident that should be called the *condition*
—and often not so much, but merely the *occasion*
—while the proper cause of the invention is to be
sought for in the co-existing state and previous
habit of the observer's mind.   I cannot bring myself to account for *respiration* from the stimulus
of the *air*, without ascribing to the specific stimula-
bility of the lungs a yet more important part in the
joint product.   To how many myriads of individuals had not the rise and fall of the lid in a boiling
kettle been familiar, an appearance daily and hourly
in sight ? But it was reserved for a mind that understood what was to be wished and knew what
was wanted in order to its fulfilment—for an *armed*
eye, which meditation had made contemplative, an
eye armed from within, with an instrument of
higher powers than glasses can give, with the logic
of method, the only true *Organum Flevristicum*
which possesses the former and better half of knowledge in itself as the science of wise questioning,*
and the other half in reversion,—it was reserved for
the Marquis of Worcester to see and have given

---

* " Prudens quæstio dimidium scientiæ," says our Verulam,
the second founder of the science, and the first who *on principle* applied it to the *ideas* in nature, as his great compeer
Plato had before done to the *laws* in the mind.

into his hands, from the alternation of expansion
and vacuity, a power mightier than that of Vulcan
and all his Cyclops : a power that found its practical limit only where nature could supply no limit
strong enough to confine it.   For the genial spirit,
that *saw* what it had been *seeking*, and saw *because*
it sought, was it reserved in the dancing lid of a
kettle or coffee-urn, to behold the future *steam-en-
gine*, the Talus, with whom the Britomart of science is now gone forth to subdue and *humanize* the
planet! When the bodily organ, steadying itself on
some chance thing, imitates, as it were, the fixture
of " the inward eye" on its ideal shapings, then it
is that Nature not seldom reveals her close affinity
with mind, with that more than man which is one
and the same in all men, and from which

> " the soul receives
> Reason : and reason is her *being!*"
>> *Par. Lost.*

Then it is, that Nature, like an individual spirit
or fellow soul, seems to think and hold commune
with us.   If, in the present contempt of all mental
analysis not contained in Locke, Hartley, or Con-
dillac, it were safe to borrow from " scholastic
lore" a technical term or two, for which I have not
yet found any substitute equally convenient and
serviceable, I should say, that at such moments
Nature, as another *subject* veiled behind the visible
object without us, solicits the intelligible object hid,
and yet struggling beneath the subject within us,

and like a helping Lucina, brings it forth for us into distinct consciousness and common light. Who has not tried to get hold of some half-remembered name, mislaid as it were in the memory, and yet felt to be there? And who has not experienced, how at length it seems *given* to us, as if some other unperceived had been employed in the same search? And what are the objects last spoken of, which are *in* the subject, (*i. e.* the individual mind) yet not *subjective*, but of universal validity, no *accidents* of a particular mind resulting from its individual structure, no, nor even of the *human* mind, as a particular class or rank of intelligencies, but of imperishable subsistence; and though not *things*, (*i. e.* shapes in outward space,) yet equally independent of the beholder, and more than equally real—what, I say, are those but the *names* of nature? the *nomina quasi νόυμενα,* opposed by the wisest of the Greek schools to *phænomena,* as the intelligible correspondents or correlatives in the mind to the invisible supporters of the appearances in the world of the senses, the upholding powers that cannot be seen, but the presence and actual being of which must be supposed—nay, *will be* supposed, in defiance of every attempt to the contrary by a crude materialism, so alien from humanity, that there does not exist a language on earth, in which it could be conveyed without a contradiction between the sense, and the words employed to express it!

Is this a mere random flight in etymology, hunt-

ing a bubble, and bringing back the film? I cannot
think so contemptuously of the attempt to fix and
restore the true import of *any* word; but, in this
instance, I should regard it as neither unprofitable,
nor devoid of rational interest, were it only that the
knowledge and reception of the import here given,
as the etymon, or *genuine* sense of the word, would
save Christianity from the reproach of containing
a doctrine so repugnant to the best feelings of humanity, as is inculcated in the following passage,
among a hundred others to the same purpose, in
earlier, and in more recent works, sent forth by
professed Christians. " Most of the men, who are
now alive, or that have been living for many ages,
are Jews, Heathens, or Mahometans, strangers and
enemies to Christ, in whose *name* alone we can be
saved.   This consideration is extremely sad, when
we remember how great an evil it is, that *so many
millions of sons and daughters are born to enter
into the possession of devils to eternal ages."—*
Taylor's Holy Dying, p. 28. Even Sir T. Brown,
while his heart is evidently wrestling with the
dogma grounded on the trivial interpretation of the
word, nevertheless receives it in this sense, and
expresses most gloomy apprehensions " of the ends
of those honest worthies and philosophers," who
died before the birth of our Saviour: " It is hard,"
says he, " to place those souls in hell, whose worthy
lives did teach us virtue on earth. How strange to
them will sound the history of Adam, when they

shall suffer for him they never heard of!"   Yet he concludes by condemning the insolence of reason in daring to doubt or controvert the verity of the doctrine, or " to question the justice of the proceeding," *which verity,* he fears, the woeful lot of " *these great examples of virtue must confirm.*"

But here I must break off.

Your's most affectionately,

S. T. COLERIDGE.

LETTER V.
To the Same.

MY DEAR D.—The philosophic poet, whom I quoted in my last, may here and there have stretched his prerogative in a war of offence on the general associations of his contemporaries.   Here and there, though less than the least of what the Buffoons of parody, and the Zanies of anonymous criticism, would have us believe, he may be thought to betray a preference of mean or trivial instances for grand morals, a capricious predilection for incidents that contrast with the depth and novelty of the truths they are to exemplify.   But still to the principle, to the habit of tracing the presence of the high in the humble, the mysterious Dii Cabiri, in the form of the dwarf Miner, with hammer and spade, and week-day apron, we must attribute Wordsworth's *peculiar* power, his *leavening* influence on the opinions, feelings, and pursuits of his

admirers,—most on the young of most promise and
highest acquirements; and that, while others are
read with delight, his works are a *religion*. A case
still more in point occurs to me, and for the truth
of which I dare pledge myself. The art of printing
alone seems to have been privileged with a Miner-
val birth, to have risen in its zenith; but next to
this, perhaps, the rapid and almost instantaneous
advancement of pottery from the state in which Mr.
Wedgwood found the art, to its demonstrably
highest practicable perfection, is the most striking
fact in the history of modern improvements achieved
by individual genius. In his early manhood, an
obstinate and harassing complaint confined him to
his room for more than two years; and to this apparent calamity Mr. Wedgwood was wont to attribute his after unprecedented success. For a while,
as was natural, the sense of thus losing the prime
and vigour of his life and faculties, preyed on his
mind incessantly—aggravated, no doubt, by the
thought of what he should have been doing this
hour and this, had he not been thus severely visited.
Then, what he should like to take in hand: and
lastly, what it was desirable to do, and how far it
might be done, till generalizing more and more, the
mind began to feed on the thoughts, which, at their
first evolution, (in their *larva* state, may I say?)
had preyed on the mind. We imagine the presence
of what we desire in the very act of regretting its
absence, nay, *in order* to regret it the more live-

lily; but while, with a strange wilfulness, we are
thus engendering grief on grief, nature makes use
of the product to cheat us into comfort and exertion.   The positive shapings, though but of the
fancy, will sooner or later displace the mere knowledge of the negative.   All activity is in itself
pleasure; and according to the nature, powers, and
previous habits of the sufferer, the activity of the
fancy will call the other faculties of the soul into
action.   The self-contemplative power becomes
meditative, and the mind begins to play the geometrician with its own thoughts—abstracting from
them the accidental and individual, till a new and
unfailing source of employment, the best and surest
nepenthe of solitary pain, is opened out in the habit of seeking the principle and ultimate aim in the
most imperfect productions of art, in the least attractive products of nature; of beholding the possible in the real; of detecting the essential form in the
intentional; above all, in the collation and construc-
tive imagining of the outward shapes and material
forces that shall best express the essential form, in
its coincidence with the idea, or realize most adequately that power, which is one with its correspondent knowledge, as the revealing body with its
indwelling soul.

Another motive will present itself, and one that
comes nearer home, and is of more general application, if we reflect on the habit here recommended,
as a source of support and consolation in circum-

stances under which we might otherwise sink back
on ourselves, and for want of colloquy with our
thoughts, with the objects and presentations of the
inner sense, lie listening to the fretful *ticking* of
our sensations. A resource of costless value has
that man, who has brought himself to a habit of
measuring the objects around him by their intended
or possible ends, and the proportion in which this
end is realized in each. It is the neglect of thus
educating the senses, of thus disciplining, and, in
the proper and primitive sense of the word, *informing* the fancy, that distinguishes at first sight
the ruder states of society. Every mechanic tool,
the commonest and most indispensable implements
of agriculture, might remind one of the school-boy's
second stage in metrical composition, in which his
exercise is to contain *sense*, but he is allowed to
eke out the scanning by the interposition, here and
there, of an equal quantity of nonsense. And even
in the existing height of national civilization, how
many individuals may there not be found, for
whose senses the non-essential so preponderates,
that though they may have lived the greater part
of their lives in the country, yet, with some exceptions for the products of their own flower and
kitchen garden, all the names in the Index to
Withering's Botany, are superseded for them by
the one name, a *weed!* " *It is only a weed!* "
And if this indifference stopt here, and this particular ignorance were regarded as the *disease*, it

would be sickly to complain of it. But it is as a *symptom* that it excites regret—it is that, except only the pot-herbs of lucre, and the barren double-flowers of vanity, their own noblest faculties both of thought and action, are but weeds—in which, should sickness or misfortune wreck them on the desert island of their own mind, they would either not think of seeking, or be ignorant how to find, nourishment or medicine. As it is good to be provided with work for rainy days, Winter industry is the best cheerer of winter gloom, and fire-side contrivances for summer use, bring summer sunshine and a genial inner warmth, which the friendly hearth-blaze may conspire with, but cannot bestow or compensate.

A splenetic friend of mine, who was fond of *outraging* a truth by some whimsical hyperbole, in his way of expressing it, gravely gave it out as his opinion, that beauty and genius were but diseases of the consumptive and scrofulous order. He would not carry it further ; but yet, he must say, that he *had* observed that very *good* people, persons of unusual virtue and benevolence, were in general afflicted with weak or restless nerves ! After yielding him the expected laugh for the oddity of the remark, I reminded him, that if his position meant any thing, the converse must be true, and we ought to have Helens, Medicean Venuses, Shakspeares, Raphaels, Howards, Clarksons, and Wilberforces by thousands ; and the assemblies and pump-rooms

at Bath, Harrowgate, and Cheltenham, rival the *con-
versazioni* in the Elysian Fields. Since then, however, I have often recurred to the portion of truth,
that lay at the bottom of my friend's conceit. It
cannot be denied, that ill health, in a degree below
direct pain, yet distressfully affecting the sensations,
and depressing the animal spirits, and thus leaving
the nervous system too sensitive to pass into the
ordinary state of feeling, and forcing us to live in
alternating *positives*, is * a hot-bed for whatever
germs, and tendencies, whether in head or heart,
have been planted there independently.

Surely, there is nothing fanciful in considering
this as a providential provision, and as one of the

---

* Perhaps it confirms while it limits this theory, that it
is chiefly verified in men whose genius and pursuits are eminently *subjective,* where the mind is intensely watchful of its
own acts and shapings, thinks, while it feels, in order to understand, and then to *generalize* that feeling ; above all,
where all the powers of the mind are called into action, simultaneously, and yet severally, while in men of equal, and
perhaps deservedly equal celebrity, whose pursuits are objective and universal, demanding the energies of attention
and abstraction, as in mechanics, mathematics, and all departments of physics and physiology, the very contrary would
seem to be exemplified. Shakspeare died at 52, and probably
of a decline ; and in one of his sonnets he speaks of himself
as grey and prematurely old ; and Milton, who suffered from
infancy those intense head-aches which ended in blindness,
insinuates that he was free from pain, or the anticipation of
pain. On the other hand, the Newtons and Leibnitzes have,
in general, been not only long-lived, but men of robust health.

countless proofs, that we are most benignly, as well
as wonderfully, constructed! The cutting and irritating grain of sand, which by accident or incaution
has got within the shell, incites the living inmate to
secrete from its own resources the means of coating
the intrusive substance. And is it not, or may it
not be, even so, with the irregularities and uneven-
nesses of health and fortune in our own case? We,
too, may turn diseases into pearls. The means and
materials are within ourselves; and the process is
easily understood. By a law common to all animal
life, we are incapable of attending for any continuance to an object, the parts of which are indistinguishable from each other, or to a series, where
the successive links are only numerically different.
Nay, the more broken and irritating, (as, for instance, the *fractious* noise of the dashing of a lake
on its border, compared with the swell of the sea on
a calm evening,) the more quickly does it exhaust
our power of noticing it. The tooth-ache, where
the suffering is not extreme, often finds its speediest
cure in the silent pillow; and gradually destroys
our attention to itself by preventing us from attending to any thing else. From the same cause, many
a lonely patient listens to his moans, till he forgets
the pain that occasioned them. The attention atten-
uates, as its sphere contracts. But this it does even
to a point, where the person's own state of feeling,
or any particular set of bodily sensations, are the
direct object. The slender thread winding in nar-

rower and narrower circles round its source and
centre, ends at length in a chrysalis, a dormitory
within which the spinner undresses himself in his
sleep, soon to come forth *quite a new creature.*

So it is in the slighter cases of suffering, where
suspension is extinction, or followed by long intervals of ease. But where the unsubdued causes are
ever on the watch to renew the pain, that thus
forces our attention in upon ourselves, the same
barrenness and monotony of the object that in
minor grievances lulled the mind into oblivion, now
goads it into action by the restlessness and natural impatience of vacancy. We cannot perhaps
divert the attention ; our feelings will still form the
main subject of our thoughts. But something is
already gained, if, instead of attending to our sensations, we begin to *think* of them. But in order
to this, we must reflect on these thoughts—or the
same *sameness* will soon sink them down into mere
feeling. And in order to sustain the act of reflection on our thoughts, we are obliged more and more
to compare and generalize them, a process that to
a certain extent implies, and in a still greater degree
excites and introduces the act and power of abstracting the thoughts and images from their original
cause, and of reflecting on them with less and less
reference to the individual suffering that had been
their first subject. The *vis medicatrix* of Nature is
at work for us in all our faculties and habits, the associate, reproductive, comparative, and combinatory.

That this source of consolation and support may be

equally in your power as in mine, but that you may never have occasion to *feel* equally grateful for it, as I have, and do in body and estate, is the fervent wish of

Your affectionate

S. T. COLERIDGE.

FROM BLACKWOOD'S EDINBURGH MAGAZINE, JAN. 1822.

Sundry
Select Chapters
From the Book of the
Two Worlds,
Translated from the Original ESOTERIC into the
Language of the
Border Land :

Comprizing the *Historie* and *Gests* of MAXILIAN, agnominated COSMENCEPHALUS and a Cousin-German of SATYRANE, the IDOLOCLAST —— a very true Novel founded on Acts, aptly divided and diversely digested into Fyttes, Flights, Stations (or Landing-places) Floors and Stories —— complete in *Numeris*, more or less.

NOTA BENE.—By default of the decypherer, we are forced to leave the blank space before " Numeris" unfilled; a part of the work, we fear, still remaining in the 𝕾𝖓𝖈𝖊𝖕𝖍𝖆𝖑𝖎𝖈 character, a sort of SANS-SCRIPT, much used, we understand, by adepts in the occult sciences, as likewise for promissory notes. We should also apologize for the indiscretion of our author in his epistolary preface (seduced by the wish of killing two birds with one stone,) in shutting up *vis a vis*, as it were, so respectable and comprehensive (not to say synodical,) a personage as THE READER with Dick Proof, corrector—of what press, we know not, unless, as we grievously suspect, he is in the employ of Messrs. Dash, Asterisk, Anon, and Company. Nor is this all; this impropriety being aggravated by sundry passages, exclusively relating and addressed to this Mr. Proof, which have an effect on the series of thoughts common to both the parties, not much unlike that, which a parenthesis or two of links, made of dandelion stems, might be supposed to produce in my Lord Mayor or Mr. Sheriff's gold chain. In one flagrant instance, with which the first paragraph in the MSS. concluded, we have, by virtue of our editorial prerogative, degraded the passage to the place and condition of a *Note.*—EDITOR.

Motto.*

" How wishedly will some pity the case of ARGALUS and PARTHENIA, the patience of GRYSELD in Chaucer, the misery

---

* Which *Posterity* is requested to reprint at the back of

and troublesome adventures of the ph*anatic* (*phrenetic?*) lovers in Cleopatra, Cassandra, Amadis de Gaul, Sidney, and such like! Yet all these are as mere romantic as Rabelais his Garagantua.   And yet with an unmoved apprehension, can peruse the very dolorous and lamentable murder of MILCOLUMB the First, the cutting off the head of good KING ALPINUS, the poisoning of FERGUSIUS the Third by his own queen, and the throat-cutting of KING FETHELMACHUS by a fiddler! nay, and moreover, even the martyrdom of old QUEEN KETABAN in Persia, the stabbing of Henry Fourth in France, the sacrilegious poisoning of Emperor Henry Seventh in Italy, the miserable death of MAURICIUS the Emperor, with a wife and five children, by wicked PHOCAS,—can read, I say, these and the like fatal passages, recorded by holy fathers and grave chroniclers, with less pity and compassion than the shallow loves of Romeo for his Juliet in Shakespeare—his deplorable tragedies, or shun the pitiful wanderings of Lady Una in search of her stray Red-cross, in Master Spenser his quaint rhymes.   Yea, the famous doings, and grievous sufferings of our own anointed kings, may be far outrivalled in some men's minds by the hardships of some enchanted innamorato in Ariosto, Parisinus, or the two Palmerins."

FOULIS's *History of the Wicked Plots and Conspiracies, &c.*

MOTTO II.

" Pray, why is it that people say that men are not such fools now-a-days as they were in the days of yore? I would fain know, whether you would have us understand by this same saying, as indeed you logically may, that formerly men were fools, and in this generation are grown wise.   How many and what dispositions made them fools? How many, and what dispositions were wanting to make 'em wise?

---

the title page, for the present, Quo' North, quo' Blackwood quo' *concessére Columnæ.*

Why were those fools? How should these be wise? Pray,
how came you to know that men were formerly fools? How
did you find that they are now wise? Who made them fools?
Who in Heaven's name made them wise? Who d'ye think
are most, those that loved mankind foolish, or those that
love it wise? How long has it been wise? How long otherwise? Whence proceeded the foregoing folly? Whence the
following wisdom? Why did the old folly end now and no
later? Why did the modern wisdom begin now and no
sooner? What were we the worse for the former folly? What
the better for the succeeding wisdom? How should the ancient folly have come to nothing? How should this same
new wisdom be started up and established? Now answer
me, an't please you."

FRANCIS RABELAIS' *Preface to his Fifth Book.*

EPISTLE PREMONITORY FOR THE READER;
but contra-monitory and in reply to
DICK PROOF, *Corrector.*

OF the sundry sorts of vice, Richard, that obtain in this sinful world, one of the most troublesome is *advice,* and no less an annoyance to my
feelings, than a pun is to thine. " Lay your *scene*
further off!!" Was ever historian before affronted
by so wild a suggestion? If, indeed, the moods,
measures, and events of the last six years, insular
and continental, or the like of that, had been the
title and subject matter of the work; and you had
then advised the transfer of the scene to Siam and
Borneo, or to Abyssinia and the Isle of Ormus—
there would be something to say for it, *verisimili-*

tudinis causá, or on the ground of lessening the improbability of the narrative. But in the history of Maxilian !—Why, the locality, man, is an essential part of the *a priori* evidence of its truth ! * *

In a biographical work, † the proprieties of place are indispensable, Dick. To prove this, you need only change the scene in the History of Rob Roy from the precipices of Ben Lomond, and the glens and inlets of the Trossacs (the Trossacs worthy to have made a W. S. but that a W. S. is only of God's making, " *nascitur non fit,*") to Snow-hill, Breckneck Stairs, or Little Hell in Westminster— by going to which last named place, Dick, when we were at the —— school, you evaded the guilt of forswearing for telling of me to our master, after you had sworn that you would go ——, if you did, —well knowing where you meant me to understand you, and where in honour you ought to have gone —but this may be mended in time.

——And lay the *time* further back ! But why, Richard? I pray thee tell me, why? *The present,* you reply, *is not the age of the supernatural.*

---

† In biography, which, by the *bi-*, reminds me of a rejoinder made to me, nigh 30 years ago, by Parsons the Bookseller, on my objecting to sundry anecdotes in a MS. Life, that did more credit to the wit and invention of the author, than to his honesty and veracity. " *In a professed biography*, Mr. P." quoth I, pleadingly, and somewhat syllabically.—" Biography, sir," interrupted he, " *Sell*ography is what *I* want."

2   z

Well, and if I admit, that the age at present is so
fully attached to the unnatural in taste, the præter-
natural in life, and the contra-natural in philosophy,
as to have little room left for the supernatural—yet
what is this to the purpose? I cannot *antedate* the
highly respectable personage, into whose company
I have presumed to bring you—I may make THE
READER sleep, but I cannot make him one of the
Seven Sleepers, to awake at my request for the
first time since he fell into his long nap over the
Golden Legend, or the Vision of Alberic! Or does
the reader, thinkst thou, believe that witch and
wizard, gnome, nymph, sylph, and salamander, *did*
exist in those days; but that, like the mammoth
and megatherim, the race is extinct? Will he accept as *fossiles*, what he would reject as specimens fresh caught—herein differing widely from
the old woman, who, as the things were said to
have happened so far off and so long ago, hoped in
God's mercy, there was not a word of truth in
them? Thou mayst think this, Richard, but I will
neither affront the reader by attributing to him a
faith so dependent on dates, nor myself, whose history is a concave mirror, not a glass case of mum-
mies, stuffed skins of defunct monsters, and the an-
omalous accidents of nature.

Thus, Richard, might I multiply thy objection,
but that I detest the *cui bono*, when it is to be a
substitute for the *quid veri*.   Nor will I stop at
present to discuss thy insinuation against the com-

parative wisdom of the sires of our great grandsires, though at some future time I would fain hear thy answers to the doubts and queries in my second motto, originally started by Master Rabelais, in that model of true and perpetual history, the Travels of Garagantua and his friends.

Without condescending to non-suit you by the *flaws* in your indictment, I assert the *peculiar* fitness of this age, in which, by way of compromising the claims of memory and hope, the rights both of its senior and of its junior members, I comprise the interval from 1770 to 1870.

An adventurous position, but for which the age, I trust, will be " my good masters"—the more so, that I must forego one main help towards establishing the characteristic epithets rightfully appertaining to its emblazonment—namely, an *exposè* of its own notions, of its own *morals* and *philosophy*. But Truth, I remember, is reported to have already lost her front teeth *(dentes incisores et prehensiles)* by barking too close at the heels of the restive fashion : a second blow might leave her blind as well as toothless. Besides, a word in your ear, Richard Proof, I do not half trust you. I mean, therefore, to follow Petrarch's * example, and con-

---

* The passage here alluded to, I should, as an elevated strain of eloquence warm from the heart of a great and good man, compare to any passage of equal length in Cicero. I have not the folio edition of Petrarch's works by me (by the bye, the worst printed book in respect of blunders I

fine my confidence on *these* points to a few dear
friends and revered benefactors, to whom I am in
the habit of opening out my inner man in the world
of spirits—a world which the eyes of " the profane
vulgar" would probably mistake for a garret floored
and wainscoated with old books; tattered folios, to
wit, and massive quartos in no better plight. For the
due nutriment, however, of scorn and vanity—which
are in fact much the same; for contempt is nothing
but egotism *turned sour*—for the requisite supply,
I say, of our social wants (Reviews, Anecdotes of
Living Authors, Table-talk, and such like provend-
er,) it will suffice if I hereby confess, that with rare
exceptions these friends of mine were all born and
bred before the birth of Common Sense by the ob-
stetric skill of Mr Locke, nay, prior to the first
creation of intellectual Light in the person of Sir
Isaac Newton—which latter event (we have Mr.
Pope's positive assurance of the fact) may account
for its universal and equable diffusion at present,
the Light not having had time to collect itself into
individual luminaries, the future suns, moons, and

---

know of, not excepting even Anderson's British Poets) and
cannot therefore give any particular reference. But it is my
purpose to offer you some remarks on the Latin Works of
Petrarch, with a few selections, at a future opportunity. It
is pleasing to contemplate in this illustrious man, at once the
benefactor of his own times, and the delight of the succeeding,
and working on his contemporaries most beneficially by that
portion of his works, which is least in account with his posterity.—S. T. C.

stars of the *mundus intelligibilis*.   This, however,
may be hoped for on or soon after the year 1870,
which, if my memory does not fail me, is the date
apocalyptically deduced by the Reverend G. S.
Faber, for the commencement of the Millennium.

But though my prudential reserve on these points
must subtract from my forces numerically, this
does not abate my reliance on the sufficing strength
of those that remain.   No ! with confidence and se-
cular pride I affirm, there is no age you could suggest, the characteristic of which is not to be found
in the present—that we are the quintessence of all
past ages, rather than an age of our own.   You recommend, you say, the Dark Ages; and that the
present boasts to be the contrary.   Indeed? I ap-
peal then to the oracle that pronounces Socrates
the most enlightened of men, because he *professed*
himself to be in the dark.   The converse, and the
necessary truth of the converse, are alike obvious :
Besides, as already hinted, in time all light must
needs be in the dark, as having neither reflection
nor absorption; yet may, nevertheless, retain its
prenomen without inconsistency, by a slight change
in the last syllable, by a mere—for "*ed*" read "*ing*."
For whatever scruples may arise as to its being an
enlightened age, there can be no doubt that it is an
enlightening one—an era of *enlighteners*, from the
Gas Light Company to the dazzling Illuminati in
the Temple of Reason—not forgetting the diffusers
of light from the Penny-Tract-Pedlary, nor the

numberless writers of the small, but luminous works
on arts, trades, and sciences, natural history, and
astronomy, *all* for the use of children from three
years old to seven, interwoven with their own little
biographies and nursery journals, to the exclusion
of Goody Two Shoes, as favouring superstition, by
one party; and of Jack the Giant-killer, as a suspicious parody on David and Goliah, by the other.

> Far, far around, where'er my eye-balls stray,
> By Lucifer! 'tis all *one milky way!*

Or, as *Propria Quæ Maribus,* speaking (*more pro-
phetico, et proleptice,*) of the Irradiators of future
(i. e. *our*) Times long ago observed, they are common, quite a *common* thing!

> Sunt *commune* Parens, Authorque; Infans, Adolescens;
> Dux; Exlex; bifrons; Bos, Fur, Sus atque Sacerdos.

So far, at least, you will allow me to have made
out my position. But if by a dark age you mean
an age concerning which we are altogether in the
dark; and as, in applying this to our own, the Subject and Object, we and the age become identical
and commutable terms; I bid adieu to all reasoning
by implication, to all legerdemain of inferential
logic, and at once bring notorious facts to bear out
my assertion. Could Hecate herself, churning the
night-damps for an eye-salve, wish for an age more
in the dark respecting its own character, than we
have seen exemplified in our next-door neighbour,
the Great Nation, when, on the bloodless altar of

Gallic freedom, she took the oath of peace and
good-will to all mankind, and abjured all conquests
but those of reason? Or in the millions throughout
the continent, who believed her? Or than in the
two component parties in our own illustrious isle,
the one of whom hailed her revolution as " a stupendous monument of human wisdom and human
happiness;" and the other calculated on its speedy
overthrow by an act of bankruptcy, to be brought
about or accelerated by a speculation in assignats,
corn, and Peruvian bark? Or than in the more recent constitutional genius of the Peninsula—

> What time it rose, o'er-peering, from behind,
> The mountainous experience, high upheaped
> Of Gallic legislation—

and " taught by others' harms," a very *un*gallic respect for the more ancient code, vulgarly called the
Ten Commandments, left the lands as it found them,
content with excluding their owners—owners of
four parts out of five, at least, the church and nobility—from all share in their representation? Or
when the same genius, the emblem and vice-gerent
of the present age in Spain, poising the old indige-
nous loyalty with the newly-imported state-craft,
secured to the monarch the revenue of a caliph,
with the power of a constable? But Piedmont!
but Naples—the Neapolitans! the age of patriotism, the firm, the disinterested—the age of good
faith and hard fighting—of liberty or death!—yea,
and the age of newspapers and speeches in Britain,

France, and Germany—the *uncorrupted* I mean;
(and the rest, you know, as mere sloughs, rather
than a living and component part, need not be
taken into the calculation)—were of the same
opinion! A dream for Momus to wake out of with
laughing!

But enough! You are convinced on this point,—
at least you retract your objection. And now what
else? Does my history require, in the way of *cor-
respondency*, a time of wonders, a revolutionary
period? Does it demand *a non-descript age?*
Should it, above all, (as I myself admit that it
should,) be laid in an age " without a name," and
which, therefore, it will be charity in me to chris-
ten by the name of the *Polypus?* An age, where
the inmost may be turned outside—and " Inside
out and outside in," I at one time intended for the
title of my history—where the very tails, inspired
by the spirit of independence, shoot out heads of
their own? (Thanks, with three times three, to
Ellis and Trembley, the first historiographers of
the Polypus realm, for this beautiful emblem and
natural sanction of the SOVEREIGNTY OF THE PEO-
PLE!) All, all are to be found in the age we live in
—whose attributes to enumerate would exhaust the
epithets of an Orphic hymn, and beggar the Gradus
ad Parnassum!— All, all, and half besides —the
feasibility of which I first learnt during the last war,
at two public dinners severally given, one by Scot-
tish, and the other by Irish patriots, where each as-

signed to their countrymen three-fourths of our whole naval and military success. In each case, *a priori*, the thing was possible, nay, probable; as each meeting the assertion passed *nem. con.* though there were eye-witnesses, if not pars-maximists present—and both were so much in earnest, that I could not find it in my heart to disbelieve either. But this is a digression. Or it may be printed as a parenthesis. All close thinkers, you know, are apt to be parenthetic.

One other point, and I conclude. You are a mighty man for parallel passages, Dick! a very ferret in hunting out the pedigree and true parentage of a thought, phrase, or image. So far from believing in equivocal generation, or giving credit to any idea as an *Autochthon, i. e.* as self-sprung out of the individual brain, or *natale solum*, whence (like Battersea Cabbages, Durham mustard, Stilton cheese, &c.) it took its *market* name, I verily suspect you of the heresy of the Præ-Adamites! Nay, I would lay a wager that the Thesis for your Doctor's Degree, should you ever descend from your correctorship of *typical* errata to that of misprints in the substance, would be: *quod fontes sint nullibi.* In self-defence, therefore, by *warrantable anticipation*, —a pregnant principle, Richard! by virtue of which, (as you yourself urged at the time) the demagogues that threw open the election of the Mayor of Garrett, hitherto vested in the blackguards of Brentford exclusively, to the blackguards of the country at large, exposed us to an invasion from the aristocracies of Tunis and Algiers! N.B. Clarendon and the Quarterly are of the same opinion—prospectively, I say, for informers, and informatively for the reader, I make known the following:

Some ten or twelve years ago, as the Vassals of the Sun, *i. e.* the Bodies, count their time, being in the world of spirits, as above mentioned, and in the Parnassian quarter, in literary chit-chat with Lucian, Aristophanes, Swift, Rabelais, and Molière, over a glass of green gooseberry wine, (since the departure of the last-named spirit, articles of French produce have been declared contraband in the spiritual Parnassia)—I read them a rough *pre-existent*, or as we say here, copy, of Maxilian. When who should be standing behind my chair, and peeping over my shoulder, (I had a glimpse of his face when it was too late, and I never saw a more Cervantic one) but a spirit from Thought-land, (North Germany I should say) who, it seems, had taken a trip thither, during the furlow of a *magnetic crisis*, into which his Larva had been thrown by —— Nic, senior, M. D.* and a Mesmerist still in great practice. Well! there would have been no harm

---

* See " Archiv des thierischen Magnetismus," edited by Professor Eschenmiayer and Co. I mentioned one of Dr. Nic's cases, with a few of Doctors Kieser's and Nasse's, and of Mr. Van Ghert's, to Lemuel Gulliver; but I found him strangely incredulous. *He* (he said) had never seen any

in this, for in such cases it was well known, that the spirit, on its return to the body, used to forget all that had happened to it during its absence, and became as ignorant of all the wondrous things it had seen, said, heard and done, as Balaam's ass. Γίνεται δ'αὖ ὄνος ὁ ὄνος ἐξαγγελιζόμενος. But unluckily, and only a few months before, Mr. Van Ghert, (who, as *privy* counsellor to the King of the Netherlands, ought to have known better) had, by metaphysical skill, discovered the means of so softening the waxen tablet in the patient's *cranium*, that it not only received, but retained, the impression from the movements of the soul, during her trance, re-suggesting them to the patient, sooner or later, sometimes as dreams, and sometimes as original fancies. Thus it chanced, that the great idea, and too many of the sub-ideas, of my *ideal* work awoke, in the consciousness of this Prussian or Saxon,——Frederic Miller is the name, he goes by——soon after the return of the spirit to its old chambers in his brain. Alas! my unfortunate intimacy with a certain well-known "Thief of Time," for which my originality had suffered on more than one former occasion, was part in fault! But, be this as it may, so it chanced, however, that before I had

---

thing like it. But what is that to the purpose? What does any one man's experience go for, in proving a negative at least? I could not even learn from him, that he had ever met with a single Meteorolithe, or sky-stone, on its travels from the volcanos of Jupiter, or the moon, to our earth.

put a single line on paper, (my time being, indeed, occupied in determining which of ten or twelve *pre-existents* I should transcribe first) out came the surreptitious duplicate, with such changes in names, scene of action, thought, images, and language, as the previous associations, and local impressions of the unweeting plagiarist had clothed my ideas in. But what I take most to heart, it so nearly concerning the credit of Great Britain, is, that it came out in *another* country, and in high Dutch ! I foresee what my anticipator's compatriots will say — that *admitting* the facts as here related, yet the Anselmus is no mere transcript or version, but at the lowest *a free imitation* of the Maxilian : or rather that the English and German works are like two paintings by different masters from the same sketch, the credit of which sketch, *secundum leges et consuetudines mundi corpuscularis*, must be assigned to the said Frederic Miller by all incarnate spirits, held at this present time *in their senses*, and as long as they continue therein ; but which I shall claim to myself, if ever I get *out of them*. And so farewell, dear Corrector ! for I must now adjust myself to retire bowing, face or frontispiece, towards THE READER, with the respect due to so impartial and patient an Arbiter from the

AUTHOR.

MAXILIAN.

Flight I.

IT was on a Whitsunday afternoon — the clocks
striking five, and while the last stroke was echo-
ing, in the now empty churches — and just at the
turn of one of the open streets in the outskirts of
Dublin—that a young man, swinging himself round
the corner, ran full butt on a basket of cakes and
apples, which an old barrow-wife was offering for
sale; and with such force, that the contents shot
abroad, like the water-rays of a trundled mop, and
furnished *extempore*—on the spur of the occasion,
as we say — a glorious scramble to the suburban
youngsters, that were there making or marring this
double holiday.   But what words can describe the
desperate outburst, the *blaze* of sound, into which
the beldam owner of the wares exploded! or the
" boil and bubble" of abuse and imprecation, with
which the neighbour gossips, starting from their
gingerbread and whiskey stands, and clustering round
him, astounded the ears and senses of the ill-starred
aggressor! a tangle-knot of adders, with all its heads
protruded towards him, would not have been more
terrific.   Reeling with surprise and shame, with
the look and gesture of a child, that, having whirled
till it was giddy-blind, is now trying to stop itself,
he held out his purse, which the grinning scold with

one snatch transferred to her own pocket. At the sight of this peace-offering, the circle opened, and made way for the young man, who instantly pursued his course with as much celerity as the fulness of the street, and the dread of a second mishap, would permit. The flame of Irish wrath soon languishes and goes out, when it meets with no fuel from resistance. The rule holds true in general. But no rule is of universal application; and it was far from being verified by the offended principal in this affray. Unappeased, or calling in her fury only to send it out again condensed into hate, the implacable beldam hobbled after the youth, determined that though she herself could not keep up with him, yet that her curses should, as long at least as her throat and lungs could supply powder for their projection. Alternately pushing her limbs onward, and stopping not so much to pant as to gain a *fulcrum* for a more vehement scream, she continued to pursue her victim with "vocal shafts," as Pindar has it, or ὡς πρῖνος ἐμπρησθείς i. e. spitting fire like a wet candle-wick, as Aristophanes !

And well if this had been all—an intemperance, a gust of crazy cankered old age, not worth recording. But, alas ! these jets and flashes of execration no sooner reached the ears of the fugitive, but they became articulate sentences, the fragments, it seemed, of some old spell, or wicked witch-rhyme:—

> Ay!—run, run, run,
> Off flesh, off bone !

Thou Satan's son,
Thou Devil's own !
Into the glass
                Pass
The glass ! the glass,
The crystal glass !

Though there is reason to believe that this trans-
formation of sound, like the burst of a bomb, did
not take effect till it had reached its final destination, the youths own *meatus auditorius;* and that
for others, the scold's passionate outcry did not
verbally differ from the usual outcries of a scold in
a passion : yet there was a something in the yell
and throttle of the basket-woman's voice so horrific,
that the general laugh, which had spread round at
the young man's expense, was suspended. The
passengers halted, as wonder-struck ; and when they
moved on, there was a general murmur of disgust
and aversion.

The student MAXILIAN—for he it was, and no
other, who, following his nose, without taking counsel of his eyes, had thus plunged into conflict with
the old woman's wares—though he could attach no
sense or meaning to the words he heard, felt himself, nevertheless, seized with involuntary terror,
and quickened his steps, to get as soon as possible
out of the crowd, who were making their way to the
pleasure-gardens, the Vauxhall of the Irish metropolis, and whose looks and curiosity converged towards him. His anxious zig-zag, however, marked
the desire of haste, rather than its attainment : and

still as he pushed and winded through the press of
the various gay parties, all in holiday finery, he
heard a whispering and murmuring, " The poor
young man! Out on the frantic old hag!" The
ominous voice and the wicked looks which the
beldam seemed to project, together with the voice—
and we are all, more or less, superstitious respecting *looks*—had given a sort of sentimental turn to
this ludicrous incident. The females regarded the
youth with increasing sympathy: and in his well-
formed countenance, (to which the expression of
inward distress lent an additional interest,) and his
athletic growth, they found an apology, and, for the
moment, a compensation, for the awkwardness of
his gait, and the more than most unfashionable cut
of his clothes.

It can never be proved, that no one of the Seven
Sleepers was a tailor by trade; neither do I take
on myself to demonstrate the affirmative. But this
I will maintain, that a tailor, disenthralled from a
trance of like duration, with confused and fragmentary recollections of the fashions at the time he
fell asleep, blended with the images hastily abstracted from the dresses that passed before his
eyes when he first reopened them, might, by dint
of conjecture, have come as near to a modish suit,
as the ambulatory artist had done, who made his
circuit among the recesses of Macgillicuddy's Reeks,
and for whose drapery the person of our luckless
student did at this present time perform the office of

*Layman.** A pepper-and-salt frock, that might be taken for a greatcoat,—but whether docked, or only out-grown, was open to conjecture; a black satin waistcoat, with deep and ample flaps, rimmed with rose-colour embroidery; green plush small-clothes, that on one limb formed a tight compress on the knee joint, and on the other buttoned mid-way round the calf of a manly and well-proportioned leg. Round his neck a frilled or laced collar with a ribbon round it, sufficiently alien indeed from the costume below, yet the only article in the inventory and sum total of his attire that harmonized, or, as our painters say, was in some keeping — with the juvenile bloom, and [*mark gentle Reader ! I am going to raise my style an octave or more*]—and ardent simplicity of his face; or with the auburn ringlets that tempered the lustre of his ample fore-

---

* The jointed image, or articulated doll, as large, in some instances, as a full-grown man or woman, which artists employ for the arrangement and probation of the drapery and attitudes of the figures in their paintings, is called *Layman*. POSTSCRIPT. Previously to his perusal of the several particulars of the student's *tout-ensemble*, I am anxious to inform the reader, that having looked somewhat more heedfully into my documents, I more than suspect that the piece, since it came from the hands of the Sartor of Macgillicuddy, had been most licentiously interpolated by genii of most mischievous propensities—the *boni socii* of the Etruscan and Samo-thracian breed; the " Robin Good Fellows" of England; the " Good Neighbours" of North Britain ; and the " Practical Jokers" of *all* places, but of special frequency in clubs, schools, and universities.

head! like those fleecy cloudlets of amber, which
no writer or lover of sonnets but must some time
or other, in some sweet Midsummer Night's Dream
of poetic or sentimental sky-gazing, have seen as-
tray on the silver brow of the celestial Dian! Or as I
myself, once on a time, in a dell of lazy Sicily, down
a stony side * of which a wild vine was creeping
tortuous, saw the tendrils of the vine pencilling with
delicate shadows the brow of a projecting rock of
purest Alabaster, that *here* gleamed through from
behind the tendrils, and *here* glittered as the inter-
space.

Yes, gentle Reader!—the diction, similes, and
metaphors, of the preceding paragraph, *are* somewhat motley and heterogene.   I am myself aware
of it.   But such was the impression it was meant
to leave.   A harmony that neither existed in the
original, nor is to be found in any portraiture

---

* The author asks credit for his having, here and elsewhere, resisted the temptation of substituting " *whose* " for
" *of which*"—the misuse of the said pronoun relative " whose,"
where the antecedent neither is, nor is meant to be represented as, personal or even animal, he would brand, as one
among the worst of those mimicries of poetic diction, by which
imbecile writers fancy they elevate their prose—*would*, but
that, to his vexation, he meets with it, of late, in the compositions of men that least of all need such artifices, and who
ought to watch over the purity and privileges of their mother tongue with all the jealousy of high-priests set apart by
nature for the pontificate.   Poor as our language is, in ter-
minations and inflections significant of the genders, to destroy the few it possesses is most wrongful.

thereof, presents itself in the exact correspondence
of the one to the other. My friend Panourgos,
late of the Poultry Counter, but at present in the
King's Bench, a descendant of the Rabelaisean Panurge, but with a trick of Friar John in his composition — acted on this principle. He sent an old
coat to be dyed; the dyer brought it home blue and
black: he beat the dyer black and blue: and this,
he justly observed, produced a harmony. *Discor-
dia concors!*—the motto, gentle Reader! prefixed
by the masters of musical counterpoint, to the
gnarled and quarrelsome notes which the potent
fist of the Royal Amazon, our English Queen Bess,
boxed into love and good neighbourhood on her
own virginals. Besides, I wished to leave your
fancy a few seconds longer in the tyring-room.
And here she comes! The whole figure of the student—She has *dressed* the character to a hair.—
You have it now complete before your mind's eye,
as if she had caught it *flying.*

And in fact, with something like the feeling of
one flying in his sleep, the poor youth neither
stopped nor stayed, till he had reached and passed
into the shade of the alley of trees that leads to the
gardens—his original destination, as he sallied forth
from his own unlightsome rooms. And scarcely,
even now, did he venture to look up, or around him.
The eruption from the basket, the air-dance of
cakes and apples, continued still before his eyes.
In the sounds of distant glee he heard but a vibra-

tion of the inhuman multitudinous horse-laugh (ἀνάριθμον γέλασμα) at the street corner. Yea, the restrained smile, or the merry glance of pausing or passing damsel, were but a dimmer reflection of the beldam's *haggish* grin. He was now at the entrance gate. Group after group, all in holiday attire, streamed forward. The music of the wind instruments sounded from the gallery; and louder and thicker came the din of the merry-makers from the walks, alcoves, and saloon. At the very edge of the rippling tide, I once saw a bag-net lying, and a poor fascinated haddock with its neb through one of the meshes: and once from the garrison at Valette, I witnessed a bark of Greece, a goodly Idriote, tall, and lustily manned; its white dazzling cotton sails all filled out with the breeze, and even now gliding into the grand port, (*Porto Grande,*) forced to turn about and beat round into the sullen harbour of quarantine.—Hapless Maxilian! the havens of pleasure have *their* quarantine, and repel with no less aversion the plague of poverty. The *Prattique* boat hails, and where is his bill of health? In the possession of the Corsair. Then first he recovered his thoughts and senses sufficiently to remember that he had given away—to comprehend and feel the whole weight of his loss. And if a bitter curse on his malignant star gave a wildness to the vexation, with which he looked upward,

> Let us not blame him: for against such chances
> The heartiest strife of manhood is scarce proof.

We may read constancy and fortitude
 To other souls—but had ourselves been struck,
 Even in the height and heat of our keen wishing,
 It might have made our heart-strings jar, like his!
                    Old Play.

Hapless Maxilian! hard was the struggle between the tears that were swelling into his eyes and
the manly shame that would fain restrain them.
Whitsunday was the high holiday of the year for
him, the family festival from which he had counted
and chronicled his years from childhood upwards.
With this vision before him, he had confined himself for the last four or five weeks to those feasts of
hope and fancy, from which the guest is sure to
rise with an improved appetite : and yet had put
into his purse a larger proportion of his scanty allowance than was consistent with the humblest
claims of the months ensuing. But the Whitsunday, the *alba dies*, comes but once a-year—to keep
it, to give it honour due,—he had pinched close,
and worked hard. Yes, he was resolved to make
much of himself, to indulge his genius, even to a
bottle of claret,—a plate of French olives,—or
should he meet, as was not improbable, his friend,
Hunshman, the Professor of Languages—*i. e.* a
middle-aged German, who taught French and Italian : excellent, moreover, in pork, hams, and sau-
sages, though the anti-judiac part of the concern,
the pork shop, was ostensibly managed by Mrs.
Hunshman, and since her decease, by Miss Lusatia,
his daughter—or should he fall in with the Professor,
and the fair Lusatia, why then, a bowl of Arrack

punch, (it is the ladies' *favourite*, he had heard the
Professor say, adding with a smile, that the French
called it *contradiction*)—Yes, a bowl of punch, a
pipe—his friend, townsman and maternal descendant
of the celebrated Jacob Behmen, had taught him to
smoke, and was teaching him Theosophy—coffee,
and a glass of Inniskillen to crown the solemnity.
In this broken and parenthetic form did the bill of
fare ferment in the anticipator's brain: and in the
same form, with some little interpolation, by way
of gloss, for the Reader's information, have we, sa-
crificing elegance of style to faith of History, delivered it.

Maxilian was no ready accountant; but he had
acted over the whole expenditure, had rehearsed it
in detail, from the admission to the concluding
shilling and pence thrown down with an *uncounting*
air for the waiter.   Voluptuous Youth!

But, ah! that fatal incursion on the apple-basket
—all was lost! The brimming cup had even
touched his lips—it left its froth on them, when it
was dashed down, untasted, from his hand.   The
music, the gay attires, the tripping step and friendly
nod of woman, the volunteer service, the rewarding
smile—perhaps, the permitted pressure of the hand
felt warm and soft within the glove—all shattered,
as so many bubbles, by that one malignant shock!
In fits and irregular *pulses* of locomotion, hurrying
yet lingering, he forced himself alongside the gate,
and with many a turn, heedless whither he went, if

only he left the haunts and houses of men behind him, he reached at length the solitary banks of the streamlet that pours itself into the bay south of the Liffey. Close by stood the rude and massy fragment of an inclosure, or rather the angle where the walls met that had once protected a now deserted garden,

" And still where many a garden-flower grew wild."

Here, beneath a bushy elder-tree, that had shot forth from the crumbling ruin, something higher than midway from the base, he found a grassy couch, a sofa or ottoman of sods, overcrept with wild-sage and camomile. Of all his proposed enjoyments, one only remained, the present of his friend, itself almost a friend—a Meerschaum pipe whose high and ample bole was filled and surmounted by tobacco of Lusatian growth, made more fragrant by folded leafits of spicy or balsamic plants. For a thing was dear to Maxilian, not for what it was, but for that which it represented or recalled to him : and often, while his eye was passing,

" O'er hill and dale, thro' CLOUDLAND, gorgeous land !"

had his spirit clomb the heights of Imaus, and descended into the vales of Iran, on a pilgrimage to the sepulchre of Hafiz, or the bowers of Mosellara. Close behind him plashed and murmured the companionable stream, beyond which the mountains of Wicklow hung floating in the dim horizon : while

full before him rose the towers and pinnacles of the
metropolis, now softened and airy-light, as though
they had been the sportive architecture of air and
sunshine.   Yet Maxilian heard not, saw not—or,
worse still,

> He saw them all, how excellently fair—
> He *saw*, not *felt*, how beautiful they were.

The pang was too recent, the blow too sudden.
Fretfully striking the fire-spark into the nitred
sponge, with glazed eye idly fixed, he transferred
the kindled fragment to his pipe.   True it is, and
under the conjunction of friendlier orbs, when, like
a captive king beside the throne of his youthful
conqueror, Saturn had blended his sullen shine
with the subduing influences of the star of Jove,
often had Maxilian experienced its truth—that

> The poet in his lone yet genial hour
> Gives to his eye a magnifying power :
> Or rather he emancipates his eyes
> From the black shapeless accidents of size—
> In unctuous cones of kindling coal,
> Or smoke upwreathing from the pipe's trim bole,
> > His gifted ken can see
> > Phantoms of sublimity.   MSS.

But the force and frequence with which our student now commingled its successive volumes, were
better suited, in their effects, to exclude the actual
landscape, than to furnish tint or canvas for ideal
shapings.   Like Discontent, from amid a cloudy
shrine of her own outbreathing, he at length gave
vent and utterance to his feelings in sounds more

audible than articulate, and which at first resembled
notes of passion more nearly than parts of speech,
but gradually shaped themselves into words, in the
following soliloquy :

"Yes ! I am born to all mishap and misery !—
that is the truth of it !——Child and boy, when did
it fall to my lot to draw king or bishop on Twelfth
Night ? Never ! Jerry Sneak or Nincompoop, to a
dead certainty ! When did I ever drop my bread
and butter—and it seldom got to my mouth without
some such circuit—but it fell on the buttered side ?
When did I ever cry, Head ! but it fell tail ? Did
I ever once ask, Even or odd, but I lost ? And no
wonder ; for I was sure to hold the marbles so awk-
wardly, that the boy could count them between my
fingers ! But this is to laugh at ! though in my life
I could never descry much mirth in any laugh I
ever set up at my own vexations, past or present.
And that's another step-dame trick of Destiny !
My shames are all immortal ! I do believe, Nature
stole me from my proper home, and made a blight
of me, that I might not be owned again ! For I
never get older. Shut my eyes, and I can find no
more difference between *eighteen* me and *eight* me,
than between to-day and yesterday ! But I will not
remember the miseries that dogged my earlier
years, from the day I was first breeched ! (Nay,
the casualties, tears, and disgraces of that day I
never can forget.) Let them pass, however—
school-tide and holiday-tide, school hours and play

hours, griefs, blunders, and mischances. For all these I might pardon my persecuting Nemesis! Yea, I would have shaken hands with her, as forgivingly as I did with that sworn familiar of hers, and Usher of the Black Rod, my old schoolmaster, who used to read his newspaper, when I was horsed, and flog me between the paragraphs! I would forgive her, I say, if, like him, she would have taken leave of me at the School Gate. But now, *vir et togatus*, a seasoned academic—that now, that still, that evermore, I should be the whipping-stock of Destiny, the laughing-stock of Fortune."   *   *

*   •   *   *   *   *   •

N.B. Of the " Selection from Mr. Coleridge's Literary Correspondence" the author said in a note to the *Aids to Reflection*, " which, however, should any of my readers take the trouble of consulting, he must be content with such parts as he finds intelligible at the first perusal. For from defects in the M.S., and without any fault on the part of the Editor, too large a portion is so printed that the man must be equally bold and fortunate in his conjectural readings who can make out any meaning at all." P. 171. edit. 1. p. 168. edit. 2. S. C.

NOTES TO LECTURE XIII.

ON POESY OR ART.

(a) p. 157.

IT has been stated elsewhere (*Biographia Literaria* Introd. p. 37.) that for many positions of this Lecture the author was indebted to Schelling's admirable Oration—*Ueber das Verhältniss der Bildenden Künste zu der Natur : Philosophiche Schriften,* p. 341—96. Here, as well as in his Lecture on the Greek Drama, Mr. Coleridge seems to have borrowed from memory. A few short sentences are taken almost *verbatim ;* but for the most part the thoughts of Schelling are mixed up with those of the borrower, and I think that, on a careful comparison of the Lecture with the Oration, any fair reader will admit that, if it be Schelling's —and that the leading thought of the whole is his, I freely own,—it is Coleridge's also. But this question every student will be able to decide for himself even without going beyond the present volume.

N. B. The title of Schelling's Discourse has been commonly translated, *On the Relation between the* Plastic *Arts and Nature ;* yet the term *Plastic* refers to Sculpture exclusively, and is never applied either by Schelling or Schlegel to Painting : and Schelling's discourse treats *der Bildenden Künste,* of the figuring or imaging Arts, in their relationship to Nature.* *Bild* is a picture, a print, as well as a graven image. The verb πλάσσω is " strictly used of the artist who works in soft substances, such as earth, clay,

---

* He says of Raphael, p. 379. " The bloom of the most cultivated life, the perfume of fancy, together with the aroma of the spirit breathe forth unitedly from his works;" and his criticism on Correggio, pp. 378-9. is remarkably genial and beautiful.

wax." Liddell and Scott. Still *die Plastik* is generally applied to carving or sculpture; but never, I believe, to the
mere expression of shape and visual appearance by painting,
drawing or printing.

(*b*) p. 157. See the next note.

(*c*) p. 160. *Phil. Schrift.* pp. 344-5. " For the imaging art
(die bildende Kunst,) in the oldest form of expression, is
styled *a dumb poetry*. The author of this definition doubtless
meant to intimate thereby that, like Poetry, it is intended to
express intellectual thoughts, conceptions, which the soul
originates, not however by means of speech, but as silent
Nature does, through form, through sensuous works independent of herself. Thus the imaging or figuring art stands
evidently as an active bond betwixt the Soul and Nature, and
can be conceived only in the vital mean — *in der lebendigen
Mitte*,—between both. Yea, since its relationship with the
Soul it has in common with every other art, and with Poetry
in particular, that (relation) whereby it is connected with
Nature and becomes, like Nature, a productive power, remains as the only one that is peculiar to it: and to this
alone can we refer a theory which shall be satisfactory to the
understanding, as well as furthering and beneficial to art."
Transl. Compare also with a passage, which will be pre-
sently quoted, in p. 352.

(*d*) p. 160. See the last note.

(*e*) p. 161. Ib. pp. 345-6. " But has not Science then always
recognised this relationship? Has not every theory of later
times even set out from the fixed principle, that Art should
be the imitatress of Nature? It has so: but what did this
broad general principle avail the artist, amid the various sig-
nifications, *(Vieldeutigheit)* of the conception of Nature, and
when there were almost as many representations of this Nature as different modes of existence?"

(*f*) p. 161. Compare with the following passage, *Phil.
Schrift.* p. 356. " How comes it that, to every cultivated sense,
imitations of the so named real, carried even to illusion, appear in the highest degree untruthful,—even convey the im-

pression of spectres; whereas a work, in which the idea is
dominant, seizes us with the full force of truth,—nay trans-
ports us for the first time into the genuine world of reality?
Whence does this arise, save from the more or less obscure
perception, which proclaims, that the idea is that alone
which lives, (*das allein Lebendige*) in Things:—that all else
is beingless and empty shadow? *Tr.*

(*g*) p. 162. Ib. p. 347. " Should then the disciple of Nature
imitate every thing in her without distinction, and in every
thing all that belongs to it, *und von jedem jedes?* Only beautiful objects, and even of these only the beautiful and perfect
should he repeat." *Tr.*

(*h*) p. 162. Compare with the following. Ib. p. 351. " We
must depart from the form in order to win it back again, to win
back *itself*, perceived as true, livingly and in the light of
understanding.   Consider the most beautiful forms, what
remains, when in thought you have abstracted from them
the operative principle? Nothing but bare unessential properties, such as extension and space-relationship. * * * * *
Nicht das Nebeneinanderseyn macht die Form,—it is not the
contiguity or mutual nearness of parts that constitutes form,
but the manner thereof, (the mode in which it takes place.)
But this can only be determined through a positive power,
dem Aussereinander vielmehr entgegenwirkende—opposed even
to that condition of space whereby things are perceived as
without one another, which subjects the variety (or mani-
foldness) of parts to the unity of an idea (*Begriff*): from the
power which works in the crystal even to that which, like a
soft magnetic stream, gives to the parts of matter in human
frames a disposition and situation relatively to one another, whereby the conception,—the essential unity and beauty
—can become visible." *Tr.* Compare with this passage the
last sentence of the first paragraph of Mr. C.'s Lecture.

(*i*) p. 163. Ib. p. 353. " This effective science is the bond
in Nature and Art between the conception and form; between body and soul." *Tr.*

(*j*) p. 163. Ib. p. 352. "The science, through which Nature works, is indeed like to no human science, which is united with self-reflection; *mit der Reflexion ihrer selbst.* In it conception is not distinct from art, nor design separate from execution." *Tr.*

(*k*) p. 164. Compare with this passage : *Ph. Schrift.* p. 353. " If that artist is to be accounted fortunate and praiseworthy beyond all others, on whom the Gods have bestowed this creative spirit, so will the work of art appear excellent in that proportion wherein it shews us, as in outline, this uncounterfeited power of creation and effectivity." *Tr.*

(*l*) p. 164. Ib. p. 353-4. " It has long been perceived that, in Art, not every thing is performed with consciousness: that with the conscious activity an unconscious power must be united, and that the perfect union and interpenetration of these two accomplishes that which is highest in Art. Works that want this seal of unconscious science are recognised through the sensible deficiency of a self-subsistent life independent of the life which produces them : while, on the other hand, where this operates, Art imparts to its work, together with the highest clearness of the understanding, that inscrutable reality, through which it appears like to a work of Nature."

" The attitude of the Artist toward Nature should frequently be explained by the maxim, that Art in order to be such, must, in the first instance, depart from Nature, and only return to her in the last fulfilment. The true sense of this appears to be no other than what follows. In all natural existences the living idea appears only as a blind agent ; were this true of the Artist, he would not be distinguishable from Nature in general. Were he to subordinate himself consciously and altogether to the actual, and repeat that which exists with servile fidelity, he would bring forth masks (*Larven,*) but no works of Art. For this cause he must remove himself from the product or creature, but only for the sake of raising himself up to the creative power and seizing that intellectually or spiritually. Hereby he rises into the domain of pure ideas ; he forsakes the creature in order to win it back again with a thousandfold profit, and in this way he will come back to Nature indeed." *Tr.*

(*m*) p. 165. Ib. p. 354. (*Next Sentence.*) " The Artist should by all means strive after that spirit of Nature which operates in the inner being of things through form and visual appearance no otherwise than as through speaking symbols,—(*jenem im Innern der Dinge wirksamen durch Form und Gestalt nur wie durch Sinnbilder redenden Naturgeist soll der Künstler allerdings nacheifern*) : and only in so far as, in his imitation, he livingly seizes this, has he himself produced anything of truth." *Tr.*

Compare also with this passage. Ib. p. 348. " The *object* of imitation was altered—imitation went on as before. In the place of Nature came the sublime works of Antiquity, from which the scholar was occupied in taking the outward form, but without the spirit that filled it." *Tr.*

(*n*) p. 166. Ib. p. 347. " When we view things not in respect to their essence, but to the empty abstract form, then they speak not at all to the inward being in ourselves—(*so sagen sie auch unserm Innern nichts*) : we must put into them our own mind (*Gemüth*), our own spirit, if they are to respond to us." *Tr.*

(*o*) p. 166. Ib. p. 355. " For works which should be the result of a combination of forms in themselves even beautiful, *einer Zusammensetzung auch übrigens schöner Formen*, would yet be devoid of beauty, inasmuch as that whereby peculiarly the work or the whole is beautiful cannot be mere form,— *nicht mehr Form seyn kann.* It is above Form,—is Being—the Universal—the look and expression of the indwelling Spirit of Nature.—*Es ist über die Form, ist Wesen, Allgemeines, ist Blick und Ausdruck des inwohnenden Naturgeistes.*"

(*p*) p. 166. Ib. p. 356-7. " By the same principle (that the conception (*Begriff*) is the sole life of things—*das allein Lebendige in den Dingen,*) we may explain all the opposed cases which are adduced as examples of the surpassing of Nature by Art. When it arrests the swift course of human years, when it unites the vigour of full-blown manhood with the soft charm of early youth, or presents a mother of grown-up sons and daughters in the perfect condition of powerful beauty, what does it but remove that which is non-essential—Time. If according to the remark of the distinguished critic (*Kenner*), each growth of Nature has but a single moment of true perfect beauty, we may also say that it has but one moment of full existence. In this moment it is what it is in all eternity : beside this there pertains to it only a becoming and a ceasing to be. Art, in representing that moment, lifts it out of time ; makes it appear in its true essence, in the eternity of its life." *Tr.*

(*q*) p. 167. Ib. p. 375-6. " But the case appears to be very different with Painting and with Sculpture. For the former represents, not like the latter, through corporeal things, but through light and colour, thus even through an incorporeal and in some measure spiritual medium." *Tr.*

(*r*) p. 168. Ib. p. 348. " But they, (the lofty works of antiquity,) are just as unapproachable ; nay, they are more unapproachable than the works of Nature; they leave us colder even than those do ; unless we bring with us the spiritual eye to pierce through the husk or veil, and perceive the operative energy within them." *Tr.*

(*s*) p. 170. Ib. p. 357. " When once we have abstracted from form all the Positive and Essential, it cannot but appear restrictive, and, as it were, hostile in respect of the Essence; and the same theory, which called forth the false ineffective Idealistic, must, at the same time, tend to the formless in Art. Form would indeed circumscribe the Essence, if it were independent of it. But, if it exists with and through the Essence, how should it feel itself restricted through that which itself creates ? Violence might be done it by a form forced on it from without, but never by that which flows from itself. On the contrary it will rest satisfied in this, and find therein its existence as self-subsistent and self-included."
Tr.

(*t*) p. 170. Ib. p. 361-2. " Winkelmann compares Beauty to water, which, drawn from the bosom of the spring, is held the purer the less taste it has. It is true that the highest Beauty is characterless ; just as we say also that the Uni-

verse has no determinate dimension, neither length, nor
breadth, nor depth, because it contains them all in a like
infinitude; or that the Art of creative Nature is formless,
because itself is subjected to no form." *Tr.*

I have now brought forward not only every sentence in
Schelling's Oration which has been adopted in the Lecture,
but also, to the best of my ability, every passage to which
the author can be conjectured to have *possibly* owed a suggestion. I have translated the extracts very literally with
more regard to exact fidelity than to idiomatic elegance: and
I am not without a hope that these specimens may induce
some readers to study Schelling's refined treatise at length
in the original. An English translation of it is named as one
of the " Catholic Series," published by Mr. Chapman, 142,
Strand. Translations are useful as aids to a rapid perusal
of the originals; taken as substitutes for them they are apt in
some measure, to mislead, and give a partially false colouring
to that which they aim to represent.

ERRATA.

NOTES OMITTED.

Vol. i. p. 146. " The art displayed in the character of
Cleopatra is profound," and Schlegel says of this heroine:
" The coquettish arts of Cleopatra are displayed without reserve: she is an equivocal creature, made up of regal
pride, womanish vanity, voluptuousness, fickleness, and
true attachment. Although the passion she feels and inspires is devoid of moral dignity, it yet excites interest as
an invincible fascination. The lovers seem formed for each
other, Cleopatra being as singular in her seductive charms,
as Antony in the splendour of his achievements." Vol.
iv. p. 20, edit. 2. Lecture xii. now xxvi.

Vol. i. p. 165. " —glorious subjects; especially Henry
I. &c., &c., and Henry VII." " This has been already
done by Ford " a reviewer suggested, " in his fine Tragedy

of *Perkin Warbeck*, brought upon the stage by Macklin in a modernized form."

Of Macklin's performance this anecdote is told by Badeley, the Actor :—" I was sitting one evening at the Cyder Cellar with Macklin, and incidentally observed, (for I was not very deeply read in theatrical history,) that I wondered there had not been a play written on the story of Perkin Warbeck. ' There has, sir,' gruffly replied Macklin. ' Indeed! and how did it succeed?' ' It was damned, sir.' ' Bless me! it must have been very ill written then—such a story! Pray, Mr. Macklin, who was the stupid author?' ' I, sir!' roared the veteran, in a tone that took away, continued Badeley, all desire to renew the conversation." Gifford's edition of Ford, vol. ii. *Introduction to Perkin Warbeck*. In the *MS. Notes to Langbaine, by Oldys*, quoted by Gifford, Macklin's " silly performance" is spoken of, as if it were no revival of Ford's play, but an original composition. It was produced in December, 1745, on occasion of the rebellion under the Pretender's eldest son; and another drama on the same story was brought out at the same time by Joseph Elderton, a young Attorney.

Vol. i. p. 258.—" seeming justification of our blackamoor or negro Othello." " I believe," says an anonymous critic, " in one edition of *Coryatt's Crudities* there is a drawing of the Venetian General, Othello, representing him *tawny*. Schlegel's reasons for Othello's blackness might be compared with Coleridge's against it." Schlegel's view of the subject is as follows : " What a happy mistake it was that led Shakespeare to convert ' the Moor,' under which name, in the original story, a baptized Saracen of the Northern coast of Africa was unquestionably meant, into a proper negro ! We recognize in Othello the wild nature of that burning zone, which produces the most violent beasts of prey, and the deadliest poisons, subdued in appearance only by love of fame, by foreign laws of honour, and by nobler and milder manners. His jealousy is not that jealousy of the heart which is compatible with the tenderest sensibility and devotedness toward the beloved object; it is that sensual frenzy, which in torrid climes has produced the unworthy confinement of women and other unnatural usages. A drop of this poison shed in his veins sets his whole blood in a ferment. The Moor appears noble, open, confiding, grateful for the love shewn him;—and he *is* all this; and, furthermore, he is a hero, who despises danger, a worthy commander of armies, a true servant of the state; but in a moment the mere physical force of passion overthrows all his acquired and habitual virtues, and gives the upper hand to the savage over the cultivated man in his nature. Even in the expression of his rage to revenge himself on Cassio, the despotism of the blood over the will betrays itself. At last, in his repentance, a genuine tenderness for his murdered wife and anguish from the sense of honour destroyed speak out of him in presence of the witnesses of his deed: and in the midst of all this he falls upon himself with the fury with which a tyrant tortures a rebellious slave. He suffers, like a double man, at once in the higher and the lower sphere into which his being is divided." Vol. iii. pp. 288, 9. Lecture xii. (xxv).

Vol. ii. p. 99.—" the crusading armaments." There must have been some mistake in the report of this passage, if not in the original conception of it; for the last crusades were undertaken in the earlier part of the thirteenth century; Dante's poetry was not produced till the beginning of the fourteenth. The error was noted in a critique on the *Lit. Rem.*

The Signature S. C. has been omitted by mistake in two or three Notes at the foot of the page in Vol. II.

THE END.

C. Whittingham, Chiswick.

Lightning Source UK Ltd.
Milton Keynes UK
UKHW020639060223
416537UK00012B/2528